George Keith

The Arguments of the Quakers

More particularly, of George Whitehead, William Penn, Robert Barclay, John Gratton, George Fox, Humphry Norton, and my own, against baptism and the Supper examined and refuted

George Keith

The Arguments of the Quakers
More particularly, of George Whitehead, William Penn, Robert Barclay, John Gratton, George Fox, Humphry Norton, and my own, against baptism and the Supper examined and refuted

ISBN/EAN: 9783337410810

Printed in Europe, USA, Canada, Australia, Japan

Cover: Foto ©Lupo / pixelio.de

More available books at **www.hansebooks.com**

THE
ARGUMENTS
OF THE
QUAKERS.

More particularly, *Ant. Johnson*.

Of
{ *George Whitehead.*
William Penn.
Robert Barclay. }
{ *John Gratton.*
George Fox.
Humphry Norton, }

And my own,
AGAINST

𝔅aptism and the 𝔖upper

Examined and Refuted.

ALSO

Some clear Proofs from Scripture; shewing that they are Institutions of Christ under the Gospel.

WITH

An *APPENDIX*, Containing *some Observations upon some Passages, in a Book of* W. Penn, *called,* A Caveat against Popery. *And on some Passages of a Book of* John Pennington, *called,* The Fig-Leaf Covering Discovered.

By *George Keith.*

1. John 4. 1. *Beloved, believe not every Spirit, but try the Spirits whether they are of God.*

Chrysost. Homil. on Matthew. *If thou hadst been without a Body, God had given thee things naked, and without a Body, but because the Soul is planted in the Body, he gives thee intelligible things in things sensible.*

London, Printed for G. Brome at the Gun at the West-End of St. Paul's Church-yard. 1698.

TO THE
READER.

Divers Weighty Reasons have induced me to this Undertaking. One whereof chiefly is; that whereas most of these Men, have not only run out with bitter Invectives against these Divine Institutions; but have Fathered their Bold Opposition to them upon the Holy Spirit, (as they commonly do their other Gross Errors) a Witness whereof, is *W. Penn*, in his Book against *Thomas Hicks*, called, *Reason against Railing*; who saith in p. 109. concerning these Institutions, *We can testifie from the same Spirit, by which* Paul Renounced Circumcision; *that they are to be rejected, as not now required*. Now if upon due Tryal, their Arguments they have used, and still use against them are found to be Vain and Invalid, Grounded upon gross Wrestings and Perversions of Holy Scripture; and that it be proved by sound Arguments, that they were, and are true Divine Institutions under the pure Gospel Dispensation ; not only their too Credulous Followers; but the Teachers themselves, such of them as are alive, may have occasion to reflect upon that Spirit, which had acted their first Leaders to oppose those things, as well as other great Truths of the Gospel ;

A 2 and

To the Reader.

and thereby discern that it was not the Spirit of God, but a Spirit of Untruth, and may judge it forth from among them, and be humbled before the Lord for entertaining it. Another Reason is, (which is indeed my chiefest Reason) That whereas I had formerly been Swayed and Byassed by the undue Opinion I had of their chief Teachers and Leaders, who had Printed Books long before I came among them, as being greatly indued with Divine Revelations and Inspirations; and that I too Credulously believed their Bold and False Asseverations; that what they had said and Printed against the *outward Baptism*, and *outward Supper*, was given forth from the Spirit of Truth in them; by means whereof, I had been drawn into the same Error, (as many other well meaning, and simple Hearted Persons have been, and still are by them) to oppose these Divine Institutions, and have in some of my Printed Books used some of the same Arguments which they had used; I having in a Measure of Sincerity (I hope) Repented, and been humbled before the Lord, for that my said Error; whereof I have given a Publick Acknowledgment in Print, in my late Book, called, *George Keith's Explications and Retractations*; and wherein I have not only Retracted my Errors in Relation to *outward Baptism* and the *Supper*; but in Relation also to divers other Particulars therein mentioned (but withal holding close to my Testimony in all Principles of Christian Faith and Doctrin, delivered by me in any of my former Books) I judged it my Duty, (besides my Publick Acknowledgment and Retractation of the Error) to endeavour according to the Ability given me of God,

To the Reader.

God, of a better Underſtanding, to undeceive and reduce from the ſaid Error, any into whoſe Hands my Books have come, Treating on that Subject; who have been deceived, or hurt by them. For as the Law of God requireth Reſtitution for any Wrong done to a Neighbour in Worldly Matters; ſo I judge it no leſs requireth the like in Spirituals. And as the Law required an Eye for an Eye; the Goſpel requireth, that whom we have in any degree been acceſſory to Blind, or Miſinform their Underſtandings, we ſhould labour to our outmoſt Ability (after we are better Enlightened our ſelves) to Enlighten and duly Inform them; ſo far as God ſhall be pleaſed to make us his Inſtruments in ſo doing, to whom it chiefly belongs. Know therefore, Friendly Reader; that what Arguments I have uſed in any of my Books againſt the *outward Baptiſm* and *Supper,* particularly in that, called, *Truth's Defence*; and in another, called, *The Presbyterian and Independent viſible Churches in New* England, *and elſewhere brought to the Teſt,* Cap. 10. and in another, called, *The pretended Antidote proved Poiſon*; and in another, called, *A Refutation of Pardon* Tillinghaſt, *who pleadeth for* Water-Baptiſm, *its being a Goſpel Precept.* As I hereby declare them to be void and null; ſo I do in this following Treatiſe ſhew the Nullity and Invalidity of them; by anſwering not only them, but divers others of other Perſons (together with them) as above named in the Title Page of this Treatiſe. And ſo far as the Arguments are the ſame, which both they and I have uſed; one Anſwer will ſerve to both; though I never was ſo blind, as not to ſee the

Weak-

To the Reader.

Weaknefs of divers Reafons of fome of their Great Authors againft thefe Inftitutions. But the Truth is, divers of their Weakeft and moft Impertinent Arguments. I never heard nor read, till of late, that Providence brought to my hand fome of their Books I never heard of before.

THE

PART I.

The CONTENTS.

SECT. I. *Containeth an Answer to the Argument of* G. W. *from* Matth. 28. 19.

SECT. II. *Containeth an Answer to his Argument, from* Mark 16. 16. *and sheweth the Invalidity of their Arguing from the Greek Words,* εις το ονομα *in* Matth. 28. *compared with* Acts 8. 16.

SECT. III. *Containeth an Answer to the Argument of* G. W. *and* R. B. *from* 1 Peter 3. 21.

SECT. IV. *Containeth an Answer to the Argument of* G. W. *and* R. B. *from* 1 Cor. 1. 17. *and an Answer to three other Arguments of* G. W. *in his Book, called,* An Antidote, *&c. from* Matth. 28. 19. *and* Gal. 3. 5.

SECT. V. *Containeth an Answer to the Argument of* W. P. *and* R. B. *from the ceasing of* John's *Baptism, and from the words* one Baptism *and* one Body, *Ephes.* 4. 4, 5.

SECT. VI. *Containeth an Answer to* W. Penn's *Arguing from Water, Bread and Wine ; their being Figures and Shadows ; their general Arguments from* Col. 2. 17. Col. 3. 1. Heb. 12. 22. *Answered, his Example of a Picture Retorted against himself.*

SECT. VII. *Containeth an Answer to the Arguments of* W. P. *and* R. B. *from* Matth. 28. 19. R. B. *his Argument, from* Gal. 3. 27. *Answered. Whether the Apostles did Baptize with the Holy Ghost : Resolved Negatively, as being Unscriptural, and without Reason so to affirm.*

SECT. VIII. *Containeth an Answer to* W. Penn's *Arguing against the Signs of Water in Baptism, and Bread and Wine in the Supper ; from his Inference that the continuance of them would be a Judaizing of the Spiritual Evangelical Worship, &c.*

SECT. IX. *Contains an Answer to* W. Penn's *Arguing ; that therefore they are to be Rejected, now the False Church hat got them.*

SECT. X. *Contains an Answer to the Argument of* W. P. *and* R. B. *from Christ's commanding the Disciples to wash one another's Feet, Anointing the Sick with Oyl, not practised by Protestants, abstaining from Blood, &c. The great use of the outward Signs to preserve the Doctrin, &c.*

SECT. XI. *Further sheweth the great use that the due practice of these outward Institutions hath to preserve the Doctrin of Christ Crucified, and Faith in him ; many of the Teachers among the Quakers, having made the Doctrin and Faith of Christ without ; not only not necessary ; but some of the chief of them having made it contrary to the Apostles Doctrin, particularly* G. Whitehead, *his Perverse Gloss, on* Rom. 10. 7, 8. *Refuted.*

SECT. XII. *Sheweth that the Spirit that Acted in* G. F. *and* G. W. *and some other first Teachers among the Quakers to oppose the Practice of Water-Baptism and the outward Supper ; was to draw People from the Faith in Christ without us. Some other Arguments against Baptism Answered.*

PART.

PART II.

The CONTENTS.

SECT. I. *Containeth a Correction of* R. B. *his great Mistake* ; That the Eating Christ's Flesh, *John* 6. *hath no Relation to Christ's outward Flesh. The Quotation of* Augustine *vindicated from his Mistake.*

SECT. II. *Containeth a Vindication of* B. Jewel's *words, on* Jos. 6. 1, 2, 3. *from the Great Misconstruction that* W. Penn *hath put on them, contrary to* B. Jewel's *intended Sense.* R. B. *his Arguments to prove that the Flesh of Christ,* John 6. 53. *hath no Relation to his outward Flesh, Answered.*

SECT. III. *Containeth a Correction of two Unsound Assertions of* R. B. *concerning Christ's Flesh and Blood.*

SECT. IV. *Sheweth* R. B's *Mistake, in saying that both Papists and Protestants tye the Participation of the Body and Blood of Christ to the outward Sign of Bread,* &c. *And his other Mistake ; that the whole end of the Paschal Lamb, was to signifie to the Jews, and keep them in remembrance of their Deliverance out of* Ægypt. *The true Sense of* Paul's *words given ;* The Bread which we break, &c. 1 Cor. 10. 16.

SECT. V. *Sheweth* R. B. *his Mistake ; as if the Cup of the Lord, and Table of the Lord,* 1 Cor. 10. 21. *did not signifie the use of Bread and Wine,* &c. *His Reasons against it proved invalid. His Argument from the Custom of the Jews using Bread and Wine at the Passover, Answered. His other Arguments, from the supposed difficulties about the time of practising it ; the sort of Bread and Wine to be used,* &c. *Answered.*

SECT. VI. *Sheweth* R. B. *his Mistake, that the Eating in these Words,* Take, Eat, &c. do this in remembrance of me, *was their common Eating. The continuance of the Supper, Argued from* 1 Cor. 11. 23. &c. *That the coming of Christ, meant in these Words,* until he come, *is his outward and last coming at the end of the World.*

SECT. VII. *Containeth three Reasons,* That by his coming, 1 Cor. 11. 26. is meant his outward coming.

SECT. VIII. *Containeth three other Reasons for the same.* R. B. *his Argument from the* Syriack *Translation, in* 1 Cor. 11. 26. &c. *Answered.*

SECT. IX. *Containeth* R. B. *his last Argument against the outward Baptism and Supper, Answered, respecting the Power to Administer them ; as whether Mediate or Immediate. The Collective Body of the Protestant Churches, may by Allusion, or an Hypothesis, be said to answer to the Church of* Sardis; *which who not blamed for Idolatry, but otherwayes. An Advice to all sincere Christians, agreeing in Fundamentals, to own one another as Brethren.*

SECT. X. *Sheweth, that many in the Protestant Churches, can give greater Evidence of their true inward Call to the Ministry, than many of the Teachers among the Quakers. Want of due Administrators, no Argument against Baptism and the Supper. An Advertisement, concerning* W. Del's *Book against Baptism. Good Advice to the Quakers, concerning those Institutions.*

SECT. XI. *Containeth some Arguments of* G. Fox, *and* Humphry Norton, *with their Answers, and some dreadful Words of* Humphry Norton, *against our Saviour's last coming ; though the Man was highly commended by* E. Burrough *and* F. Howgil. *Great Teachers among the Quakers.*

SECT. XII. *Containeth some Scripture Proofs, shewing that Baptism and the Supper are Institutions of Christ.*

PRAT.

PART I.

SECT. I.

An Impartial Examination, and Refutation of their Arguments against Water-Baptisme.

IN a Book of *George Whitehead*'s, whose Title is, *The Authority of the true Ministry in* Baptizing *with the Spirit, and the Idolatry of such Men as are doting about Shadows and Carnal Ordinances* ; [here note his severe Charge] p. 13. he bringeth three Reasons or Arguments to prove that in the Commission which *Christ* gave to his Discipless, in *Matth.* 29. 19. *Mark* 16. 18. *Water-Baptisme* was not intended, but the *Baptisme* of the Spirit.

His first Argument is, *If the Baptisme which* Christ *commanded in* Matth. 28. 19. Mark 16. 16. *was a* Baptisme, *without which a Man cannot be saved ; then it was not the* Baptisme *of* outward Water, (*for* Water-Baptisme *is not of necessity to Salvation, neither is there any stress for Salvation laid upon it*) *but it was that* Baptisme, *without which Men cannot be saved, which* Christ *commanded,* Matth. 28. *therefore not* Water-Baptisme, *I prove* (saith he) *the Minor Proposition thus* : *No man can be saved without being* Baptized *into the* Name *of* God, *and his Son* Christ Jesus, *for his* Name *is the word of* God *by which Salvation comes, and by no other* Name, *and the* Lord *is one, and his* Name *one, and it was into his* Name, *that the Disciples were commanded to* Baptize *People.*

Ans. Here *G. Whitehead* would appear to be some body in Logick (though it is judged by many of his Brethren to be little better than a piece of the black Art) but he has in this sufficiently discovered his Ignorance, both in true Divinity and true Logick. The Fallacy of his Argument is in this apparent, that in his supposed Proof of that he calleth the *Minor Proposition*, he confoundeth *Baptisme* into the *Name*, and the *Name* it self, for *saith he*, his *Name* is *the word of God* by which Salvation comes. But though Salvation cometh by the word of *God*, and none can be saved without that Word, yet it doth not follow, that none can be saved without such a *Baptisme* as the Apostles did Baptize with into the *Name* of that Word ; for as they were to Baptize

B   into

[2]

into the *Name* of the *Lord Jesus Christ*, and in the *Name* of the Father, *&c.* So they were to Teach in that *Name*, but this proves not that they were not to teach outwardly, and they were to work Miracles in that *Name*; it doth not therefore follow that they were not to work outward Miracles visible to Men's outward sight. Again, *G. Whitehead* useth the *Name word of God*, in a too narrow and limited Sense; for the full *Name* of *Christ* is not the *word only*, but *the word made Flesh*, or the *word having assumed the true Nature of Man*, and that by the *Name* of *Christ* here is understood the *Name* of the *Man Christ* who was Crucified, is clear from *Paul's* words to the *Corinthians*: *Was* Paul *Crucified for you, or were ye Baptized into the* Name *of* Paul ? Signifying, that they were Baptized into the *Name* of *Christ* Crucified, which hath a necessary Relation to the *Man Christ*, and to *Christ* considered as truly as *Man*, as *God*, and thought *the word is a Name* proper to the *Son*, yet it is not the *Name* either of the *Father*, or of the *Holy Ghost*, for that were to confound, and wholly to destroy the distinction of the *Relative Properties* of *Father, Son*, and *Holy Ghost*, which was the *Sabellian Heresie*. The Minor thereof of his Argument is Fallaciously proved by him, and his Assertion is false, *viz.* That the *Baptisme* without which Men cannot be saved was the *Baptisme* which *Christ* Commanded to the Apostles, if by the words *cannot be saved*, he means, *absolutely impossible*; for he hath not in the least proved that it was not *Water-Baptisme* which *Christ* Commanded; but whereas his Argument seemeth to depend on this, that becomes *Water-Baptisme* is not *absolutely necessary* to Salvation, therefore *Christ* did not Command it. But he should learn better to distinguish things *absolutely necessary* to Salvation, and things *necessary in some respect*, and very profitable, though not of *absolute necessity*, and the like distinction *G. Whitehead* must allow with respect to his and his Brethrens Ministry, Preaching, and Writing which they suppose *Christ* has Commanded them, and yet he will not say his and their Ministry Preaching and Writing is *absolutely necessary* to any Man's Salvation. Besides it doth *absolutely* contradict *G. Whitehead's* declared Principle concerning the *Sufficiency of the Light within every Man to Salvation without any thing else*; to affirm that Men could not be saved, unless the Apostles had Baptized them according to *Christ's* Command, even supposing it had been the Baptisme of the Spirit, which the Apostles had been Commanded to Administer; for this World have made the Salvation of Men depend upon the Ministry of Apostles, and their Successors in the outward Exercise.

[3]

ercife of their Spiritual Gift of Preaching and Prayer; now before the Apoftles Adminiftred this *Baptifme* (fuppofe it be that of the *Spirit*) the Men to whom they were fent had the *Light* in them, which was *fufficient to Salvation without any thing elfe*, according to G. *Whitehead*'s Doctrine, and confequently without all Miniftry of the Apoftles; and had they never heard or feen the Apoftles, or any other Men, had they given due Attendance and Obedience to the light within, that that would have faved them (according to G. *Whitehead*'s Divinity) without any other *Baptifme*, outward or inward, that the Apoftles could Adminifter unto them.

SECT. II.

Next, as to his fecond Argument from that in *Mark* 16. 16. *He that believeth and is baptized fhall be faved*; thefe words do not prove that this was not *Baptifme with Water*; for its a true Affertion, he that *believes* and is *Baptized* with Water fhall be faved; but it will not prove, that therefore *Baptifme with Water* is of *abfolute neceffity* to Salvation, the moft it proveth, is, that *Baptifme with water*, when and where it can be duly had is a *means of Salvation*, as outward Hearing, and Reading in the Holy Scriptures are means of Salvation, yet not of fuch *abfolute neceffity*, but that Men may be faved without them; even as it may be truly faid, he that believeth, and frequenteth the Meetings of the Faithful fhall be faved, and yet in divers Cafes Men may be faved without frequenting fuch Meetings, as when they are hindred by Sicknefs, or Imprifonment, or fome other Reftraint, as when living in a Country where no fuch Meetings are to be found, and that the *Baptifme* mentioned, *Mark* 16. *is not that which is of abfolute neceffity to Salvation*, is evident from the following Words, where the word *Baptized* is omitted; for *Chrift* did not fay, *be that is not baptized fhall be damned, but he that believeth not fhall be damned*; the varying of the Expreffion fufficiently proveth that he did not mean the inward *Baptifme*, but the outward; and whereas not G. *Whitehead*, but W. *Penn*, and R. *Barclay*, argue from the Particle in Greek, that fignifieth in Englifh *into*, that therefore it muft be the *Baptifme with the Spirit*, it is indeed very weakly and fallacioufly argued, for the fame Greek Particle is found Acts, 8. 16. where it is faid, that thefe of *Samaria*, who were Baptized *into the Name of the Lord Jefus* had not *received the Holy Ghoft*, when fo Baptized, till for fome time after, that *Peter* and *John* came unto them, the Greek Particle, εἰς τὸ ὄνομα is the fame here, and in

B 2 *Matth.*

Matth. 28. 19. And any who have but a little skill in Greek know, that the Greek Particle εἰς hath often the same signification, with the Greek Particle ἐν, and signifieth as well *in*, as *into*, so that their so arguing is built on a Grammatical Quibble that is altogether groundless. And for them to argue, that it was not *Water-Baptisme*, which Christ commanded to the Apostles, *Matth.* 28. 19, because of the words *Baptizing into the name*, &c. with as much colour of reason they might argue, that when in *James* 5. 14. It is said anointing them with Oyl in the name of the Lord, that the *anointing* there meant was not an *outward anointing* but an *inward*, and that the *Oyl* was not outward but inward.

Again, whereas *G. W.* saith on this second Argument, for the Saints were saved by that *Baptisme, which was not the putting away the filth of the Flesh, but the answer of a good Conscience*, 1 Pet. 3. 21. Therefore it was not *Water-Baptisme* which Christ commanded in *Matth.* 28. &c. I answer, that doth no wise follow that therefore it was not *Water-Baptisme*.

SECT. III.

AND because I find that *Robert Barclay* in that Chapter of his Printed *Apology*, reprinted by his Son *Robert Barclay* at *London*, 1696, doth much insist upon this place in *Peter*, as if it did effectually prove that *Water-Baptisme* is no *Gospel Institution*, and it is a common Text the Teachers among the Quakers bring to oppose *Baptisme with Water*; therefore I think fit the more fully to examine the Arguments brought by him from this place against it. But in the first place, I do apologize for my medling to answer or correct any Passages in the Books of *R. Barclay*, whom as I did greatly love and esteem, and who, I believe, was one of the soundest Writers among the People called Quakers, so I do truly honour his memory, believing that as to the main, he was a true Christian, though in divers things, he was byassed and misled, as I also was, by the too great esteem that he had, and too great credit he gave, (as I also did) of those called his *Elders*, whose *gross perversions* and *misinterpretations* of Holy Scripture, we both did upon their *Authority* take for *Divine Inspirations*; and I hope it may be a *just Apology* to me, and defence against the injurious Clamours of some, that may and will object it against me, as a breach of Friendship, to censure or correct any thing of that my *deceased Friend: That I do no otherwise in this Case; than*

I would

I would be done by; for, if after my decease, (as well as before) any Friend of mine should censure and correct any Passages in any Books of mine that did justly need such *Censure and Correction*, I and all that love me should take it, as a *true act of Friendship*; it being the best way to cover the Faults of our Friends, or were it of our Parents, to *correct them*, and though Men may be dear to us, yet *Truth* ought to be more dear; nor do I thus censuring and correcting what I judge amiss in *R. B.* on these Heads, do any more wrong to him, than I do to my self, whom I have impartially censured, and now again do, freely declaring, that whatever I have said, or writ any where against *Baptisme with Water*, and the *Outward Supper*, as being no Gospel Institution was erronious, and which therefore I retract and correct. And where I have used divers of the same Arguments, which *G. W.* and *R. B.* hath used, which I find *R. B.* hath been more large upon than I have any where been in any of my Books; therefore I shall rather consider these Arguments as brought by him, than by me, especially for this cause, that he is judged by many of the Quakers to have writ more forcibly against these matters than most have, or then I have done.

R. B. thus argueth from 1 *Pet.* 3. 21. (see pag. 16. of his *Sons Edition* called *Baptisme and the Supper substantially asserted*) The *Apostle* (saith he) *tells us first negatively, what it is not*, viz. *not a putting away of the filth of the Flesh, then surely it is not a washing with Water, since that is so.*

Answer, That the *Baptisme* there described is not a putting away the filth of the Flesh is granted, but it doth not follow, that therefore it is not *Water-Baptisme*, for though *ordinary washing with Water* is a doing away *Bodily filthiness*, yet *Baptisme with Water* is not, nor ever was, nay not *John's Baptisme with Water*; for *John* did not say that he *baptized* his Disciples to *wash away* the *filth* of their Bodies, but unto Repentance. The description of *Baptisme* here given by *Peter*, is taken from the *end*, as is very common both in Scripture and elsewhere, to describe a *thing* from *its end*; now the *end of Water-Baptisme*, as it was commanded by Christ, *Matth.* 28. 19. was not to *put away the filthiness of the Flesh*, but to signifie the *inward washing by the Blood and Spirit of Christ* upon the Soul and Conscience, the which when so washed is a good Conscience, and the effect of that inward washing is the answer of a good Conscience; and indeed to me it is evident, that *Peter* in this description of *Baptisme* first

nega-

negatively, what it is not, doth refer by way of comparison to the *legal purifyings* under *Moses Law*, *by Blood*, and the *Ashes of an Heifer with water sprinkling the Unclean*, which as the Author to the *Hebrews* saith, *sanctified to the purifying the Flesh*, Heb. 9. 13. and yet even this *washing* was not to *cleanse* the Body from *natural filth*, but from the legal uncleanness that Men had on divers occasions, as when they touched a dead Body they were *legally unclean*, and because of that they were not to come into the *Tabernacle*, until they were *cleansed* with this *water* of *purifying sprinkled* on them. But the *Baptisme with water* under the Gospel, had not that but a greater signification, and being duly received had a greater and more *noble effect*) *viz*. to *signifie* the *spiritual cleansing by Christ*, and to be a *means of Grace*, far greater than under the Law.

Again p. 17. He thus argueth, *If we take the second and affirmative definition, to wit, that it is the Answer or Confession of a good Conscience*, &c. *then* Water-Baptisme *is not it, since as our Adversaries will not deny*, Water-Baptisme *doth not always imply it, neither is it any necessary consequence thereof.*

Answ. This Consequence also is not good, because though *Water-Baptisme* in the *literal sense* strictly taken, without any *Metonymy* is not the *answer of a good Conscience*, as the *Lamb was* not the *Passover*, but a signification of it, yet the *Lamb* is called in Scripture the *Passover*, by a *Metonymy* of the Sign put for the *thing signified*, that is very common in Scripture, as in other Authors, so the *Baptisme with water, metonymically* may be called, the *answer of a good Conscience*, being the *thing signified* thereby. That he saith, their Adversaries will not deny, that *Water-Baptisme* doth not always *imply it*, neither is it any *necessary consequence* thereof; in that he was under a mistake, for they will say, and do say, that *Water-Baptisme* doth always imply it, to such as *duly and worthily receive it*; and that it is always a *necessary consequence* or concomitant thereof upon due and well qualified Receivers. And if nothing appear to the contrary by words or actions, but that the receivers are duly qualified (tho' some of them be not such really) yet in the judgment of Charity, even according to *Scripture rule*, they are called such, as *Paul* calleth these of the *Churches* to whom he writ *Saints*, and yet no doubt all were not *real Saints* in the *Churches*, though by Profession they were such.

Again,

Again, whereas pag. 18. he argueth thus: Peter *calls this here which saveth the* Antitypos, *the Antitype, or the thing figured, whereas it is usually translated, as if the like figure did now save us,* thereby infinuating, that *as they were saved by Water in the Ark, so are we now by* Water-Baptisme, *but this Interpretation* (he faith) *crosseth his sense.*

Answ. His Argument from the Greek word used by *Peter, viz. Antitypos* (he should have said ἀντίτυπον in the neuter gender) is indeed altogether *weak and groundless*, as if it only signified the thing and could not be understood of the Figure of the thing, the contrary whereof appeareth from *Heb.* 9. 24. where the holy Places made with hands are called ἀντίτυπα, *i. e.* the Antitypes of the true, which are truly translated the Figures of the true holy Places made without hands.

Again, whereas he argueth, *that* Water-Baptisme *is not meant* (p. 19.) *in* 1 Pet. 3. 21. *that the* Baptisme *there mentioned, is said to save us; but Protestants deny it to be absolutely necessary to Salvation.*

Answ. Nor hath this Argument any force, for though it is not *absolutely necessary* to Salvation, yet that it is in *God's ordinary way*, where it can be duely had, and by whom it is duely received one of the *ordinary. means* of Salvation; it is truly said to save as the *Doctrine of the Gospel* outwardly Preached by the Ministry of Men, is *saving by way of means*, and as the Holy Scriptures are said by *Paul* to be able to make wise unto Salvation, through Faith in *Christ Jesus*, and said *Paul* to *Timothy*, 1 *Tim.* 4. 16. *Take heed unto thy self, and unto thy Doctrine, continue in them, for in doing this, thou shalt both save thy self and them that hear thee:* And as concerning the means of Salvation, though all of them, when really given of God, are *very profitable*, yet all are not *alike necessary*, nor *alike given*, nor *afforded* unto all; some, yea, many never perhaps heard the *Gospel* truly Preached unto them by the *Voice* of Man, yet having the Scriptures read unto them, that hath proved an *outward means* of their Salvation, the Lord working inwardly by his *Grace* and *Spirit*, to make the same effectual to them. And as at times the *Book* of the Holy Scriptures supplieth the defect of a *Vocal Ministry*, so at times, a *Vocal Ministry* doth supply the want of the Book of the Scriptures; and thus, though *Baptisme* and the *Supper* outwardly administred are *means of Grace* and Salvation, when *duly received*, yet they are not *so necessary*, as the Doctrine of the Gospel, as outwardly delivered by Men, and the Books of the Holy Scripture.

If any shall object, that it is better to keep to the *literal Sense* of the words in *Peter*, than to run to the *Metonymy*, which ought not to be done, but in case of *necessity*; I answer what way soever, the *Baptisme* in 1 *Pet.* 3. 32. be taken, as suppose for the *Baptisme of the Spirit*, yet such whoso take it must run to a *Metonymy*, for the *inward* Baptisme *of the Holy Spirit*, is not the *Answer* or *Confession* of a *good Conscience*, otherwise than by a *Metonymy* of the Cause, for the effect. The *Answer* or *Confession* of a *good Conscience*, being the *effect* of the *inward Baptisme* and operation of the Spirit, and not *the inward* Baptisme *it self*. And indeed such *Figures and Metonymycal Speeches* are very frequent in Scripture, to which for not well adverting, many are drawn into most false Interpretations of Scriptures, and most hurtful Errors, as the *Papists* by taking the words of *Christ*, *this is my Body*, in a mere *literal Sense*, without any *Metonymy*. To conclude upon this Argument, the most that with any colour or shadow of Reason can be inferred from this place, in 1 *Pet.* 3. 21. is that *Water-Baptisme* alone, neither doth, or can save any without the inward *Baptisme*, or operation of the Spirit; all which is readily granted, nor yet doth the inward *Baptisme*, though joyned to the outward save, without any thing else, but both the *inward Baptisme*, and *outward* do save us, as *Peter* plainly declareth by the *Resurrection of Jesus Christ from the Dead*, nor need the inward and outward *Baptisme* be strictly called *two Baptisms*, more than *England*, and a *Map* of *England*, are called *two England*'s, or the *Law* writ in the Heart, and the same *writ in* Paper, are two *Laws*. And thus I hope I have fully examined and answered to the Argument, both of G. *Whitehead*, and *R. B.* from 1 *Pet.* 3. 21. as the impartial intelligent Reader may perceive.

SECT. IV.

THE third Argument used by G. *Whitehead*, is the same for Matter that is used by *R. B.* in the Treatise above cited, p. 30. which they bring from *Paul*'s words, 1 *Cor.* 1.17. *where* Paul *said, that Christ sent him not to baptize, but to preach the Gospel.* The *reason of that Consequence* (saith *R. B*) *is undeniable, because the Apostle* Paul's *Commission was as large as that of any of them.* And whereas it hath been answered to this, by them who holds that *Baptisme with Water* is a *Gospel Institution*, from *Matth.* 28. 19. that the Sense of *Paul*'s words is, that he was not sent *principally* to Baptize, *not* that he was not sent at all, as

where

where it is said, *Hof. 6. 6. I desired mercy, and not sacrifice.* But this parity *R. B.* doth except against, *because this place is abundantly explained by the following words, and the knowledge of God more than burnt-offerings.---But there is no such words added in that of* Paul. And against this manner of interpreting *Paul's* words, he thus argueth, *else we might interpret by the same rule all other places of Scriptures, the same way, as where the Apostle saith,* 1 Cor. 2. 5. *That your faith might not stand in the wisdom of men, but in the power of God, it might be understood, it shall not stand principally so. How might the Gospel by this liberty of interpretation be perverted?*

Anf. As we are not to Interpret all other Places of the like Phrase so, else great harm would follow in giving *false Interpretations of Scripture,* so we ought to Interpret diverse places of Scripture, *so,* to wit, by adding the word, *only,* or *more,* or *principally,* otherwise the like harm would follow, as where it is said, 1. *John* 3. 18.----*Let us not love in word, nor in tongue, but indeed and in truth,* and *Rom.* 2. 13. *For not the hearers of the law are just before God,* &c. *John* 14. 24. *The word which you hear is not mine, but the Fathers which sent me.* Matth. 15. 24. *I am not sent, but to the lost sheep of the house of Israel,* John. 4. 42. *We believe not because of thy saying.* Matth. 10. 20. It is *not ye* that speak, &c. In these and diverse the like places of Scripture, the word *principally,* or *more,* or *rather,* though not expressed, is understood; and there is a good Rule whereby to know when any such word, when not expressed, is necessarily understood, as when without *any such word* understood, or implyed, when not expressed, it would contradict some other place of Scriptures, or any true consequence from Scripture, or true Reason, as is manifest in the present Case, for *Paul* telleth in the same Chapter, that he Baptized some of the *Church* of *Corinth,* which he ought not to have done without a Commission; for as to what is alledged, that he and others did Baptize by *Permission,* and not by *Commission,* as when he Circumcised *Timothy,* it was by *Permission,* and not by *Commission,* which conceit I grant I had formerly entertained as well as *R. B.* being swayed by the assumed Authority of them we esteemed our Elders, pretending they did so Interpret the Scriptures by Divine Inspiration. But finding their Pretences to be palpably false in many other things of greater weight, occasioned me to examine their pretended Inspirations in this also, which (I desire to praise God for his true Illumination) I found to be false. Now that *Paul's* Circumcising *Timothy* was not by *Commission,* is certain, because

C   some-

sometimes afterwards he did earnestly oppose the practice of it, but we never find that he, or any else in Scripture opposed the practice of *Baptisme with Water*, or spoke so slightly of it, as he did of *Circumcision*; he did not say, if any of you be *Baptized*, *Christ* should profit you nothing, as he said, if any of you be *Circumcised*, and he submitted to *Baptisme* himself, and received it. *Acts 9. 18.* compared with *Acts 22. 16.* Though I find that *W. Penn* calleth it in question, whether this was *Baptisme* with *Water*, which bespeaketh as great inadvertency in him, as when he had printed in his *Christian Quaker*, that *Jesus Christ* was born at *Nazareth*. And as for *Paul's* saying, he *thanked* God he Baptized none of the *Corinthians*, but such and such, it only proveth that he judged *Preaching* to be his *principal work*, as indeed it was; for had he *Baptized* all to whom he Preached, and who were Converted by his Ministry, it would have been too great a hindrance to his *Preaching*; and as *Paul* Preached to many whom he did not *Baptize*, so did the other Apostles; therefore we find not either *Peter*, or *John*, or any of the other Apostles after our Saviour's Resurrection, *Baptized* all to whom they Preached, but left it to be done in great part by others; and whereas some have argued, that if *Baptisme* had been a *Gospel Precept*, Paul *would not have said, he thanked God he had Baptized so few of them*: This Argument hath no force, for he did not thank God, *simply* that he did not *Baptize*, but that he had *Baptized* so few of them, lest they should say, *he had* Baptized *in his own* Name, which sheweth, that the occasion of the Division that was among the *Corinthians* at that time was about *Baptisme*, and that they had too much an eye to those who had *Baptized* them, so as to denominate themselves after them. And whereas, R. B. saith, p. 32. 33. *Let it from this be considered how the Apostle Excludes* Baptizing, *not Preaching, though the abuse (mark) proceeded from that, no less than from the other*; *for these* Corinthians *did denominate themselves from those different Persons, by whose Preaching (as well as from those by whom they were* Baptized*) they were Converted*; *as by the 4, 5, 6, 7. and 8 Verses of the third Chapter may appear.*

Ans. But that the Preaching of these different Persons was the occasion of this *Division* among the *Corinthians*, doth not appear from the Verses Cited, nor any where else, for *Paul*, and *Apollo* Preached the same Doctrine to them; but we no where find that there Preaching occasioned any Division; but suppose it had, on the supposition, that some of the *Corinthians* might esteem the Preaching of the one, more powerful than the Preaching of another; yet that proves not that

Paul

Paul Excluded *Baptizing*; the moſt it proves, is, that he preferred, his *Preaching* to his *Baptizing*, as being the greater and more principal Work enjoyned to him.

Page 33. *And yet for to remove that Abuſe* (ſaith R. B.) *the Apoſtle doth not ſay, he was not ſent to Preach, nor yet doth he Rejoyce that he had only Preached to a few, becauſe Preaching being a* ſtanding Ordinance *in the Church, is not becauſe of any Abuſe that the* Devil *may tempt any to make of it, to be forborn by ſuch as are called to perform it by the Spirit of God.*

Anſ. All this is exceeding weak Reaſoning, and proceeds upon a falſe Suppoſition; that becauſe *Baptiſme* was abuſed, therefore it was ſimply to be forborn, or laid aſide; no ſuch thing appears mentioned in Scripture; for though *Paul Baptized* but a few of the *Corinthians*, he did not tell them that few were *Baptized* by any others. But the contrary appears from his words, that all the *believing Corinthians* were *Baptized*, though not by him, yet by ſome other, 1 *Cor.* 1. 13. *If ſome of them had not been* Baptized *at all, it had been improper for him to ask them were they* Baptized *in the* Name *of* Paul? And though Preaching be the greater Ordinance, as practiſed by the Apoſtles, and is not ſimply to be forborn, yet occaſions might and may happen that might cauſe it to be forborn at ſome certain time and place: As ſuppoſe, ſome had certainly informed *Paul*, that if he *Preached* at ſuch a place, and at ſuch a time, ſome that did lay wait for him, would lay hands on him and kill him; on this Advertiſement, who will ſay, but *Paul* might feel in himſelf, not only a Liberty to forbear going to *Preach* at ſuch a place, and at ſuch a time, but even a *Neceſſity* laid on him not then to go; for we find, that not only *Paul*, when he underſtood that ſome ſought his Life, did ſeek to eſcape; but our *bleſſed Lord himſelf* for a certain time did withdraw from ſuch as fought his Life, becauſe his time to ſuffer was not then come. And as in that caſe, upon ſuch certain Information, *Paul* might have lawfully forborn to have *Preached* to People at that place when his Life was in danger; ſo the Report being confirmed, that ſuch a Deſign was laid againſt him, he might have *lawfully rejoyced* and *thanked God*, that he did not go to *Preach* at that place, at that time. And many the like Examples might be brought to prove, that *Preaching* it ſelf may Lawfully be forborn, though not ſimply, yet at ſome occaſion which might render the *forbearance* of it at ſome certain place and time, both *Lawful* and *Neceſſary*; and ſuppoſe a Preacher did foreſee that his *Preaching* at ſuch a place, at ſuch a day, ſhould occaſion by *accident* ſome *Schiſm* or *Division* among sincere Professors of the Christian Faith, he might very lawfully forbear to do it at that time, yea it were his Duty to forbear, and he might very *justly rejoyce and thank God*, that he did not Preach to them in that place, and at that time; this needed not to have been so largely insisted upon, but for their sake, who through their great Ignorance and Prejudice) lay so great stress on this sort of Argument; as because *Paul thanked God, he had* Baptized *but a few of the* Corinthians, *therefore* Baptisme *is no Gospel Institution*; the weakness of which consequence, I suppose is sufficiently manifest: On the contrary a good Argument may be brought for *Water-Baptisme*, that seeing the abuse of it at *Corinth*, or any where else, was no cause or occasion of laying it aside to any, but that it was universally practised on Believers in the Apostles Days, insomuch that it cannot be instanced where any Church, Family, or Person that did believe was not *Baptized*, that therefore it was practised by Divine Institution, and not by Permission, such as *Circumcision* was; for neither *Circumcision*, nor any other *Jewish Rite* was universally practised, as *Baptisme* was; the above-said Argument, taken from *Paul*'s words, *he thanked God he* Baptized *none but such and such*, I find used by *W. Penn*, in his Book, called *Reason against Railing*, p. 110. to which let the above mentioned Answer serve.

But I find some new Arguments used by *G. Whitehead*, in his *Antidote*, to prove that *Baptisme* with *water* was not commanded to the Apostles, *Matth.* 28. 19. p. 120. *Lo I am with you always, to the end of the World* (saith he) *what for? to enable them to* Baptize *with* Water? *No that many can do without him, or the least sense of his Presence.*

Ans. Of all the Arguments I ever heard against *Baptisme* with *water*, this is one of the weakest, and too much favouring of Profanity, that (*saith he*) many can do without him, but can they do it in Faith without him, and in true Obedience to his Command? This Scoff of his, has equal weight against *John*'s *Baptisme*, when in force, which he grants was with *water*; and thus, as *G. Whitehead* argueth, *John* could, and did *Baptize* without *Christ*'s inward Presence, and the least sense of it, and it has the like force against all External Acts of Religion commanded of *God*, both under the Law and Gospel; for all External Acts simply considered, as such without regard to Faith, or the inward Frame of the Mind, can be done as much without *Christ*, as *Baptisme* with *water*; but none of them can be done as they ought without him. Hath *G. Whitehead* forgot *Christ*'s Saying to his Disciples;

without

without me ye can do nothing; that he hath so boldly contradicted him, to say, they could *Baptize* with *water* without him. This is more Prophane and Scandalous, than what *Samuel Jennings* said at a Monthly Meeting in *Philadelphia*, for which he was reproved by diverse in the Meeting, and of which there is an account in Print. *To do our own Business as Men, we need not the help of the Spirit, but to do* God's *Business we need it*: But here according to *G. Whitehead*, when *John Baptized* with *water*, which was *God's* Business, it being commanded of God, he could do that without him.

Another Argument of his in the same Page, is, *It is not go Teach, and then* Baptize *them with* Water, *but go teach all Nations,* Baptizing *them; and there was a Divine and Spiritual* Baptisme *immediately attending and present with their Ministry.*

Ans. This Argument is also weak, and grounded upon a Quibble, because it is not said, *go Teach, and then* Baptize, *but go Teach,* Baptizing, *&c.* Because the word *Baptizing* is a Participle; but this hath not the weight of a Feather, it is so light, and yet with such light airy Stuff they have deceived many: For as the word *Baptizing* is *a Participle*, both in the *Greek* and *English*; so the word Translated *go*, set before *Teach*, in the *Greek* is a Participle πορευθέντες going (or having gone) Teach. Now by the like Argument, because it is not said, first go, and then Teach, but going, Teach; therefore every foot of their way, where ever they went through, tho' they were not in sight or within hearing of any People, before they came to them, they were to Preach; and by the like Argument, where it is said, *Mark.* 1. 5. *And, were all Baptized of him in the river of Jordan, confessing their sins.* It is not said, they first Confessed, and then were *Baptized*, or they were first *Baptized*, and then Confessed, according to *G. Whitehead*, in the very first instant are of *Baptizing*, they confessed their Sins, and neither before nor after. But that there was a Divine and Spiritual *Baptisme* that attended their Ministry to some, will not prove that they did *Baptize* them with the Divine and Spiritual *Baptisme*, which was the Work of *God*, and of *Christ*, and promised by *Christ* to the Apostles and other Believers; but was never commanded them to give it to others.

His Third Argument, is from *Gal.* 3. 2. *Received ye the spirit by the works of the law, or by hearing of faith,* &c. *he therefore that ministreth to you the spirit, and worketh miracles among you, doth he it by the works of the law, or by the preaching of faith?*

Ans.

Anf. He taketh it for granted; that by him that worketh Miracles among them, and Miniſtreth the Spirit unto them, is to be underſtood, *Paul*, or ſome other Man, by whom they were Converted? But *Paul* it could not be, for the words being in the Preſent Tenſe, implyeth a preſent Miniſtration of the Spirit, when *Paul* wrote that Epiſtle unto them; but *Paul* was then at *Rome*, as the end of the Epiſtle ſheweth, nor was it any other Man, becauſe they were already Converted, and had received the Spirit, before he writ that Epiſtle unto them. Therefore it is moſt proper to underſtand this; *he* to be *Chriſt*, who is the only furniſher and ſupplyer of the Spirit, together with *God*, unto the Faithful; the *Greek* word ἐπιχορηγῶν, is rendred *Prebens Suppeditans*, by *Paſor*, and doth properly ſignifie the Principal Efficient from χορηγὸς *dux chori* the Captain of the *Chorus*; but this is *Chriſt* who ſupplyeth and giveth the Spirit to the Saints, and neither *Paul*, nor any other Man. And that the Apoſtles were Miniſters of the Spirit, doth not ſignifie that they gave the Spirit, or *Baptized* with the Spirit, but that they were aſſiſted and guided by the Spirit in their Miniſtry; and that *God* accompanied their Miniſtry with his (not their) giving the Spirit unto ſuch who believed their Doctrine.

SECT. V.

I Proceed in the next place, to examine all the other Arguments I find uſed by *W. Penn*, and *R. Barclay*, againſt theſe Divine Inſtitutions that ſeem to have any ſhadow of weight.

The Firſt Argument I find uſed by *W. Penn*, *in his Reaſon againſt Railing*, in p. 107. is, *firſt, ſaith he, we know, and they confeſs that they were in the beginning uſed as Figures and Shadows of a more hidden and Spiritual Subſtance.* 2. *That they were to endure no longer than till the Subſtance was come.* Now the time of the Baptiſme *of the Holy Ghoſt,* Chriſt's *only* Baptiſme *therefore called the* one Baptiſme, *has been long ſince come, conſequently the other, which was* John's, *was fulfilled, and as becomes a fore-runner ought to ceaſe; the like may be ſaid of the Bread and Wine; for as there is but* one Baptiſme, *ſo there is but* one Bread. This ſame Argument for Matter, but in different words, is uſed by *R. B.* in the above ſaid Treatiſe, p. 7. 8.

Anſ.

[15]

Anfw. The Conclusion they both draw, *viz.* that *John's Baptisme* is ceased, may be granted, and yet it will not follow that *Water-Baptisme,* as it was practised by the Apostles and other Ministers after *Christ*'s Resurrection and Ascension is ceased; seeing there is great ground to distinguish betwixt *John*'s *Water-Baptisme,* and the Apostles, in divers weighty respects; as first the Man *Christ,* after he rose from the Dead, having all Power given him in Heaven and in Earth, Commissioned the Apostles to *Baptize,* and that with *water,* as shall be afterwards proved more fully, but *John* had not his Commission from the Man *Christ, &c.* 2. *John* did only *Baptize* them of his own Nation, and was only sent to *Israel,* but the Apostles Commission reached to all Nations. 3. *John* though he taught them to believe in him who was to come, to wit, '*Christ*'; yet he required not Faith in *Christ,* as any condition to qualifie his Disciples to receive his *Baptisme*; but the Apostles required Faith in *Christ Jesus* in all the Men and Women, as a condition qualifying them to receive their *Baptisme.* 4. We do not find that the Holy Ghost was given or promised, to them who received *John's Baptisme,* but the promise of the Holy Ghost was given to such as did duly and worthily receive the Apostles *Baptisme,* therefore *John's Baptisme* was called the *Baptisme of Repentance.* 5. It seems greatly probable, that some who had received *John's Baptisme* were again Baptized with the Apostles *Baptisme, Acts* 19. 3. 4, 5, 6. But whereas they both argue, from *John's* Words, I must decrease, but he must increase; it hath a further understanding, than barely as in relation to *John's Baptisme,* for it is said, *John* 4. 12. that *Jesus* made and Baptized more Disciples than *John,* tho' *Jesus* himself Baptized not, but his Disciples; thus, *John* decreased, and *Christ* increased, when both *Water-Baptismes* were in force, that *Christ* had more Disciples than *John,* even when *John* was living, at which he rejoyced; and as the number of Christ's Disciples increased above the number of *Johns,* before *John's* decease, so still after, and will encrease; and so will the Glory and Honour of Christ encrease above *John,* to the end of the World. But whereas they both argue, as they think so strongly both against *Water-Baptisme,* and the *outward Supper,* because of the Scripture Phrase, *one Baptisme,* and *one Bread,* which I confess did formerly carry some weight with me, and I have so argued in some of my former Books; but I have sufficiently seen the weakness of that Argument, as well as other Arguments brought both by them and me, against these Divine Institutions.

tutions. But let it be confidered, how things are faid to be one in divers fenfes and acceptations. God is one in the higheft fenfe, yet this doth not infer that there is no diftinction of the Father, Son, and Holy Ghoft, in their *relative Properties*, which are incommunicable; and *Chrift* is one, and yet this doth not prove that *Chrift* hath not two *Natures*, one of the *Godhead*, another of the *Manhood* moft glorioufly united. 3. Faith is one, yet there are divers true fignifications of Faith in Scripture, as 1. the faving Faith, 2. the Faith of Miracles which every one had not who had the faving Faith, 3. Faith objectively taken for the Doctrine of Faith, either as it is outwardly Preached or Profeffed, as in *Rom.* 1. 5. *Gal.* 3. 2. *Acts* 24. 24. Now if one fhould argue, becaufe the Scripture faith, there is one Faith, *Eph.* 4. 5. that confequently there is but one Faith, and that is the Doctrine of Faith outwardly Preached and Profeffed, and confequently deny Faith as it is an inward Grace and Virtue of the Spirit in the Hearts of true Believers, his Argument would be falfe, fo on the other hand, if another fhould argue, true faving Faith, that is, of *abfolute neceffity to Salvation*, is an inward Grace or Vertue of the Holy Spirit in the hearts of true Believers; and therefore there is no Doctrine of Faith to be Preached or Profeffed, his Argument fhould be alfo falfe, and as falfe is this way of reafoning, that becaufe the *Baptifme* is *one*, therefore that *one Baptifme* is only the inward of the Spirit, excluding the outward *Baptifme of Water*, or as to fay therefore it is only the outward *Baptifme of water*, excluding the inward *Baptifme of the Spirit*. Now, as the one Faith mentioned *Ephef.* 4. 5. Suppofe is meant the inward Grace or Virtue of Faith in the hearts of all True Believers, doth not exclude the Doctrine of Faith, outwardly Preached and Profeffed; fo nor doth the inward *Baptifme of the Spirit*, fuppofe there meant, *Eph.* 4. 5. exclude the outward *Baptifme of Water*, both being true and one in their kind, as the inward Grace of Faith is fpecifically one in all true Believers, but numerically manifold, even as manifold as there are numbers of Believers, fo the Doctrine of Faith is one in its kind, though confifting of many parts; therefore to argue as *W. Penn* doth, that *Baptifme* is one in the fame fenfe as God is *one* is very inconfiderate, which would infer that though God is *one* in fpecie, yet that there are as many Gods numerically as Believers. And notwithftanding that in *Ephef.* 4. 5. it is faid there is one *Baptifme*, yet it is not faid there or elfewhere, that there is but one *Baptifme*; for another place of Scripture mentions *Baptifmes* in the Plural Number, *Heb.* 6. 2. And indeed as weak as their Argument againſt *Water-Baptiſme* is from the Scripture words *one Baptiſme*; no leſs weak is their Argument againſt the outward Supper, practiſed with Bread and Wine, in commemoration of our Lord's Death, becauſe of the Scripture words, *one Bread*, 1 Cor. 10. 17. for in that ſame verſe, *Paul* tells of *one Bread* in a very different ſignification, even as far as the Church of *Chriſt* is not *Chriſt*; *we* (ſaid he) *being many are* one Bread; but doth it therefore follow that there is no other *Bread* than the Church; nay, for they are all partakers of that *one Bread*, which is *Chriſt*, and there is a *third Bread* that he mentions in the ſame Chapter, which is neither the one nor the other, *one Bread*, and that is the outward *Bread* that they did eat, *v.* 16. *the bread which we break, is it not the Communion of the body of Chriſt?* Even as *Chriſt* ſaid concerning the outward Bread; that it was his Body, to wit, Figuratively (ſo by the like Figure it was the Communion of his Body) but not the Body it ſelf, which too many have been ſo fooliſh, as to imagine, that the outward *Bread* was Converted into *Chriſt's* real Body, and as if *Paul* had foreſeen that many would become ſo fooliſh and unwiſe, as ſo to imagine; therefore to caution againſt any ſuch folly, he had ſaid, I ſpeak as to wiſe Men; judge ye what I ſay. But whereas, many of the People, called *Quakers*, by *Bread*, in that part of the Verſe; the *Bread* which we break, is it not the Communion of the *Lord's* Body? Will have to be mean t, not the outward Elementary *Bread*, but the Body of *Chriſt* it ſelf, in this they are under a great miſtake; for that would render the words to have a moſt abſur'd Senſe, as to ſay, the Body of *Chriſt* is the Communion of his Body; but the Body is one thing, and the Communion of that Body is another, and it were as little ſenſe to underſtand it thus; the Body of *Chriſt* is a Figure of the Communion of his Body; therefore the true ſenſe of the words is the outward *Bread* which we break is a Figure, or Sign of the Communion of the *Lord's* Body: But theſe Men are under another great Miſtake, as if by the *Lord's* Body, here were not meant his outward Body that was Crucified, and Raiſed again; but the Life, which is the Light in them, and in every Man, whether Believer, or Unbeliever. But of this great Error, I ſhall have occaſion hereafter to take notice, only at preſent let it be remembred, that by the Body of *Chriſt*, in theſe above-mentioned words, is to be underſtood the Body of *Chriſt*, that was outwardly Crucified, Dyed, and roſe again, and is a living Glorious Body, which

D   is

is the Body of the second *Adam*, the quickning Spirit, of the Virtue of which, all true Believers partake; and by their having the Communion of his Body (whether when eating the outward Bread, so that they eat with true Faith, or when they do not eat, yet believing; for the Communion of his Body is not confined to the outward eating) they have the Communion of his Spirit also, and enjoy of the manifold Spiritual Blessings of Grace, Life, and Light, sent and conveyed into their Hearts, by and through the glorified Man, *Christ Jesus*, who hath a Glorified Body; and though this Communion of *Christ's* Body is hard to be expressed, or to be demonstrated to Man's reasonable understanding, yet by Faith it is certainly felt and witnessed, with the blessed Effects of it, causing an encrease in Holiness and Divine Knowledge and Experience in all true Believers; nor is there any thing in this Mystery, or any other Mystery of the Christian Religion, that is contradictory to our reasonable understanding. But yet a little further to let them see the folly of that Argument from the Scripture Phrase, *one Baptisme, and one Body*; when *Paul* saith, *Eph.* 4. 4. There is *one Body and one Spirit*; it doth not bear this Sense, as if the Church were but one numerical Body, or one single Man, or as if there were no Body of the Man, *Christ* in Heaven, though some of their Teachers have so falsely argued; that because the Body of *Christ* is one, therefore *Christ* has no Body but his Church, and as false should their Arguing be; there is but one Spirit, and that Spirit is the Holy Ghost; therefore the Man *Christ* hath no Soul or Spirit of Man in him, and therefore Believers have no Spirits or Souls of Men in them that are Created Rational Spirits, both which are most false and foolish consequences; also when the Scripture saith, there is one Father, and one is your Father; it would be a very false consequence to infer, that therefore we have never had any outward or visible Fathers, and as false a consequence it is, from one invisible *Baptisme* of the Spirit, to argue against any outward and visible *Baptisme*, or from the outward visible *Baptisme*, being one in its kind to argue against the invisible and inward *Baptisme*, which is one in its kind also; this is an Error called by Logicians, a Transition from one kind to another, as because there is one kind of Animal on Earth, called a Dog, therefore there was not any thing else so called; whereas, there is a Fish that hath the same Name, as also a Star in Heaven.

SECT.

SECT. VI.

BUT whereas *W. Penn*, in his above mentioned Argument faith, *first we know, and they confess, that they were in the beginning used as Figures and Shadows of a more hidden Spiritual Substance.*

Ans. In this he is very short and defective in his Expreſſion, they were both appointed and uſed in the beginning, I mean from the time of *Chriſt's* Reſurrection and Aſcenſion, to be Figures and Signs of *Chriſt's* outward Body that was broken for us on the Croſs, and his Blood that was outwardly ſhed. In the firſt place, and conſequently of the inward Graces of the Spirit, and Benefits coming to Believers by his outward Body and Blood, and by the Man *Chriſt* wholly conſidered, both in Soul and Body; and whereas he faith, 2. They were no longer to endure, than till the Subſtance was come: All this ſheweth *W. Penn*'s great Miſunderſtanding of the Nature of theſe Inſtitutions, both of *Baptiſme* and the Supper, as if they only ſignified ſome inward hidden Virtue, which he calls a more hidden and ſpiritual Subſtance that was to come; and ſo were only as he calls them in his *Defence of his Key*, called, *a Reply to a pretended Anſwer*, &c. *Prenunciative and forerunning Signs*, but were not *commemorative Signs*, as well of things paſt, as of things preſent; for this is utterly falſe, that *water* in that *Baptiſme* which the Apoſtles, uſed after *Chriſt's* Reſurrection and Aſcenſion was prenunciative, and not commemorative; for on the contrary it was not ſimply prenunciative, but commemorative, as commemorating and ſignifying the Blood of *Chriſt*, that had been ſhed outwardly for the Remiſſion of our Sins, and the ſame commemoration and ſignification had the Wine, in the practiſe of the Lord's Supper, and the Bread that was broken in the Supper, ſignified (after *Chriſt's* Death and Reſurrection) his Body that was outwardly broken on the Croſs, and that outward practiſe was Inſtituted by *Chriſt* for a Memorial of his Death and Sufferings, which all true Believers in *Chriſt* ought to have freſh and lively in their Minds; to which the outward practiſe both of *Baptiſme* and the Supper is of great uſe; and the more frequent the practiſe of the Supper is, being duly uſed, as with Faith, Reverence, and Devotion, the more profitable it is. Therefore ſaid *Chriſt, as oft as ye eat this bread,* &c. As if one did ſay, as oft as ye Pray with true Faith and Fervency, it turns the more to your Spiritual Advantage. And though the Spirit of *Chriſt* in true Believers is the great and principal rememberer unto them, yet he oft doth remember them, in the ufe of that outward Practife, ufing it as a means, and bleffing it unto them, even as the Spirit ufeth the frequent outward Inftitutions and Exhortations that Minifters give to Believers as a means, and blefleth that outward means unto them alfo, the more to quicken and enlighten them; and as *Peter* faid, to ftir up the pure mind in them, by way of remembrance, which was the end of his Epiftles, and alfo of *Paul*'s Epiftles unto the Churches; and therefore it is but weakly and falfly argued by many of the People, called *Quakers*, and their Teachers; the Spirit in them is their remembrancer, and they have the more hidden and invifible fubftance in them; and therefore there is no ufe of thefe outward Signs to them; for this Argument has the fame force againft all outward Teaching, and External Acts of Worfhip. And indeed, as I have oft obferved and confidered the chiefeft Arguments ufed by thefe Men, againft thefe outward Practifes of the outward *Baptifme*, and the Supper may be as much brought againft all outward Teaching, and External Acts of Worfhip, and againft all ufe of Books, yea, of the Holy Scriptures themfelves; and the like may be faid of thefe Arguments, that are commonly in the Mouths of the People, called *Quakers*; *that Bread, and Wine, and Water are carnal things, and vifible, which may be touched, tafted, handled; whereas the Scripture faith, touch not, taft not, handle not, which are all to perifh with the ufing, and the kingdom of God is not meat and drink, but righteoufnefs, peace, and joy in the Holy Ghoft? Again, we look not at things feen, for they are temporal, but at the things unfeen, which are eternal*; and Col. 3. *If ye be rifen with Chrift, feek the things which are above, and fet your affection on things above, not on things on the earth; but Water, Bread and Wine, are things on earth; and let no man judge you in meats and drinks*, Col. 2. 17. *which are a fhadow of things to come, but the body is of Chrift?* All thefe, and the like Scriptures (I fay) may with as great fhow of reafon be brought againft all good Books, and outward Teachings, Inftructions, Exhortations, yea, againft the Books of the Holy Scriptures, which *G. Fox* hath called the Carnal and Earthly Letter, that he touched, and handled, as much as *Water*, *Bread*, and *Wine*, and is vifible; and confequently by their Argument, is not to be look'd into, nor is the Scripture, nor the beft of words uttered in Speech, or Written, the Kingdom of God, or the hidden invifible Subftance, as neither *Water*, *Bread* and *Wine*, yet all thefe have their ufe, when duly ufed on a Spiritual Account; for as words fignifie, and

hold

hold forth *Chrift*, and the inward and fpiritual Benefits that Believers have by him, to the outward hearing, fo do thefe other hold forth *Chrift*, and his fpiritual Bleffings to their Sight, Taft, and Feeling; for which reafon, antient Writers did call the outward *Baptifme* and Supper, *verbum vifible*, i. e. the *vifible word*. God having fo appointed it in his Wifdome, that the Knowledge of Divine and Spiritual things, after a fort fhould be given to us by outward Signs and Symbols, that affect our Senfes, and by our Senfes, as by fo many Doors and Windows fhould be let into our Souls, by means whereof, through the inward Operation of the Holy Spirit, the inward and Spiritual Faculties of our Souls and Minds are awakened and enabled to apprehend the Spiritual things themfelves, whofe Symbols and Emblems thefe outward Elementary things are. And none of thefe Scriptures above mentioned, have any relation to the outward *Baptifme* and Supper, which were the Inftitutions of *Chrift*, but to fuch outward things, the obfervations of which were after the Commandments and Doctrines of Men, as not only the *Jewifh* Rites, but *Gentile* Cuftoms and Traditions, alfo were touching Meats and Drinks, and other things, which the Apoftle calls, *Col.* 2. 20. 21, 22. *the Rudiments of the world*, which as they are of a perifhing nature, fo the ufe and fervice of them; but fo is not the ufe and fervice of the outward *Baptifme* and Supper, which is a holy Commemoration of our *Lord's* Death and Sufferings, and of the great benefits we have thereby, tending to excite our ardent Love and Affections to him, and to raife them up to afcend to him in Heaven; therefore though true Believers at *Chrift's* command ufe the outward things, yet neither their Minds, nor Affections are fet on them, but on him, and the heavenly Bleffings they have by him; which holy Commemoration we fhould not let dye or perifh in us, but keep alive for our fpiritual Benefit and Advantage; and as concerning, *Colof.* 2. 17. The things there mentioned, are called fhadows of things to come, fuch as the Types of the *Mofaical* Law were; but *Water-Baptifme*, and the Supper, which the Chriftians were enjoyned to practice, were fimply, not fhadows of things to come, but are commemorative Signs of *Chrift*, as he hath already come in the Body that was prepared for him, and of his Body and Blood which he hath given for us, together with the fpiritual bleflings of Grace, Life, and Light that we have by him, to make us conformable to him in holinefs, as well as to give us the pardon of our Sins, and to juftifie us, and give us a right to eternal Life. But it bewrayeth ftill great in confideration

fideration in *W. Penn*, to argue againſt the outward *Baptiſme* and Supper, as he doth in his *Defence of his Key*, above-mentioned, p. 154. *They that perſonally* (faith he) *enjoy their deareſt Friends, will not repair to their Pictures, though drawn never ſo much to the life, to quicken their remembrance of them.* His ſimilitude of a *Picture*, to which he compareth the outward *Baptiſme* and Supper is a good Argument againſt him, the Saints on Earth have not the Man, *Chriſt*, perſonally preſent with them, they have not his Body that ſuffered Death for them, and roſe again a preſent object to their outward ſight; therefore did he in his great love appoint theſe outward Signs to be a Memorial of him, until they ſhould have himſelf Perſonally preſent with them, as they will certainly have in the time appointed, and to as little purpoſe is his arguing in that ſame page, *That the true Believers were come to Mount Zion, Heb.* 12. 22. *and ſit in heavenly places in Chriſt Jeſus, which muſt be an attainment above ſigns of inviſible grace, being the life and ſubſtance of Religion; and ſo the Period and Conſummation of Types, Shadows, and ſuch ſort of Signs or Significations as are in queſtion.* Anſwer, It is a great Miſrepreſentation of the State of the Queſtion in *W. Penn*, ſo to place it as well as a weak Argument, as becauſe true Believers are come to Spiritual Attainments above Signs of inviſible Grace; that therefore there is no uſe of Signs in Religious Matters. Why then doth he ſpeak and writ ſo much in Religious Matters, for all his Words and Writings are but Signs; and he thinketh that his Brethren are come to higher Attainments than theſe Signs, yea, why doth he kneel in Prayer, and diſcover his Head when he Prayeth; what are theſe but Signs? And why ſo much ſtrife and contention about *G. Fox*'s Papers of Church Orders, and Womens Dreſſes? Are not his Brethren come to higher Attainments than theſe outward things? But it is an obſervation of many, that after *G. Fox* had taught his Followers to throw down the outward Inſtitutions of *Chriſt*, he ſet up among them his own, and ſo did perſuade them to exalt them; that whoever did not comply therewith, were to be judged by his zealous Admirers to be Apoſtates; thus *Phariſee* like, ſetting up Humane Traditions above Divine Precepts, and in ſo'doing, *W. Penn* has had no ſmall ſhare, who hath as eagerly promoted *G. Fox*'s Inſtitutions about outward things, as he hath laboured to throw down the Inſtitutions of *Chriſt*.

SECT.

SECT. VII.

TO avoid the Argument for *Water-Baptifm*, it being an Inſtitution of *Chriſt* from *Matt.* 28. 19. *Go teach all Nations*, Baptizing *them into the name* &c. he ſaith, *but no water is mentioned* page 106. Reaſon againſt Railing; *and therefore he concludes in the next* p. *that* Chriſt *commanded the Apoſtles to* Baptize *with the* Holy Ghoſt, *and the like evaſions is made by* R. B. *in the aboveſaid Treatiſe* p. 26. *where he putteth them who underſtand it of* Water-Baptiſme *to prove, that* Water *is here meant ſince the Text is ſilent of it*.

Anſ. As *water* is not mentioned, ſo nor is Baptizing with the *Holy Ghoſt* mentioned, and at this rate of arguing uſed by them, nor muſt Baptizing *with the Holy Ghoſt* be underſtood, which yet they ſo inconſiderately affirm muſt be meant here.

But *R. B.* thinks to prove, that *Baptiſme* with the *Holy Ghoſt* is here meant, arguing from the literal ſignification of the Text, which we ought not to go from, except ſome urgent neceſſity force us thereunto; but no ſuch urgent neceſſity forceth us thereunto.

Anſ. The literal ſignification of the Text, is not *Baptizing* with the Holy Ghoſt; but on the contrary, the word *Baptizing* literally ſignifieth to Waſh with Water or Dip into Water; *Yea* R. B. *grants* p. 49. *If the etymology of the word ſhould be tenaciouſly adhered to, it would militate as well againſt moſt of their Adverſaries as the Quakers*. When it is transferred from the literal ſignification to a Metaphorical, as to ſignifie the Inward and Spiritual *Baptiſme* with the Holy Spirit, it is never when ſo transferred applied to Men, as having any command ſo to *Baptize*, but wholly and only to *God* and *Chriſt*. I challenge any Man to give but one inſtance in all the Scripture, where *Baptizing* with the Spirit is ever referred to Men, either by way of Precept or Practiſe, as if ever any Man but the Man *Chriſt*, did *Baptize* with the Holy Spirit, or were commanded ſo to do; the quibble from the Greek Particle εἰς is anſwered and refuted above, as alſo his arguing from the word *one Baptiſme*; and whereas he ſaith the Name of the Lord is often taken in Scripture for ſome thing elſe than a bare ſound of words or literal expreſſion, even for his Virtue and Power. I anſwer and ſo is it oft taken otherwiſe, as the Name of God in Scripture ſignifieth himſelf, ſo the *Name* of *Chriſt* ſignifieth *Chriſt*, and that both conſidered as he is *God* and *Man*, and yet one *Chriſt*, and that to be

Baptized

Baptized into the *Name* of the *Lord Jesus* did not fignifie the *Baptifme* of the Holy Ghoft; I have proved already out of *Acts* 8. 16. Befides the *Name* of the Father is not the Holy Ghoft, as neither is the *Name* of the Son, for as the Father is neither the Son, nor the Holy Ghoft; fo, nor is the *Name* of the Father, nor the *Name* of the Son, the *Name* of the Holy Ghoft, as they are diftinguifhed by their relative properties, fo by thefe *Names*, though the *Name God* belongeth to each of them, and who are one only *God* blelled for ever. But that he further contends, that the *Baptifme* commanded here in *Matth.* 28. 19. is *Chrift*'s own *Baptifme*. I anfwer, *Chrift*'s own *Baptifme* whereof *John* makes mention, andof which he is the author and giver, is indeed the *Baptifm* with the Holy Ghoft, which he promifed unto the Apoftles to give them, and accordingly did perform; but we no where find that ever he promifed to give them Power, to give it to others, or commanded them to give it, that is wholly an unfcriptural Phrafe, and fcandalous, if not Blafphemous, to fay, that poor mortal Men hoever fo Holy could give the *Baptifme* of the Spirit, this is to give to them what was proper only to *God* and *Chrift*: why did *John* fay, *he that comes after me fhall Baptize with the Holy Ghoft*: he did not fay, they who fhould come after me, but he, intimating none had that Power and Dignity but *Chrift*, who was *God* as well as Man, and as he was *God* had this power belonging to him, and which did belong to no Men nor Creature whatfoever; and thus indeed the *Baptifme* with the Spirit is *Chrift*'s *Baptifme*, not which he commanded Men to do, but which he promifed to do, altho' the *Water-Baptifme* which he commanded his Apoftles to practife in his *Name* is alfo his, in a fecondary fenfe, as the Apoftles teaching is his, becaufe commanded by him; yet when we fpeak of *Gods* teaching according to the fenfe of that Scripture, they fhall all be taught of *God*, it is not meant the outward teaching of Men, but *Gods* inward teaching in Mens hearts; As touching his third Reafonto prove that *Baptifme* with the Holy Ghoft is meant Matth. 28. 19. *The Baptifme which Chrift commanded his Apoftles, was fuch that as many as were therewith baptized, therewith did put on Chrift, but this is not true of Water-Baptifme.*

Anf. As concerning that place of Scripture, *Gal.* 3. 7. from which this Argument feems to be taken, the place it felf reftricts it to the believing *Galatians*, as v. 26. *For yee are all the Children of God by faith in Chrift Jefus*, and all fuch as beings *Baptized* with outward *Water*, put him on by a publick Profeffion, fo by true Faith they inwardly put

put him on. To make a publick Profession of *Christ* by *Baptisme* of *Water* is to put him on, in a common Phrase of speech, as when a Man is said to put on the *Souldier*, the *Magistrate*, by putting on the Garment of a *Souldier* or *Magistrate* in which sense *Jerome* said, *Romæ Christum indui*, i.e. *at* Rome *I put on Christ*, signifying that he was there *baptized*, and it is to be noticed how *Paul* generally in his Epistles to the Churches he wrote to, calls them Saints, they being so by profession, though there might have been Hypocrites among them, and as by outward profession Men are said to be Saints, so they may be said to have put on *Christ*, when nothing by Word or Deed can appear to the contrary in a judgment of Charity.

As to his 4th. Argument that *Baptisme* with *Water* was *John*'s *Baptisme*, I have above shewn, that *John*'s *Water-Baptisme*, and the *Water-Baptisme* commanded to, and practised by the Apostles after *Christ*'s Resurrection, differed in many respects, and tho' both required Repentance as a condition in order to receive the *Water-Baptisme*, yet the later required Faith in *Christ* Crucified and Raised again, as a condition in order to receive *Baptisme*, but the former did not require that Faith. Again his arguing from their not using that form of *Baptism*, *In the Name of the Father, of the Son, and of the Holy Ghost*, who did *Baptize* with *Water* in those days of the Apostles, is as defective as his otherways of arguing on this Head.

But how doth he prove that they used not this Form? Why because *in all these places, where Baptizing (with water) is mentioned*, there is not a word of this Form, and in two places *Acts* 8. 16. and 19. 5. *that it is said of some that they were Baptized in the Name of the Lord Jesus*. But it ought to be considered, that oft in the Scriptures what is not exprest, is understood, yea that very Form expressed 8. 16. is comprehensive of the other, and if no more be expressed by him that is the Administrator, if he be found in the Faith, and that the person to be *Baptized* hath a sound Faith, that Form is sufficient, it is not exprest that the Eunuch gave any other confession of his Faith before he was *Baptized*, but that *Jesus Christ* is the Son of *God*, but will it therefore follow, that he believed no other Article of the Christian Faith but that, and confessed no other. In his further Essay to defend his assertion, that *Christ* commanded the Apostles to *Baptize* with the Spirit, he saith, Baptisme *with the Spirit*, *tho' not wrought without* Christ *and his Grace, is instrumentally done by men fitted of God for that purpose, and therefore no absurdity follows, that* Baptisme *with the Spirit should be expressed as the action of the Apostles*; for tho' it be Christ by his

E

Grace

Grace that gives Spiritual Gifts, yet the Apostle Rom. 1. 11. *speaks of his imparting to them Spiritual Gifts, and he tells the* Corinthians, *that he had begotten them thro' the Gospel,* 1 Cor. 4. 15. *To convert the heart is properly the work of* Christ, *and yet the Scripture oftentimes ascribes it unto Men, as being the Instruments, and* Paul's *commission was to turn Men from Darkness to Light.*

Ans. I acknowledge such like answers I had formerly given in some of my former Books to the like Objection; but I am come to see the weakness and defect of it; in order therefore to detect the fallacy of this assertion, that the Apostles might be as well said to *Baptize* with the Spirit, as to Beget, to Convert, to Impart some Spiritual *Gift,* &c. Let it be considered that *Baptisme* with the Holy Spirit, is not only another thing than Conversion, or imparting some Spiritual *Gift,* &c. that it is incomparably greater; for *Baptisme* with the Spirit is equivalent to the mission of the Spirit, and his Inhabitation in Believers, and his being given to them; all Spiritual *Gifts* of Faith, Conversion, Regeneration, however so true and real, are but works and effects of the Spirit, with whom Men may be said Instrumentally to work; but the giving the Holy Spirit, to which *Baptisme* with the Holy Spirit is equivalent, is of a higher Nature, than any or all these Spiritual Gifts, differing as much as the Giver differs from his Gifts: For as to Create is only proper to *God* and *Christ,* and the *Holy Ghost*: to Redeem by way of Ransome and Satisfaction to Divine Justice is only proper to *Christ,* without any concurrence of Men or Angels, so to *Baptize* with the Holy Ghost or endue therewith, or give or send the Holy Ghost, is only proper to *God* or *Christ* and not to Men so much as Instrumentally, there is no such Phrase to be found in all the Scripture, as that any Man did *Baptize* with the Holy Ghost, in any case or sense, we ought not to allow such odd Phrases so forrain to Scripture, otherwise the greatest absurdities might follow, and a Power of Creating and Redeeming might be given to Men at this rate, by adding the word Instrumentally, but as we are to allow no *Instrumental Creators or Redeemers,* so no Instrumental giver of the Holy Ghost or *Baptizers* with the same. The Holy Ghost is *God* himself, and it is too arrogant and wild to say, that Men who in respect of *God* are as Worms, can give their Creator and Maker. The Scripture indeed tells us, that the Holy Ghost was given thro' the laying on of the Apostles hands, *Acts* 8. 16. and sometimes in Preaching, and sometimes in Prayer, the Holy Ghost was given; but it was never said, that

that Men gave it or *Baptized* with it. Besides, at this rate, they may say, the Teaching that *Christ* commanded *Matth.* 28. 19. was not outward Teaching but inward, and then call it Instrumental; but what sense would be made of such an assertion, the Apostles were sent not to Teach outwardly but inwardly, by Instrumental Teaching; and one might argue as strongly, that it was not outward Teaching that *Christ* meant, *Matth.* 28. 19. why, not the least word is mentioned of outward Teaching, therefore it is not understood but only inward Teaching. If it be fit to answer, this wild inference thus, the Teaching there commanded must needs be outward, because its only Mens work to Teach outwardly, and *Gods* work to teach inwardly; the like answer is as proper to be given in relation to *Baptisme*, as it is Mens work to *Baptize* outwardly with *Water*, so it is the work of *God* and *Christ* to *Baptize* inwardly with the Spirit. And if Men be resolved to quibble and embrace any wild notion, rather than the simple Truth, had there been express mention made of *water*, *Matth.* 28. 19. that quibbling Spirit would have made a new objection, and still argued it was not material or outward *water*, but inward and Spiritual, because in many places of Scripture, *water* signifieth not outward material *water*, but inward and Spiritual.

SECT. VIII.

THERE is yet another Argument used both by *W. Penn* and *R. B.* against both *Water-Baptism* and the *Supper* in common. I shall recite it in *W. Penn*'s words (being the same in effect with these of *R. B.*) Thirdly *faith* W. Penn, *they were but the more noble among the Meats and Drinks, and diverse washings that the Apostles said, were but shadows of the good things to come; for I would not that any should be so sottish as to think that Christ came to abolish those shadows of the Jews, and institute others in their room, by no means. He came to remove, change and abolish the very nature of such Ordinances, and not the particular Ordinances only, to wit, an outward Shadowy and Figurative Religion; for it was not because they were Jewish Meats and Drinks, and diverse washings, but because they were Meats and Drinks, and outward washings at all, which never could nor can cleanse the Conscience from dead works, nor give eternal Life to the Soul, else wherein would the change be? A continuance of them, would have been a judaizing of the Spiritual Evangelical Worship, the Gospel would have been a state of Figures, Types and Shadows, which to assert or Practice, is as much as in such lies to pluck it up by the roots.*

Anf. This whole way of Arguing proceeds upon a supposed Foundation that is false, and because the Foundation is false, therefore is his Superstructure also; both which I shall briefly show: First, His supposed Foundation is false, *viz.* No Signs that is no outward things that are Symbolical, or Significative of greater and more excellent things do by any means belong to the Gospel, and Christian Religion, otherwise (as he argueth but very weakly) there would be no change, and no difference betwixt the *Jewish* Religion and the Christian, or betwixt Law and Gospel; but this doth by no means follow. For allowing that some Signs belong to the Gospel, yet there is not only a change and difference betwixt them two, but a very great change and difference, even as much as betwixt the Light of the Twilight, and the clear Light of the Sun after he is risen, or betwixt the Sun in the Morning, and the Sun when he is high in the Firmament; and if he will have the outward *Baptisme* and *Supper*, called Shadows as well as Signs; is there no difference betwixt the Shadow that the Sun casts early in the Morning, when he is but low above the Horizon, and when he is high; we know that the higher the Sun riseth, the Shadow is the less, yet still there is some Shadow; however high the Sun riseth until he come to the Zenith, or Vertical Point, at which Point there is no Shadow, but this never happeneth to us in these Northern Parts; and to apply the similitude of the Sun and Shadow to the case in hand; admit the Sun to be *Christ*, as he enlighteneth the Christian Church, or the best Christian Congregation that ever was on the Earth; did any such Church or Congregation know that Divine Sun to be risen upon them so high as the Vertical Point in this Spiritual Sense? Is not that rather the State that is reserved to the future Life? When the Shadows shall flee away, *Cant.* 2. 17. and 4. 6. What was the State of the Church in the Apostles days, after they had received plentiful Illuminations of the Holy Ghost? Did not *Paul* say concerning himself and them, now we see darkly as in a Glass, *tanquam in ænigmate* the seeing Face to Face, being reserved to the future State after Death; and as he said again, we walk by Faith, not by Sight; which is to be understood comparatively; for though it is granted that the Saints while living in the mortal Body have often sweet and precious sights and tasts of the glory of *God* and of *Christ*; yet it is not so always with them and their highest Illuminations of Knowledge do admit.

admit of some defects and obscurities, and the condition of a mortal State, as it implyeth somewhat of Shadow, with reference to their defects and shortness, in respect of the much higher and more full and perfect Attainments of glorified Saints and Angels. So in this State of the mortal Body, Shadows and Symbolical things may be, and are really of that Service to them, as the Shadow of a Curtain is, that is interposed betwixt the brightness of the Sun, and the frail sight of our mortal Bodies; And what are all words but Signs, *verba sunt signa rerum & conceptuum*; words are Signs of Things and Thoughts: So are words properly defined by Logicians and Philosophers. Now if the Gospels Dispensation under Christianity be all life and substance, and nothing else; then not only all Books and Letters, but all words possible to be uttered by the Mouths of Men, must be rejected from having any use in Gospel Worship, and instead of silent Meetings at times, there must be no other Meetings but silent Meetings; nay, nor any Meetings at all of Bodies of Men and Women outwardly Assembled; for by *W. Penn*'s way of Arguing, there is no use of them; such Meetings of Bodies reach but to the sight, and all that is or can be seen is but Carnal, and cannot reach to the Soul; all Meetings must be only within, and all Teaching within, and all Prayer and Worship within, and nothing without. But if it be granted that outward words, though Signs may be useful for the encrease of spiritual Knowledge, by the same reason the outward signs of *God's* appointment may be useful also; yea, in some sort they are more useful, when the signification of them is understood; for Example, *water* in *Baptisme* hath a nearer resemblance to the thing signified by it, than any words whatsoever; for words signifie only by humane Institution, but visible signs that are not words, bear some similitude and Analogy to the things signified, and are as it were so many Hieroglyphicks of Divine Mysteries. In short, the difference betwixt the Judaick and the Christian Dispensation stands not, as *W. Penn* would have it, that the Judaick Dispensation was an outward Figurative and shadowy Worship, and Religion, and that the Gospel hath nothing of outward in it, nothing of Figure, sign, or shadowy; for in both these Descriptions he is under a great mistake, the Judaick Religion had substance, Life and Vertue, and an inward Glory belonging to it as really as the Christian, yea, the very same in Nature; and therefore it is not a fit Definition he gives of the Judaick Dispensation and Religion; that it was an outward Figurative and shadowy Worship and Religion, the outward
part

part of it was as the shell and Cabinet, but it had an inward part that was as the Kirnel and Jewel, as all the Faithful did know, who were under that Dispensation, while it stood in force. Again, it is as really an Error on the other hand to define the Christian Dispensation to be all inward, all Life and Spirit, and Substance; that is, too Chymical and Subtile, and no wise Suits with a mortal State at least; for as our natural Bodies cannot Eat and Drink all Spirit, but require a Food more Bodily; so our Christian Religion requireth a Bodily part as well as a Spiritual. And such who through an ignorant Presumption throw away the Bodily part of the Christian Religion, lose the Spiritual, or rather never find it, but in place of the true Spirit of Christianity embrace an inward Shadow and Imagination, and oft an Antichristian Spirit, and such, I have known who had been once very Zealous in the *Quakers* way, who upon such ignorant Presumption, would come to no Meetings, hear no outward Teaching, nor joyn in any External Act of Worship; alledging all was inward, and they needed no outward thing, and God was only to be Worshipped in the inward, which are the true and proper Consequences of *W. Penn*'s Reasonings here; His Distinction of Prenunciative and Commemorative Signs I have above examined, and shewed that *Water-Baptisme*, and the outward Supper are not meerly Prenunciative but Commemorative, as commanded to be practised after *Christ's* Resurrection. The true distinction betwixt the Judaick and Christian Dispensation and Religion, consists in these following Particulars: That the Judaick Dispensation and Religion had much more of outward Figurative and Shadowy things than the Christian, the former had much, as best suited to that Time and State, the latter had but little in comparison to the former. As for Example, the Figures and Shadows of the Law were indeed many, perhaps some hundreds there were of the *Mosaical* Laws, commonly called Ceremonial, relating to Meats and Drinks, Washings or *Baptisms*, Persons, Places and Times, as Days, Weeks, Months and Years; but the Symbols and Signs under the Gospel are but few, as *Water* in *Baptisme*, and *Bread* and *Wine* in the Supper, kneeling or standing up in Prayers, and the Men uncovering their Heads may be called Decent Religious Signs of our Worship. Secondly, The Typical and *Mosaical* Precepts were not only many, but considerably chargeable and painful; the multitude of their Sacrifices were a great charge, and the Males coming there every year to *Jerusalem*, very Laborious, Circumcision of the Male Children painful, but *Water-Baptisme* and the Supper very easie,

easie, and with very little charge, and little or no pain; which chargeable and painful Service of the Law among other things, occasioned *Peter* to call it a Yoak; which neither they nor their Fathers were able to bear, *Acts* 15. 10. *And God in his wisdom saw it meet to put that yoak upon them, as suiting to that legal and typical state; and our deliverance from that Yoak is a great blessing of God.* Thirdly, These Signs and Shadows of the Law did not near so clearly and plainly hold forth *Christ*, and the Spiritual Blessings of Remission of Sins, Justification, Adoption, Sanctification, and Glorification through *Christ*; as these few plain Signs and Symbols of *water* in *Baptisme*, and *Bread* and *wine* in the *Supper* do; the words in the Form of *Baptisme* do plainly express that Great Mystery of the Father, Son, and Holy Ghost, and how these three are concerned in the things signified by the outward *Baptisme*; as namely, in the Pardon of our Sins; the Father giveth it, the Son purchaseth it, the Holy Spirit in our Hearts persuadeth us of it: Again, the form of words in the Institution of the *Supper*, *take, eat, this is my body*, &c. *and this cup is the new Testament in my blood shed for the remission of the sins of many; drink ye all of it.* There are no such plain and clear Forms of Speech holding forth *Christ* and the Spiritual Blessings we have by him, that were annexed to, or used with any of the Figures and Shadows of the Law. Fourthly, The Figures and Shadows of the Law in the use of them, had not that Plenty of Grace, and Divine and Spiritual Influence of the Holy Ghost, accompanying them generally to Believers under the Law, as doth generally accompany Believers under the Gospel; for as *Paul* declareth, it was reserved unto the days that were to come after the Judaical Dispensation was ended, wherein *God* was to shew the exceeding Riches of his Grace; and in the latter Days, *viz.* under the Gospel the Spirit was to be poured forth, as was accordingly fulfilled; and on these Accounts, especially the two last, it is, that *Baptisme* with *water*, and the outward *Supper* ought not to be numbred among the Carnal Ordinances of the Judaick Dispensation; for though the material things in some part be the same, yet the manner so differing, and the Grace and Spirit more plentiful abundantly, as is above declared, gives just cause, that the outward *Baptisme* and the *Supper*, when duly Administred, as they ought to be, and were in the Apostles Days, should not be numbred among the Carnal Ordinances, nor yet so called, but rather Spiritual; for things receive their denomination from the greater and better part: Holy Men in Scripture are called Spiritual though

having

having Bodies of Flesh; and why may not things be called Holy and Spiritual, that are used and practised by Ho'y Men wholly for a Holy End; although the things themselves be Material and External: All which being considered, it will plainly appear how weakly and rawly, both *W. Penn*, and *R. B.* have argued in this Point, and what an Impertinent Consequence *W. Penn* hath made, to infer, that to allow *Water-Baptisme*, and the outward *Supper* to belong to the Gospel, is to make the Gospel a State of Figures, Types and Shadows, which doth no more truly follow, than to allow, that because *W. Penn* hath a Body of Flesh and Blood; that therefore he is a Carnal and Bloody Man; or because the *Quakers* have Flesh and Blood as other Men; therefore there Church is a Carnal and Bloody Church; and as raw and defective is *R. B.* his way of Reasoning, p. 25, 26, 27. of the above said Treatise; that where the Author is the same, the Matter of Ordinances is the same, and the end the same; and having the same effect, they are never accounted more or less Spiritual, because of their different times. For all this is not a sufficient enumeration, to prove the one not to be more Spiritual than the other; there are diverse other great Considerations or Arguments, besides these mentioned by him so generally and overly; as in the respects above mentioned, relating to their Form and Manner, and greater Efficacy, because of the greater plenty of Grace, accompanying the latter than the former, and having greater and more excellent Effects; for who that knows, what a true Christian is, but will say he is far beyond an ordinary Religious *Jew* that had some degree of Faith in the promised *Messiah*; the Scripture comparing the *Jew* and the Christian, as the Child and the Man. And who but will say, that the true Gospel way of Ministry, as it was in the Apostles Days, and wherein they were excercised in Preaching and Prayer, did far excell the Ministry of the ordinary sincere *Jewish* Priests and Scribes, although they had one Author, and one Doctrine for Substance, and one end in their Ministry at large and in general, and also one effect in general and at large, *viz.* to instruct in Righteousness such as heard them. And though in one sense the *Jewish Baptisms*, and that practised by the Apostles after *Christ's* Resurrection had one Author, *viz.* God, yet in another sense there was a considerable difference, it being *God* or the word Incarnate, or *Christ God* Man that was the Author of the latter, but not of the former. And though the *Jewish Water-Baptisms*, and the Christian *Water-Baptisme*, which is but one, do agree in relation to t nd in some sort, yet there is a great difference in that very respect; for the' the remote end of the *Jewish Baptisms* was to signifie Remission of Sin through Faith in *Christ*; yet the proximate, or next end of those *Baptisms* was to make them legally clean, so as to be allowed to come into the Congregation of the *Jewish* Church; but the end of the Christian *Water-Baptism*, even proximately and nextly considered, is to signifie Remission of Sins, and the spiritual Cleansing by *Christ*, and also to indicate such *Baptized* Persons, and recognize or acknowledge them to be Members of the Church of *Christ*, that is more excellent and honourable as far as the Christian Dispensation excelled the *Judaick*. But that they farther argue, that *Water-Baptism* cannot reach the Conscience to cleanse it from Sin; that therefore it ought not to be practised; and because *Bread* and *Wine* in the *Supper* cannot nourish the Soul; therefore ought it not to be used in the *Supper*; they might as well have argued against the brazen Serpent, that the *Jews* at *God's* command should not have looked to it when they were poisoned with the Serpents in the Wilderness; because there was no inherent Virtue in that piece of Brass to effect any Cure; and they might argue as well against *Naaman's* going to wash in *Jordan* to be cured of his Leprosie. I know none that plead for *Water-Baptism*, and the outward *Supper*, that think there is any inherent Virtue in these outward things, either to wash or feed the Soul; the Virtue is wholly in *Christ*, whose Grace, Power, and Spirit doth accompany the due and right use of these things, as they are practised in Faith, and in Obedience to *Christ's* command. And the like way they might argue against all vocal Ministry which abounds among the *Quakers*; for no words have any inherent Virtue in them to Cure or Cleanse the Soul, or profit any more than *Water*, or *Bread* and *Wine*; it is only the Grace and Spirit of *Christ*, when it goeth along and accompanieth these outward things, whether Words, or those outward Elements, that is effectual, and maketh the use of them effectual; without which they are all but as empty Cisterns that can hold no Water.

SECT. IX.

ANother Argument of *W. Penn* against the outward *Baptism* and *Supper* is, *that therefore they are to be rejected now the false Church has got them; yea the Whore hath made Merchandize with them, and under such Historical Shadowy and Figurative Christianity, has she managed her Mistery of Iniquity unto the beguiling thousands, whose simplicity the Lord will have a tender regard to.* Ans. In this way of Arguing also he is very inconsiderate, for his Reason is of equal force against the Holy Scriptures, and all the Doctrinal and Historical part of *Christ*'s coming in the Flesh, his Death and Sufferings, &c. Why! the false Church has got all this, and makes Merchandize therewith, and therefore the Bible and the whole Historical and Doctrinal part of *Christ*'s coming in the Flesh, and his Death and Sufferings must be rejected; also all Preaching, and Praying, and Meeting together, and all external Acts of Worship must be rejected, for the same reason, because the false Church has got them all. Tho' I think it may be said, the false Church has not got either *Baptisme* or the *Supper*, in the true Administration of them; but rather a false show and likeness of them: But what hinders that the true Church may not Practise these things aright, tho' the false Practise them amiss? Should the abuse of any thing commanded by God, take away the use of it? Must Meat, Drink and Cloathing be rejected, because that many abuse them?

But he continueth to argue against them p. 110. *Reason against Railing.* Let it be considered that no other Apostle recommends these things, nor *Paul* himself to either the *Romans*, the *Corinthians* (in his first Epistle) the *Galatians*, *Ephesians*, *Philippians*, *Colossians*, *Thessalonians*, *Hebrews*, nor to *Timothy*, *Titus* and *Philemon*. Ans. If so it were that in none of these Epistles *Paul* had mentioned them, nor any other of the Apostles, which yet is not so, for I have answered it at large, what was objected from *Peter*, 1 Pet. 3. 21. as that *Water-Baptisme* is not there meant; and in the Epistle to the *Romans*, *Galatians*, *Ephesians* and *Colossians*, and in that to the *Hebrews*, *Baptisme* is mentioned, and he hath not proved that it is not *water-Baptisme* that is there meant, yet it will not follow, that therefore they are to be rejected, seeing other places of Scripture mention both the command and practice of them, so that he cannot instance one, professing Christianity, that was not *Baptized*, any where in the Scripture, after the command of *Baptism* was given by *Christ* to the Apostles; suppose there were but one Text in all the Scripture, that clearly proveth some Doctrin of the Christian Faith, were not that enough for its proof? As that one Text, that God is a Spirit is it not sufficient to prove the truth of it? And we find, but one Text of Scripture, and that is in *John* 6. that mentions the eating of *Christ's Flesh*, and drinking his *Blood*, in order to eternal Life, is not that one place enough to prove that Truth?

Ano-

Another Argument he ufeth is, p. 110. *Reaf.* &c. *That the Gentile Spirit hath treden them under foot fo long, being part of that outward Court of Religion given to them, which were left out at the meafuring of the Evangelical Temple of God,* Rev. 11. 1, 2.

Anf. It was not the outward Court, but the Holy City that the Gentiles did tread under feet: The outward Court indeed, as with refpect to that time, was not to be meafured, but left unmeafured, to-wit, during the time of the great Apoftacy. But this argueth, there was an utter Court; the not Meafuring of it feems to fignifie, that it was fhort and defective of the juft Meafure, that was originally belonging to it, as it was in the Apoftles dayes, and for a long time afterwards, until the great Apoftacy began, at leaft for the fpace of three Hundred Years and upwards from our Saviours Refurrection; But this is fo far from proving, that outward *Baptifme* and the *Supper,* fuppofe they were a part of the outward Court, were no Inftitutions of *Chrift* under the *Gofpel,* that it proves they were, for the outward Court was a part of the Temple, under the Law, and fignified that the Church of *God* under the *Gofpel* was to have that which by way of Analogie anfwered to it, as accordingly it had till the great Apoftacy came in, that made it to be for a time to be left unmeafured. But we find that in *Ezekiel,* the Temple, there defcribed, Chap 42, is defcribed with its outer Court, and is meafured; which Temple there defcribed, it not any material Temple, but the Church of *God* as it fhall be raifed up after the Apoftafie, which fhall have her outward Court in its juft meafure; and feeing the *Quakers* take themfelves to be the Church come out of the Wildernefs, and got free from the Apoftafie, and that *Water-Baptifme* and the *Supper* belongs to the outer Court, as *W. Penn* will have it; by the fame, or like Argument, they ought to reftore the true and due practice of them. But why may not their Ecclefiaftick Difcipline be reckoned as much belonging to the outer Court, as *Water-Baptifme* and the *Supper?* and if fo, why have they fet up that, (that is as much outward as *Baptifme* and the *Supper*) and not the other, which has far lefs fhow of warrant than the other?

SECT. X.

THE laft Argument *W. Penn* ufeth, or at leaft the laft that I fhall bring, and I think I have omitted none, either of his, or of *R. Barclay,* that I could find, that feem'd to require an Anfwer, is

taken

taken from Christ's *washing his Disciples Feet, and commanding them to wash one anothers Feet;* and James *commanding to anoint the Sick with Oyl; and the Apostles commanding to abstain from blood and things strangled; and that the believers sold their Possessions, and had all things common,* p. 111. Reason against Railing; *from which he infers; that seeing they who plead for the continuance of* Water-Baptism, *and the* Supper, *do not practise those things; therefore, nor should they practise the other. And the like Reasoning doth* R. B. *use in the above said Treatise, called by his* Son, Baptism and the Supper *substantially asserted; insisting upon that of* Christ's *washing the Disciples Feet, in several Pages of that Treatise, from p. 94, to 99, and on that of anointing with Oyl,* p. 115.

Ans. Upon a due consideration of things; this last Argument will have as little force as any of the former against the *outward Baptism,* and the *Supper.* That *Christ* commanded the Disciples to wash one anothers Feet, giving them an Example from his own Practice; as it was an Act of great Love and Humility in him so to do by his Example, he did enjoyn to his Disciples to practise the like Acts of Love and Humility one to another; so that what was here enjoyned the Disciples by *Christ*, was not any commemorative Sign of his Death and Sufferings, but a real Act of Love and Humility which is not tyed or confined to that particular Action that was peculiar to that Country, and an ordinary practice among the People of that Country; for the Country being hot, they used Sandals on their Feet, by occasion of which, their Feet; who used to Travel (as *Christ* and his Apostles frequently did) needed washing, not only for making them clean, but for refreshment; and when they came to lodge or stay at a place after Travel, it was usual for Travellers to have Water brought, and their Feet to be washed; as in *Gen.* 18. and 19. and what was done to them in bringing Water, and having their Feet washed; was a real Act of Love and Kindness in them that received them into their Houses, though they performed not that Office themselves, but caused it to be done by their Servants, which was a servile Act, and more usual to Servants than to Masters. But if done by the Master of the House, or by one that was not a Servant, was an extraordinary Act of Love and Humility; so here was nothing in all this of Ceremony, Sign or Figure, but all a real Act and Office of excessive Love, and most profound Humility in our Blessed *Lord* towards his Disciples, and by this exemplary Act of his, he both taught and commanded them to perform both that, and also other the like Acts and Offices of Love and Humility towards one another, which they were to do simply as

Acts

Acts of singular Virtue after his Example; and not as any Symbolical or Commemorative Sign of *Chrift's* Death and Paſſion; and accordingly we find it numbred among the Virtuous Acts of ancient Chriſtian Widows and Matrons, 1 *Tim.* 5. 10. *If ſhe have waſhed the Saints Feet:* And the like was that Cuſtom of giving a Cup of cold Water (or of cold, as the word is beſt Tranſlated) to Travellers, which was a great Act of Kindneſs and Hoſpitality in thoſe hot Countries; but none of theſe Actions, the one of waſhing the Feet, the other of giving a Cup of cold, is any ordinary Act of Friendſhip, Love, or Humility, hereaway in cold Countries, where there is either no ſuch ordinary occaſion, or uſual Cuſtom: For to do any ſuch thing hereaway, would be rather a Ceremony, than any ſubſtantial Act of either Love or Humility. But in all caſes, when occaſion is found for one Chriſtian to perform the equivalent Acts of Love and Humility towards another, or others, the Command of *Chriſt* is no doubt obligatory. But to make a Ceremony of that which was then no Ceremony, but a ſubſtantial Act of Love and Humility were altogether improper and impertinent. Next, as that in *James*, recommending the Anointing the Sick with Oyl; nor was this commanded to be done as any ſymbolical Act, or commemorative Sign, but as a mean that *Chriſt* had appointed his Diſciples to uſe towards the Sick, when he gave them power of healing them miraculouſly, *Mark* 6. 13. The abſtaining from Blood and things ſtrangled, was certainly a part, if not of the Ceremonial Law; yet of the poſitive and Judicial Laws given by the *Jews*, which the Apoſtles thought fit to enjoyn to the believing *Gentiles* at that time, to prevent the giving of Scandal to the believing *Jews*, who would have taken offence at the *Gentiles* for ſo doing. And that the practice of abſtaining from eating Blood, continued among the Chriſtians until *Tertullian's* time, is clearly evident, out of his Apology for the Chriſtians; where anſwering that abominable Charge againſt the Chriſtians, that they did eat the Blood of Infants, ſhewed that they were ſo far from that, that they did abſtain from the Blood of Beaſts. Now this abſtaining from the Blood of Beaſts, and things ſtrangled, belonging to the poſitive *Judicial* Laws given to the *Jews*; the Apoſtles might, and no doubt did ſee cauſe to enjoyn that Abſtinence to the believing *Gentiles* for a time, to prevent the Scandal of their Brethren who believed of the *Jews*. But notwithſtanding the Apoſtle *Paul* doth plainly teach, that whatever was ſold in the Shambles might be eaten; and that nothing was now unclean (provided it be not unwholſome and prejudicial to Health, as some things are) for said he, every Creature of God is good, being Sanctified by the Word of God, and Prayer, and to be received with Thanksgiving. And lastly, as to that of having Community of Goods, it was only practised at *Jerusalem*, and was a voluntary Act, not enjoyned to them, or any others; and therefore doth not oblige Christians to practise it; nor do the *Quakers* practise it more than any others. But when it was practised, it was not any symbolical Act, or commemorative Sign of *Christ's* Death and Sufferings, and of the spiritual Blessings that Believers have thereby; such as *Baptism* and the *Supper* was; and therefore to argue from the ceasing of that, or any other of the above-mentioned things, their ceasing is altogether impertinently and groundlesly argued. Before I close this Head of *Baptism*, I think fit to take some notice of this Title given by the Son to his Fathers Treating against the outward Baptism and the Supper, *Baptism and the Lord's Supper substantially asserted*. A Man might as well having writ a Book against all outward Teaching and Ministry, and against all vocal Prayers, and all external Acts of Worship, and against all outward Meetings of the Bodies of Believers, give it this Title; *True Teaching and Ministry, true Prayer and Worship, true assembling together, substantially asserted*; and all this by throwing aside all outward Teachings of Men, however so well divinely Gifted and Qualified, and all outward Ministry, and all external Acts of Worship and outward Assemblies of Persons, and telling us the true substantial Teaching and Ministry is only inward; the true substantial Worship is inward; and the true substantial Assemblies and Congregations of Believers is only inward in the Heart and Spirit; which manner of dealing, as it would not a little tend to the decay, if not rather the total destruction of the inward and substantial parts of all these things; so it is against the Practice of the People called *Quakers*, who are as much for outward Teaching, and an outward Ministry after their own way, and external Acts of Worship in outward Meetings and Assemblies, and other outward Forms of Church Discipline and Government, set up by their Leaders, and especially by *G. Fox*, as any other People, divers of which outward Forms set up by them, and greatly contended for against others of their Brethren, who said, they saw no need of them, but thought the inward Principle abundantly sufficient without these outward things, have less ground from Scripture than the practie of *Water-Baptism*, and the outward *Supper* have. And if only the substance of things must be regarded,

garded, and all useful and convenient adjuncts and accidents of them rejected and thrown off; then all the *Quakers* (at this odd way of arguing) may throw away their Cloathing and go naked; pretending they are no substantial Parts of them, but only accidental; and by the like Reasoning they may throw away their Estates and worldly Goods, as being no substantial Parts of them as they are Men, or rational Creatures. But what hurt Religion would suffer, by throwing off, and laying aside all outward Teaching, and all outward Acts of Worship, all sober and intelligent Persons, that have the least true sense of Religion, do know. And though the true Christian Religion may consist without these External Things of *water-Baptism*, and the *Supper*, as in respect of its Essentials, and Men and Women may be true Christians without them, and they may be more tollerably wanted at certain occasions, than outward Teaching, and other External Parts of Religion, as where they cannot be practised without great mixtures of Superstition and Idolatry, as in Popish Countries, or other Places where they cannot be duly had and practised according to their due Institution, or where fit and due Administrators are wanting to Administer them; yet all this is no Argument against their being divine Institutions, and really serviceable to all, who can have the due and right use of them; they being proper and useful means to preserve the Christian Doctrin Faith and Religion in the World, as duly practised as useful Appendices and Concomitants to the outward Ministry and Preaching of the Word; and it is not to be questioned, had the right and due practice of them been continued among Professors of Christianity, and a due regard had been preserved among them, chiefly and primarly to the things signified by them, and secondarily to the outward Signs, so that all possible care had been used, that *Power and Form* had gone along together, and all scandalous and unworthy Persons plainly known to be such, as well as ignorant Persons, not duly instructed in the Essentials of Christian Religion had been excluded and debarred from the use of them; that the continuance of them in the manner, as above described, would have been of singular use to have preserved the Christian Doctrin, Faith and Religion, sound and free from the great Corruptions that have crept in to the great Corrupting and Adulterating both the Doctrin and Worship as it hath been for many Ages past among Professors of Christianity; as it hath been already proved, and yet may be further proved against them.

SECT.

AND it is morally imp.ssible, that any People practising these things duly, having their true and proper Signification truly and faithfully taught them, and inculcated into them on all occasions when they are used, as well as at other convenient Seasons, ever could or can lose the Doctrin and Faith of *Christ* Crucified, or that that Doctrin and Faith can ever be made as an indifferent thing among them, as it is made by many of the People, called *Quakers*; yea, not only so, but by some of their chief Teachers and Leaders, now bearing great Sway among them; as a thing not only, not very necessary, but contrary to the Apostles Doctrin, *Rom.* 10. Witness some very express Passages in a Book of *G. Whitehead*'s, and *George Fox* the younger; called, *Truth defending the Quakers and their Principles*----Writ (say they) *from the Spirit of Truth in* G. Whitehead, *and* G. Fox *the younger.* (Judge, Christian Reader, if these Men have not belyed the Spirit of Truth, to father such gross Untruth, and Antichristian Sayings upon the Spirit of Truth as are contained in these Passages, hereafter to be quoted, and many others of the like nature that might be produced out of that vile Pamphlet, above named) *Printed at* London, *for* Tho. S mmons, *at the* Bull *and* Mouth, *near* Aldersgate, 1659.

In p. 65 of that Book, they bring in one *Christopher Wade*, saying, *Christopher Wade* affirmeth that our blessed Saviour doth instruct Men to lay fast hold of, and to abide in such a Faith which confideth in himself, *being without Men* To this they answer.

Ans. *That's contrary to the Apostles Doctrin, who Preached the Word of Faith that was in their Hearts, and the Saints Faith stood in the Power of God, which was in them.* Note Reader, this Assertion of *C. Wade,* blamed by them, as being contrary to the Apostles Doctrin, is so far from being contrary thereunto, that there can be nothing more agreeable, as appeareth in the words of the Apostle *Paul* in the very next verse following; where after mentioning the word of Faith, in Verse 8, which was nigh in the Mouth, and in the Heart; he adds in the 9th and 10th verses. *That if thou shalt confess with thy mouth the Lord Jesus, and shalt believe in thy heart that God hath raised him from the dead; thou shalt be saved; for with the heart man believeth unto righteousness, and with the mouth confession is made unto salvation.*

Again,

Again, They bring in *C. Wade* (see there page 66) saying, *C. Wade*, p. 14. hath affirmed that the *Lord* hath bought us, and Redeemed us with the precious Blood of his Humanity; and faith, your imagined *Christ* being a mere Spirit, never had any Humane Blood to Redeem you with; and to prove it, he brings 1 *Pet.* 1. 19. now see their Answer.

Ans. That Scripture, 1 *Pet.* 1. *Hast thou perverted, as thou hast done other Scriptures, to thy own destruction; for there he witnessed to the blood of the Lamb, which redeemed them from their vain conversation;* but doth not tell of humane Blood to Redeem them with. For that which is Humane is Earthly; but *Christ* whose Blood is Spiritual, is *Lord* from Heaven; and he is not an imagined Spirit, but a true Spirit. And what say'st thou to this? Was that Humane Blood, which *Christ* faith, *except a man drink he hath no life in him;* and which cleansed the Saints from all Sin, who were Flesh of *Christ's* Flesh, and Bone of his Bone? Note, Any intelligent Reader cannot but know that *Christopher Wade* by the Blood of *Christ's* Humanity, meant the Blood of the Man *Christ* that was born of the Virgin; and by the Humanity, he meant the Manhood of *Christ*, which of late years *G. Whitehead* hath in Print owned, even the words Humanity of *Christ*; and yet never to this day hath retracted his vile Doctrin in this and other his Books, whereof I have given some account in my first and second Narrative, &c. at *Turners-Hall.* Nay, it is below him to retract any Errors that would reflect upon his Infallibility; he is not changed, *as God is the same, and Truth is the same, so the* Quakers *are the same,* and by consequence so is *G. Whitehead* the same, as *John Pennington* hath affirmed in one of his late Prints.

Again, In p. 23. of that abovementioned Book, they answer a Question thus?

Q. 43. When you tell us that you have Faith in *Christ;* do you mean *Christ* whose Person is now ascended into Heaven above the Clouds; or do you mean only a *Christ* within you?

Ans. Here thou wouldst make two *Christ's,* a *Christ* whose Person is above the Clouds, and a *Christ* within, but how provest thou two such *Christs?* We have Faith in that *Christ* that descended from the Father, who is the same that ascended far above all Heavens, that he might fill all things; and this *Christ* we witness in us who is not divided. Note, I need not make any Commentary on these words; the Man that asked the Question did not in the least insinuate that there were two *Christ's,*

G but

but 'tis plain it was *G. Whitehead*'s Sense; that to own *Christ*, whose Person is now Ascended unto Heaven above the Clouds, and to own *Christ* within, is to make two *Christs*: But seeing there is but one *Christ*, that is, only (according to *G. Whitehead*'s Notion) within, and not a Person now Ascended above the Clouds; it is plain, he doth not own any such Person Ascended into Heaven above the Clouds, nor Faith in any such Person; and no wonder that he oppose Faith in *Christ's* Person without us, when he opposeth the Being of any such Person; for the object of Faith being destroyed or denyed, the Act of Faith must be destroyed or denyed also; both which we see he hath plainly done in this Book; and if in some of his latter Books he seems to be of a better Faith; yet who can believe him to be sincere, until he retract and comdemn the vile Errors in this and other of his former Books which have infected thousands of the poor ignorant People, called *Quakers*, whom he hath led into this Ditch of Unbelief? and yet for danger of loosing his Reputation of Infallibility, and of being found from the beginning; he will not do any thing to confess his former Ignorance and Unbelief, which might be a great means to lead that poor People out of that Ditch, into which he had formerly led them. And how he will answer it at the great Day of Judgment for this great Sin and Neglect, to make amendment, so as to correct his former gross Errors, and labour to undeceive those whom he had formerly deceived; he has great need to consider it; and I sincerely wish that a Heart may be given him to do it, and that by true Repentance he may be humbled before the *Lord*, and obtain forgiveness. But he hath given us a very late Instance that he is not changed really in his false Faith and Persuasion from what he was when he wrote that Book, near 40 years past, which instance is this. He hath blamed *G. K.* for undervaluing the Light within, as not sufficient to Salvation, or not sufficient without something else, that is *Christ Jesus* without us, Suffering and Dying outwardly for us, as in his late Antidote, Printed 1697. p. 28. compared with p. 27. *ad finem.* Judge Reader, of what little necessity or value he makes of the Man *Christ* without us, and of his Death and Sufferings, Resurrection and Intercession in Heaven, by this most unsound Notion of his, for which he hath got a late Patron and Assistant, a Clergy Man of the Church of *England* formerly, though not in present Office, one that calleth himself *Edmund Ely*'s, who hath Printed lately two half Sheets in Vindication of *G. Whitehead*'s vile Error, and blaming my Christian Assertion: The

Title

[43]

Title of one of his half Sheets being this; *G. Keith*'s saying that the Light within is not sufficient to Salvation without something else proved to be contrary to the Foundation of the Christian Religion. These two half Sheets are printed and sold by *T. Soule* the *Quakers* Printer, next door to their Meeting-house in *White-heart* Court in *Grace-church-street*, 1697. By which it appears they are very fond of this Patron to their Cause, and particularly that *G. Whitehead* is so, by the Commendation he gives of him in his late printed Antidote.

However this may seem to some an improper Digression; yet if they well consider the occasion of it, they will (if Impartial) acknowledge it both proper and convenient.

SECT. XII.

AND hereby it may easily appear what Spirit hath Acted the first Teachers that appeared among the *Quakers*, as chiefly *G.F.* and *G.W.* to oppose so keenly and earnestly the practice of those two Divine Institutions of *Water-Baptism* and the *Supper*; namely, to draw People into a forgetfulness of all Faith in *Christ* without us, as he dyed and rose again, and is Ascended into Heaven; for the proper Memorials of *Christ* Crucified, being rejected and laid aside as well as the Doctrin it self not only, not Preached but opposed, as contrary to the Scripture, the drift and aim of that Spirit that hath Acted them both against the one and the other, is plainly manifest, and how its opposing the Doctrin of Faith in the Man *Christ* without us, is the great cause of its opposing these external Practices which are such proper means, together with the Doctrine to propagate and preserve the true Christian Faith in the World. And indeed upon that Hypothesis, or Foundation laid by their principal Teachers, that there is no need of Preaching Faith in the Man *Christ* without, for Remission of Sin, and eternal Salvation; but the only thing needful is the Light within, as it universally enlighteneth all Mankind, either to be Preached, or Believed, as a late Writer against them hath well observed, these outward Practices of *Water-Baptism*, and the outward *Supper* are useless and insignificant Formalities, for they were never appointed to signifie Remission of Sin, Justification, and Salvation, only by obedience to the Light within; excluding the necessity of Faith in the Man *Christ* without us; whose alone Obedience unto Death for us, is the only meritorious Cause of the Remission of our Sins, of Justification, and eternal

G 2   nal

nal Salvation; and of all that inward Grace and Virtue of the Holy Spirit whereby we are inwardly Sanctified, and made meet to receive that eternal Inheritance. But though the Spirit that first appeared to Act in these Men, the first Teachers and Leaders of that People, did prove it self to be Antichristian, by opposing the Memorials of *Christ* without us; yet many simple and honest hearted People knew nothing of this design, and however in part leavened with that Spirit in respect of its opposition to these outward Institutions of *Baptism* and the *Supper*; yet by *God's* great Mercy were preserved from being prevailed upon by it, to oppose the Doctrine and Faith of *Christ* as he outwardly Suffered, Dyed, and Rose again, and is in Heaven, our Intercessor, among whom I can justly and uprightly number both *R. B.* and my self; both of us having been preserved found in our Faith, as touching the Faith in *Christ* without us, however otherwise hurt and byassed by them, in relation to these two outward Institutions of *Baptism* and the *Supper*; and my Charity leads me to believe that, if *R. B.* had lived in the Body to this day, to see the ill effects that his Writing against these Divine Institutions have had, and the bold opposition that many have of late, more than formerly made to the necessity of the Faith in *Christ* Crucified, and the Preaching of it even here in Christendom, since the Question hath been more distinctly stated betwixt my Opposers and me, touching the necessity of the Faith asserted by me, and opposed by them, he would have plainly seen and readily acknowledged his Error in Writing against these Divine Institutions.

There is yet another of their Teachers, who is of late years become a Person of no small Note among the Quakers, *viz. John Gratton,* whom I cannot well pass without observing his Ignorant and Inconsiderate way of Arguing against these Divine Institutions, especially as touching one of his main Arguments he hath framed from a most false and perverse Understanding of that place in *Heb.* 6. 1, 2. *Therefore leaving the Principles of the Doctrin of Christ, let us go on to Perfection*; where in his Book called *John Baptist decreasing,* Printed many years ago, and Re-printed in the year 1696, he layeth the Foundation of his Argument against *Water-Baptism,* upon the word in that place LEAVING, which he hath caused to be Printed more than once in his Book in Capital Letters (for a Monument it will be of his gross Ignorance, and yet bold Presumption thus to pervert the Holy Scripture) from thence inferring that *Water-Baptism* is to be left off and laid aside; for thus he argues, p. 47. of the last Edition, 1697. If they had

[45]

had been commanded by *Christ* to have been used to the Worlds end; then why should *Paul* (for so I call that Author) have been so earnest at that day, which was soon after *Christ's* Ascension, to have had them then *to leave them*, and to go on to a more Manful, Powerful, perfect State? Ans. At this rate of Arguing, not only *Water-Baptism*, but the *Baptism* of the Holy Spirit is also to be left; for the Author mentions the Doctrin of *Baptisms* in the Plural Number; which *John Gratton* most unfairly and falsly quotes in the Singular, *Baptism* for *Baptisms*: Also by the same Argument, *Repentance from dead works and faith towards God, the resurrection of the dead and eternal judgment*, are all to be left off from being Preached or Believed: But the true Sense is obvious, of the word leaving, *i.e.* not to Treat, or Write upon these first Principles further at present, but to Treat of other things; as when a Man hath laid the Foundation of a House, he goeth on to Build a Superstructure upon it.

And as Ignorant and Impertinent doth he discover himself to be in his other Treatise (preceeding the other) of *Baptism* and the *Supper*; where from the Word *Elements*, used in *Gal.* 4. 3, 9. he concludes that *Water-Baptism* is one of these beggerly Elements *Paul* opposed; because *water* is an Element; and after this rate divers others of their Teachers have Argued; but the Word Translated Elements there, *Gal.* 4. 3, 9. hath no relation to the *Water-Baptism*, nor to the Element of *water*; but to Principles and Doctrins of the *Jews*, relating to the *Jewish* Rites and Ceremonies; the *Greek* Word, ϛοιχεῖα, is applyed no less to the Principles of the Christian Doctrin of *Christ* and Oracles of *God*; which therefore by his Argument, being Elements, are to be thrown aside. As for his other Arguments in those two Treatises against the outward *Baptism* and the *Supper*; they are no other that I can find, but such as are above mentioned in my Reply to those of *William Penn*, and *Robert Barclay*, and therefore one Answer will serve both to them and him.

PART.

PART II.

SECT. I.

The Arguments against the outward Supper *examined and Refuted.*

Thus having finished my Examination, and Refutation of the Arguments of the above mentioned Persons against *Water-Baptism*, and the outward *Supper* in general, I think fit to bring to the like Examination, what *R. B.* hath more particularly Argued against the outward *Supper*; as being not any longer to continue, but until *Christ's* inward coming, to arise in their Hearts, and give a plain Refutation of the same.

In the beginning of the Chapter, or Head, wherein he discourseth concerning the Body and Blood of *Christ*, although he saith truly, that the Communion (*i. e.*) the Participation thereof is inward and Spiritual; yet he was under a great mistake, to affirm that the said Body and Blood of *Christ*, whereof true Believers do participate, is only inward; which he afterwards explains to be that Light and Seed in every Man; as he expresseth plainly in several places, as p. 61, of the above said Treatise, and p. 65, where he saith----and that *Christ* understands the same things here, (*viz. John 6.*) by his Body, Flesh, and Blood, which is understood, *John* 1. *by the light that enlighteneth every man, and the life,* &c. And p. 77. he chargeth it to be an Error to make the Communion, or Participation of the Body, Flesh and Blood of *Christ*, to relate to that outward Body, Vessel, or Temple that was Born of the Virgin *Mary*, and walked and Suffered in *Judea*; whereas it should relate to the Spiritual Body, Flesh and Blood of *Christ*, even that Heavenly and Celestial Light and Life, which was the Food and Nourishment of the Regenerate in all Ages, as we have (said he) already proved.

Ans. In this he was in a great Error, to make the Eating, or Participation of *Christ's* Flesh and Blood to have no relation to *Christ's* outward Body of Flesh and Blood that was Born of the Virgin, and Suffered Death for our Sins on the Tree of the Cross. For the Regeneration of Believers, and Justification, with all the Spiritual Blessings of Life and Light, and inward Divine Virtue and Might, wherewith they

they are inwardly Refreshed and Nourished by *Chrift*, hath a moft near and immediate Relation to *Chrift's* outward Body and Blood, and to his coming in that outward Body; becaufe that moft Holy and Perfect Obedience of *Chrift* which he performed in that Body, and became Obedient to the Death of the Crofs, was and is the procuring and meritorious Caufe of all that inward Grace, Virtue, Light and Life, whereby Regeneration was wrought in any, in any Age of the World, either before or fince *Chrift* came in the Flefh, as well as it was and is the procuring and meritorious Caufe of their Juftification, and the Remiffion of their Sins. For *Chrift* Died as well for the Sins of thofe who lived in the Ages before he came in the Flefh, as fince, and they had the fame Benefits by his Death, and by his Body and Blood, that we have; the fame inward Grace and Light to Regenerate them, as the fame Mercy and Favour to Juftifie them, and give them the Remiffion of their Sins, which they received through Faith in *Chrift*, as he was to come in the Flefh without them; and whole *Chrift* is the Food of true Believers; I mean *Chrift*, not only confidered as the Word fimply, but as the Word made Flefh. And having taken or affumed the Seed of *Abraham*, and the true Nature of Man into fuch a high Union, as that the Godhead of the Word, and the Manhood affumed thereby is but one *Chrift*; and as fuch is the Food of all true Believers, both as he outwardly came in the Flefh, and as he is inwardly come the Light and the Life in them; and Believers Eating of *Chrift*, is their Believing in him, and by their Faith being United to him, and he to them; fo that he dwells in them, and they in him. And though it may be owned, that Believers Feeding upon *Chrift's* Light and Life, Metaphorically and Allegorically fpeaking, that Light and Life may be called according to Scripture, Meat and Drink, and Flefh and Blood of *Chrift*, as it hath many other fuch Metaphorical Names; fuch as, Milk, Honey, Wine, Marrow and Fatnefs, Oyl, *&c*. All which Names are given, becaufe of Men's Weaknefs; and that they have not proper Words to exprefs Divine Things by; yet that ought not to make us reject and lay afide *Chrift's* outward Body of Flefh and Blood from having any Relation to the Saints feeding upon him. Nor do the Arguments brought by *R. B.* here, prove in the leaft what he intends, as the following Examination of them will fufficiently (I hope) manifeft. He begins with a Quotation out of *Auguftine*, in his Tractat, *Pfalm* 98. *The words which I fpeak unto you are fpirit and life, underftand fpiritually what I have fpoken; ye fhall not eat of*

this

this body which ye see, and drink this blood which they shall spill that shall crucifie me. I am the living bread which have descended from heaven; he called himself the bread which descended from heaven, exhorting that they might believe in him, &c. Ans. It is evident from these last Words, that by *Eating*, *Augustine* meant in one Sense Corporal *Eating*, and in another Sense Believing, as elsewhere *Tract. 25. ad cap. 6. Johan. Hoc est opus Dei*, ut quid paras dentem & ventrem? crede & manducasti: Credere enim in eum, hoc est, comedere panem & vinum, qui credit in eum manducat eum; in *English* thus, *why preparest thou thy Teeth and Belly? believe and thou hast eat; for to believe in him is to eat the Bread and Wine; who believeth in him eateth him.* Both these Quotations are good against the *Papists*; who hold that Believers eat the Body of *Christ* Corporally with their Mouths; but say nothing against this Spiritual Way of Eating *Christs* Body, but plainly confirm it: The plain Sense therefore of *Augustin's* Words, Quoted by *R. B.* is this; *Ye shall not eat Corporally with the outward Mouth, the Body of Christ which ye see, but ye shall eat it Spiritually, that is, believe with a sincere Faith, which the Spirit of God worketh in you; that Christ shall give his Body that ye see (speaking then to the* Jews*) to be broken for you, and his Blood, even the Blood of that Body to be shed for you.* And in so Believing ye shall eat my Body, and drink my Blood, that is, ye shall be united to me, and I to you, that I shall abide in you, and ye shall abide in me; which Sense doth evidently agree with our Saviour's Words, *John* 6. 29, 47. And indeed to Exclude Christ's outward Body of Flesh and Blood, from having any Relation to this place of Scripture, as no way concerned in the Sense of these Words of it, *John* 6. 53. is plainly to Exclude *Christ* as he outwardly came in that outward Body, from being the Object of our Christian Faith; for seeing Eating here signifieth Believing by *Agustine's* Quotation, approved by *R. B.* if this Spiritual Eating, which is our Believing, respects not the Body of *Christ* that was outwardly Slain; then *Christ* as he came and Suffered in that Body, is no Object of the Christian Faith, which is most absurd; and none that is in the least acquainted with *Augustin's* Writings, can say it ever was his meaning, to deny the Body of *Christ* that was outwardly Slain, to be any wise Concerned in the Christian Faith; for *Augustine* was a most zealous Asserter of the Necessity of *Faith* in *Christ*, as he came in that Body, in order to our Salvation, against the Heresie of *Pelagius* who denied it, and Writ many Books against that Heresie, now Revived by many of the *Quakers* Teachers; tho what *R. B.* hath Writ here, I impute

pute to his Inadvertency, and do not charge him with the *Pelagian* Herefie for the fame, becaufe from other Places of his Writings, I can prove that he made the Faith of *Chrift's* giving his Body to be Slain for us, neceffary to our Salvation, and a part of the Chriftian Belief.

SECT. II.

AND as Inadvertent and Miftaken as *R. B.* was in his Quotation of *Auguftine*, concerning *Chrift's* Flefh and Blood; no lefs hath *W. Penn* been, [p. 314. *of his Rejoynder to* J. F.] in his Quotation of Bifhop *Jewel*, in his Sermon upon *Jof.* 6. 1, 2, 3. Who fpeaking of what *Chrift* was to the *Jews* in the Wildernefs, fays thus: *Chrift had not yet taken upon him a Natural Body, yet they did eat his Body; he had not yet fhed his Blood, yet they drank his Blood?* St. Paul faith, *all did eat the fame Spiritual Meat; that is, the Body of Chrift, all did drink of the fame Spiritual Drink, that is, the Blood of Chrift; and that as truly as we do now.* And whofoever did then fo Eat, lived for ever, I think (faith *W. Penn*) a Pregnant and Apt Teftimony to *Chrift's* being the *Chrift* of *God* before his coming in the Flefh. *Anf.* But this doth not prove that by *Chrift* here, *B. Jewel* meant only the Light within in thefe *Jews*, and by his Body and Blood only, that Light within, or Seed or Principle, as *W. Penn* would have it. All that are in the leaft acquainted with the Doctrine of the Church of *England*, of which *B. Jewel* was a Zealous Defender, as in his Apologie for the fame appeareth, or with *B. Jewel's* Writings, know well that the Senfe which *W. Penn* hath here put on *B. Jewel's* Words, never came into his Remoteft Thoughts; but it is no wonder that he fhould fo mifunderftand and mifconftrue *B. Jewel's* Words, when he doth fo ufe the Scriptures themfelves. *B. Jewel's* Senfe is Obvious; *Chrift* had not taken upon him a Natural Body, yet they did Eat his Body, *viz.* by Faith, believing that in the time appointed of *God*, he would take a Body, and give up that Body to be Slain for their Sins; he had not yet fhed his Blood, yet they drank his Blood, *viz. By faith believing, that after he fhould take flefh and blood in the fulnefs of time, he would give his blood to be fhed for the remiffion of their fins; and by this faith all the faithful among them had Chrift dwelling in them by his fpirit; and did know and witnefs his fpirit to regenerate and fanctifie them, to quicken and refrefh them, and nourifh them, as meat and drink doth refrefh and nourifh the body of man.* As for his Quotations out of *Jofhua Stryg*, and others; its no wonder he doth fo Magnifie them, feeing its but too evident the *Quakers* have sucked that Poisonous Milk out of the Breasts of such Men who have been in the same Errors before them. But to return to *R. B.* his Arguments, whereby he laboureth, but to no purpose, to prove that the Flesh there mentioned, *John* 6. 53. &c. hath no Relation to his outward Flesh. First, saith he, (p. 63) *because that it is said, both that it came down from Heaven; yea that it is he that came down from Heaven.* Now all Christians at present, generally acknowledge that the outward Body of *Chrift* came not down from Heaven; neither was it that part of *Chrift* which came down from Heaven.

Anf. 1. By Himself that came down from Heaven, who is called by *Paul* the second *Adam*, the *Lord* from Heaven, Heavenly, the quickning Spirit, cannot be meant the inward Principle of Light in Men, abstractly considered from the Fountain of it, which dwelt in the Man *Chrift*, but chiefly the Light as in him; and consequentially that which Men receive out of his Fulness, according to their several Measures: And as our Regeneration and Salvation have a necessary Dependance on that fulness of Light, Life and Grace that dwells in him, out of which we receive our several Measures; so they have a necessary respect to the Man *Chrift*, both Soul and Body, in which that fulness dwelleth; because the Soul and Body of *Chrift* (even his outward and visible Body) was concerned in that great Work of our Redemption, in what he did and Suffered for us. Therefore *God* hath Exalted the same Man *Jesus Chrift* both in Soul and Body, in Unity with his Godhead, to be a Prince and Saviour to give Repentance and Remission of Sin, Grace and Glory, and all Spiritual Blessings to all that shall be saved. This, ancient Writers have explained by the Example of a red hot Iron exceedingly burning and shining; the *Fire* and *Light* in the same answering to the *Godhead*, and the *Iron* answering to the *Manhood*. Now when this fired Iron burns, or lightens any Stick of Wood that is applied to it; it is not the Fire only without the Iron, nor the Iron only without the Fire; but both joyntly that have an Operation upon the Wood to Kindle and Lighten it; even so, it is the Godhead of *Chrift* in Unity with his Manhood (consisting of Soul and Body,) that wrought that outward Redemption for us, and doth inwardly produce in us the blessed Effects of it by his Spirit, in Renewing and Sanctifying us, Justifying us, and giving us Eternal Life and Glory.

Anf. 2. Because *Chrift's* outward Body of Flesh was Miraculously Conceived by the Power of the most High, and in that respect had a

Hea-

Heavenly Original, as well as that it was really the Woman's Seed, and part of the Virgins Subſtance; therefore it may be ſaid to be from Heaven, and to be Heavenly as well as Earthly, as Wheat and Barly, and other Grains that Grow in *America*, which come Originally from *England*, are called *Engliſh* Grain, even in *America*, though they are alſo *American* Grain, being produced out of the Soil of *American* Earth. Secondly, ſaith he, p. 63. and to put the Matter out of doubt, when the Carnal *Jews* would have been ſo underſtanding it, he tells them plainly, *v.* 53. *It is the Spirit that quickneth, the Fleſh profits nothing*. Anſ. Nor doth this prove his Aſſertion; the Error of the Carnal *Jews* was, that they ſuppoſed *Chriſt* meant they were to eat his Body Corporally with their Bodily Mouth; but if they had underſtood that he meant not a Corporal Eating, but a Spiritual and Metaphorical, they had not erred in ſo thinking; his Quotation approved by him out of *Auguſtine*, proves that by eating here, *Chriſt* meant believing in him, as he was to Dye for the Sins of the World, and as he was to give his Body to be broken for them, and his Blood to be ſhed for the Remiſſion of the Sins of all that ſhould believe in him, and for the giving Eternal Life to them both in Soul and Body. Thirdly, (Saith he) p. 63. 64.) *This is alſo founded upon moſt ſound and ſolid Reaſon; becauſe that it is the Soul, not the Body that is to be Nouriſhed by this Fleſh and Blood; now outward Fleſh cannot Nouriſh nor Feed the Soul; there is no Proportion nor Analogy betwixt them; neither is the Communion of the Saints with God, by a Conjunction and mutual Participation of Fleſh, but of the Spirit; he that is joyned to the Lord, is one Spirit, not one Fleſh; for the Fleſh (I mean outward Fleſh, even ſuch as was that wherein* Chriſt *lived and walked, when upon Earth; and not Fleſh, when tranſpoſed by a Metaphor, to be underſtood Spiritually) can only partake of Fleſh, as Spirit of Spirit; as the Body cannot Feed upon Spirit, neither can the Spirit Feed upon Fleſh*. Anſ. Here alſo he Argueth very Weakly and Fallaciouſly; that which deceived him, and occaſioned his great Miſtake, which he embraced as a ſolid Reaſon; was by Arguing from the ſtrict literal Senſe of Nouriſhing and Feeding, to the Metaphorical and Figurative; which all true Logicians, and Maſters of ſolid Reaſon will ſay is unlawful, as alſo to Argue from the *natural Feeding* or *Nouriſhing* to the *ſpiritual*. To his Argument then I anſwer; outward Fleſh cannot Feed the Soul Naturally, I grant; Spiritually and Metaphorically, I deny; now the Eating, Feeding, and Nouriſhing meant, *John* 6. 53. is not Natural, but Spiritual and Metaphorical; the Word Eating

ting fignifieth Believing. And whereas he fpeaketh of the Feeding of the Spirit, or Soul of Man, that it cannot be the Flefh of *Chrift* that can Feed it, but the Spirit, fo as to be its Food; by Food here we muft underftand it Metaphorically, even as *R. B.* hath confeffed; that the Spirit of *Chrift* is not properly, but Metaphorically called Flefh. So the Souls of Believers Feeding upon the Spirit of *Chrift*, is alfo Metaphorical; for if by the Spirit of *Chrift*, he meant the Godhead; how can the Godhead, which is an *Infinite Being* in all refpects be the Food f the Soul or Spirit of Man that is Finite, ftrictly or literally underftood without a Metaphor? much more may I ufe his Argument againft his own Affertion; there is lefs Proportion or Analogie betwixt the Infinite Creator, and the Soul that is a Finite Creature, than is betwixt the Flefh of *Chrift* and the Soul. Befides, if we argue from the ftrict and literal Nicety of the Words *Food*, *Feed*, and *Nourifhment*; that which is the Food and Nourifhment of a Body, becomes a part of its very Subftance and Being; fhall any therefore conclude that becaufe *God* is the Food and Nourifhment of the Souls of the Saints; that therefore he becomes a part of their Souls? We know *George Fox* was blamed for faying the Soul was a part of *God*, or of the Divine Effence; furely it is as juftly blame-worthy for any to fay that *God* is a part of the Soul; therefore when *God* or his Spirit is faid to be the Souls Food, it is not to be underftood Strictly and Literally, but Metaphorically and Figuratively; as when *David* faith, my Soul thirfteth after *God*. But if it be faid, that not the *Godhead*, but that which *R. B.* calleth the *Vehicle* of the *Godhead*, is the moft proper and immediate Food of the Souls of Believers, as a certain Divine Emanation, or Efflux; nor can that Strictly and Literally, without a Metaphor be called the Souls Food; for that Divine *Emanation*, or *Efflux*, doth not become any part of the Souls Subftance, but is more Noble than the Soul, of any Saint, upon the Hypothefis; that there is fuch a thing, (which to difpute, is forrain to the prefent Queftion) for the Soul of Man in its own Nature is capable of Sin, and finful Defilements, which this Divine Seed, or Principle in the Soul is not; therefore it can never be Convertible into the Souls Subftance. The Feeding of the Soul, therefore in whatever Senfe we take it is Metaphorical, and not to be meafured or determined by the Feeding of the Body, yet beareth fome Analogy or Similitude thereunto, as all Metaphors do to the things, from which they are transferred; for as what Feeds the Body, doth Refrefh and Comfort it, maketh it Lively and Vigorous,

Fat

Fat and Beautiful, and doth strengthen it, and is united with it; So the Spirit of *Christ*, and his Divine Influences in the Souls of Believers have the like Effects in them, they do wonderfully Refresh and Comfort them (and that most sensibly) make them Lively and Vigorous, Fat and Beautiful, and do mightily strengthen them, and make them Fruitful in Divine Virtues and Fruits, and are United with the Soul.

SECT. III.

BUT there are two other things that need Correction, in these foregoing Words of *R. B.* the first is, that he saith it is the Soul, not the Body that is to be Nourished by this Flesh and Blood; this is a great Mistake; though the Bodies of the Saints are not to be Nourished by *Christ*, as with natural Food that is Corruptible; yet seeing it is by him that the Bodies of the Saints shall be raised up at the Resurrection of the Dead to partake of Life Everlasting; therefore he is truly said to be that Food that Perisheth not, that Feedeth both the Souls and Bodies of the Saints to Life Everlasting; and though their Bodies Dye, yet because by the Power of *Christ's* Resurrection (as his Body was Raised from the Dead, so on the account of his Resurrection) their Bodies shall be Raised to Eternal Life. Therefore their Bodies as well as their Souls are truly said to be Nourished by him. The second is that he saith, *neither is the Communion of the Saints with God by a Conjunction, and mutual Participation of Flesh, but of the Spirit; he that is joyned to the Lord is one Spirit, not one Flesh*. Ans. The Communion indeed of the Saints with *God*, is not by any natural Conjunction, or Union of *Christ's* Body that was outwardly Slain with the Saints, yet a Mystical and Relative Union there is, as really, or rather more really, as is betwixt the Husband and the Wife, who are said to be one Flesh. This is a great Mystery, said *Paul*, but I speak concerning *Christ* and the Church; who according to *Paul's* Doctrine, as they are one Spirit, so they are one Flesh: And as elsewhere he said, we are of his Flesh, and of his Bone; and forasmuch as the Children were partakers of Flesh and Blood, he took part of the same; wherefore he is not ashamed to call them Brethren. Now in this *R. B.* was in a great Error; that by his thus excluding the Flesh of *Christ's* outward Body from being any means of the Saints Communion with *God*, he excludes the said Body of *Christ* from being any necessary part of the Mediator; and at this rate of his Arguing, only the Divine Light or Seed in Men is the

Medi-

Mediator betwixt *God* and Men; but according to the Doctrine of the Apostle *Paul*, the Mediator of *God* and Men (who is one) is the Man *Christ Jesus*, and by the Man *Christ Jesus*, is understood in Scripture, not the Spirit only, nor the Soul of his Manhood only, but the Body also, together with the Soul, even *Jesus Christ* made of the Seed of *David*, according to the Flesh: And as really as there is a Relative Union betwixt Brethren, and near Kindred with respect to their Flesh and Blood; on which account it is said, Concerning *Joseph*, Gen. 37. 27. *He is our Brother and our Flesh*, and 2 *Sam.* 5. 1. *The Tribes of Israel said unto David, behold we are thy Bone and thy Flesh*: So believing *Gentiles*, as well as believing *Jews* may say concerning the Man *Christ*, who is the *Seed of the Woman*; of whom, to wit *Eve*, we are all descended, *we are his Bone and Flesh*; and because he hath taken Flesh and Blood like unto us, therefore in that very respect, he is compleatly qualified and fitted to be our Mediator, and High Priest with *God*, by whom (because of the true Nature of Man, consisting of a true reasonable Soul, and true and real Body of Man, which the Eternal Word is united unto) we have Communion with *God*. His fourth and last Argument hath the like Defect with the former. That which Feedeth upon it shall never Dye, but the Bodies of all Men once Dye. *Ans.* Men are said in Scripture to Dye; though the Soul Dyeth not, yet Men are said to Dye, because the Vital Union of the Soul with the Body is Dissolved; which being but for a Time, and that a very small Time, as a Moment, in respect of Eternity, and after that their Bodies shall be raised up again, and Vitally be United to their Souls; therefore by the contrary Argument, by the Flesh of *Christ*, that the Saints Feed upon, must be meant in part his outward Body of Flesh, now Glorified, which is a Glorious Spiritual Body; because the Resurrection of *Christ's* Body, is the Ground of the Saints Hope wrought in them by the Spirit of *Christ*, that their Bodies shall be raised up, and shall together with their Souls inherit Eternal Life. And to conclude this whole Matter; when *Christ* said, it is the Spirit that Quickneth, the Flesh profits nothing. His meaning is, that according to their Carnal and Fleshly Sense; it doth not profit; as if he had said, it would profit you nothing to Eat my Flesh, as ye imagin by the Bodily Mouth, but to Eat it Spiritually, and by Faith, this doth profit; but to take the Words, the Flesh profits nothing in the Sense that some take them, is most Blasphemous; as to say, *Christ's* outward Body of Flesh profits nothing to our Salvation; for this would make his Coming and Death for us in the Flesh to have been in vain; and also would render our Faith Vain, that he did so come; yea, so

neces-

[55]
neceſſary was *Chriſt's* coming in the Fleſh for our Salvation; that it is by his Fleſh and Soul, Conſtituting his Manhood, that we have his Spirit; the Man *Chriſt* is that Olive Tree (conſiſting of Soul and Body, United Perſonally to the Godhead of the Eternal Word) which giveth us the Oyl of the Holy Spirit, and poureth it into our Hearts; and as in the Natural Olive Tree, it is by its Body that we have of its Oyl, or Spirit; and when we Eat of its Oyl, we are ſaid to Eat of the Tree; becauſe the Tree yields us its Oyl; even as when we Eat of an Apple, or Drink the Fruit of it, or of the Vine; we may be ſaid to Eat of the Apple-Tree and Vine-Tree; the Fruit being what the Tree naturally yields; ſo the Man *Chriſt*, conſiſting of Soul and Body, is that Precious Olive-Tree, and Vine-Tree, that yields us the Oyl and Wine of the Holy Spirit, and pours it into our Hearts who Believe in him, and Love him, and as Effectual as his Soul and Fleſh of his Manhood is now to Believers for their receiving the Spirit by the ſame, ſince he came in the Fleſh, no leſs Effectual it was to Believers before he came in the Fleſh, even from the beginning of the World, according to *B. Jewel's* Words, he was not come in the Fleſh, yet they Eat his *Fleſh*; to wit, by *Faith*; he had not Shed his Blood, yet they Drank his Blood, *viz.* by Faith; and both his Fleſh and his Blood, before it had any viſible Being, or Exiſtence, together with his Soul was Effectual to Believers in all Ages, for their Reception of the Spirit, and all Spiritual Bleſſings of Juſtification, and Sanctification, *&c.* as well before he came in the Fleſh as ſince: And thus he was the Lamb Slain from the Foundation of the World, whoſe Death was of the ſame Efficacy from the beginning, and will be to the end of the World, to all that believe in him. And as *God* is the giver of the Spirit, and of all the Graces of the Spirit; ſo he giveth it to Believers by and through *Chriſt*, even the Man *Chriſt*, who is both the Procurer, and Diſpenſer of all that Grace that *God* giveth unto them; and though Men moſt properly Eat the Meat, and Drink the Drink that is bought with Money; yet in ordinary Speech, by a common Metonymy, they are ſaid to Eat and Drink the Money that buyeth it; as the Poor Widows two Mites were called her Living; ſo after ſome ſort, though the inward Life and Spirit of *Chriſt*, be the moſt immediate Food of the Souls of Believers; Yet becauſe the Fleſh of *Chriſt*, as it was broken for us, and his Blood as it was Shed for us, is the Price and Purchaſe Money which hath procured to us the inward Life and Spirit of *Chriſt*, with the various Graces and Gifts thereof; therefore we are ſaid, to Eat his Fleſh,
and

and Drink his Blood, by the like Metonymy. But there is much more in this Great Myftery, than can be demonſtrated by thefe Similitudes and Examples, or any others of the like Nature.

SECT. IV.

P. 77. *R. B.* chargeth it as another Error, which he calleth a General Error, wherein he faith, they all agree, *viz.* both Papifts and Proteftants, in tying this Participation of the Body and Blood of *Chriſt* to that Ceremony ufed by him with his Difciples in the breaking of Bread, *&c.* As if it had only a Relation thereto, or were only enjoyed in the ufe of that Ceremony; which it neither hath, nor is.

Anf. For any to tye the Participation of *Chriſts* Body and Blood to the outward Eating in the *Supper*, as above mentioned, is indeed a great Error. But it was a great Miftake in him, and too raſh'y charged in general by him, upon both Papifts and Proteftants, their being guilty of that Error. For it can be ſhewn, that fome of the Popiſh Writers have affirmed the contrary, and delivered it as the common Faith of their Church; that true Believers partake of *Chriſt's* Fleſh and Blood, although they Dye before they receive the outward *Supper*; for which Lombard, *Lib.* 4. *Diſt.* 9. citeth *Auguſtine*, faying, *Lib. de med. pæn. Nulli ambigendum eſt*, &c. 'No Man ought to doubt 'that any Man is then a partaker of the Body and Blood of the *Lord*, 'when he is made a Member of *Chriſt*; nor is he Alienated from the 'Communion of that Bread and Cup, although before he Eat that 'Bread, and Drink the Cup; being Conſtituted in the Unity of the 'Body of *Chriſt*, he depart out of this World; for he is not deprived 'of the benefit of that Sacrament, when he is found to have that which 'that Sacrament fignifieth. And as for the generality of Proteftants, I know not, nor ever knew any that fo tyed the Participation of *Chriſts* Body to the outward *Supper*, as he mentioneth. They fay indeed, it is a Means of Grace, and of our Communion of the *Lord's* Body; but not the only means, or fo abfolutely neceffary, as without it, none have that Communion.

Another great Miftake I find in *R. B.* p. 81. of that Treatife, where he faith; as for the Paſchal Lamb, the whole end of it is fignified particularly, *Exod.* 13. 8. 9. to wit, that the *Jews* might thereby be kept in remembrance of their Deliverance out of *Egypt*. Anf. That is indeed

[57]

deed mentioned as an end of it, but not the whole end of it; for the end of the whole Law was *Chriſt*; whereof that Command of the Paſſover was a part; but that the Paſſover was a Type of *Chriſt*, particularly as he was to be Slain for their Sins; is plain, out of *Paul*'s Words, 1 *Cor.* 5. 7. *Let us keep the feaſt*, &c. *for our paſſover is ſlain for us.* Now as the *Jews* were to Eat the Fleſh of the Paſſover; ſo the Believers in *Chriſt* are to Eat his Fleſh; even that Fleſh that was Slain; to wit, by Faith, as is above declared; but not by any Corporal Eating; and why did *John* the Evangeliſt apply theſe Words of the Paſſover to *Chriſt's* Body; *a bone of him ſhall not be broken?* This plainly proveth that the Paſſover was a Type of *Chriſt*; and therefore one great end of it, was to hold him forth to their Faith.

In p. 87. *R. B.* ſaith, let it be obſerved, that the very expreſs and particular uſe of it, according to the Apoſtle, is to ſhew forth the *Lord's* Death, *&c.* But to ſhew forth the *Lord's* Death, and partake of the Fleſh and Blood of *Chriſt*, are different things; from whence he infers, as his following Words ſhew that this Practice of the outward *Supper*, hath no inward or immediate Relation to Believers, Communicating, or Partaking of the Spiritual Body and Blood of *Chriſt*; or that Spiritual *Supper*, ſpoken of, *Rev.* 3. 20.

Anſ. This Conſequence doth not follow, that Practice of the outward *Supper*, had not only that end, to Commemorate and ſhew forth the *Lord's* Death, but had other great ends alſo; as another was to ſignifie their Communion of *Chriſt's* Body, as not a bare Sign, but as a means of that Communion; though not the only means, or ſuch a means, as if the ſaid Communion were tyed thereto; another erd was to ſignifie their Union and Communion one with another; both which ends are plainly held forth in theſe Words; *The bread which we break is it not the Communion of the Lord's Body*; &c. *and we being many, are one bread, and all are made partakers of that one bread.* And though *R. B.* denyeth that by Bread in thoſe Words, *the bread which we break is it not the communion of the Lord's body*, is to be underſtood the outward Bread; yet I have above proved it to be the outward Bread that was uſed in the *Supper*; for to underſtand it of the *Lord's* Body, were to make it Non-ſenſe; is to ſay the Body of *Chriſt* is it not the Communion of his Body? Whereas the true Senſe is Obvious, taking it for the outward Bread. The Bread which we break, is it not a Sign of the Communion of the *Lord's* Body, *&c.* And ſuch a Sign that is a means, whereby our Communion of the *Lord's* Body, and of the Spiritual

Bleſ-

Blessings we have thereby, is confirmed to us, and an increase of Grace is Exhibited unto us, as it is duly Administred and Received.

SECT. V.

Page 83. He puts a very false and strained Sense upon these Words; *ye cannot drink the cup of the Lord, and the cup of Devils; ye cannot be partakers of the Lord's table, and of the table of Devils,* 1 Cor. 10. 21. which shews (saith he) that he understands not here the using of *Bread* and *Wine*; because those that do Drink the Cup of Devils and Eat of the Table of Devils (yea, the Wickedest of Men) may partake of the outward *Bread*, and the outward *Wine*.

Ans. By the *Lord*'s Table, is not meant, barely and simply the Signs of *Bread* and *Wine*; but as they do signifie, and are Means Exhibitive of the Spiritual Blessings understood thereby. The Wickedest of Men may indeed receive the *Bread* and *Wine*; but they are not to them any Significative, or Exhibitive Signs and Means of these Spiritual Blessings, which are the things signified and intended; and are the Kirnel, without which the bare outward Signs are mere Shells, and broken Cisterns. Again, Let us distinguish betwixt what is *de jure*, i. e. of Right, and what is *de facto*, i. e. in Fact. Wicked Persons, though in Fact they may receive the outward Part, yet they have no Right to it. The manner of Speech used here by *Paul*, is like that of *James*; doth *the same fountain send forth sweet water and bitter? How then can the same tongue bless God and curse men? My brethren, these things ought not to be.* And when as *Paul* said elsewhere; *no man can say Jesus is the Lord, but by the Holy Ghost*; he may outwardly say the Words, but he hath no Right to say them, nor can his saying them profit him without the Holy Spirit. But that by the Table of the *Lord*, and the Cup of the *Lord* here, are to be meant the outward things of *Bread* and *Wine*; as above described, is evident from the Antithesis, or Opposition he makes betwixt the Table of Devils, and the Table of the *Lord*, and betwixt the Cup of Devils and the Cup of the *Lord*. Now the Table of Devils, and the Cup of Devils, were outward things, to wit the outward Offerings of Meats and Drinks, that the *Heathens* offered to their Idols, and to Devils. Therefore also by the Table of the *Lord*, and the Cup of the *Lord*, were meant the outward things of *Bread* and *Wine*; not barely and simply as such, but as Signifying and Exhibiting the Spiritual Things, above-mentioned.

oned. His Arguing against this Institution, from the one *Bread* is answered above, Part 1. Sect. 5.

Page 87. and 89. He gives a most jejune and strained, as well as false Sense upon these Words, the Table of the *Lord*, as (saith he p. 89.) he that esteemeth a Day, and placeth Conscience in keeping it, was to regard it to the *Lord*, and so it was to him, in so far as he was to Dedicate it unto the *Lord*, *the Lord's Day* ; he was to do it worthily. *Ans.* We find no Day called the *Lord*'s Day, upon any such account; nor did *Paul* call the Cup in the *Supper*, the *Cup of the* Lord, on any such Supposition of Men's esteeming it to be commanded, when it was not really commanded; but it is plainly apparent, *Paul* call'd it the *Cup of the* Lord, because he commanded it as the House of the *Lord*, the Law of the *Lord*, &c. and the Command is extant ; *drink ye all of it*, Matth. 26. 26, 27. Besides in this he palpably runs into a contradiction to what he had said a little before, in p. 83. For there he will not have the *Bread* and *Wine* to be the Table of the *Lord*, and Cup of the *Lord* ; because wicked Men cannot partake of the Table of the *Lord*; and yet now here he grants they may, and thereby Eat and Drink Damnation. And as jejune and strained, as well as false is the Gloss he puts on these Words, *he that eateth and drinketh unworthily, eateth and drinketh his own damnation, and is guilty of the body and blood of the Lord*; as if they signified no more than what these Words import, *Rom.* 14. 23. *He that doubteth is damned, if he eat, because he eateth not of faith*; which had only a Relation to Meats that might lawfully be Eaten ; but if he that did Eat them, did think them forbidden, he Sinned, and so was Condemn'd in his own Conscience. For the Word *Damned and Damnation*, in both places do not signifie any Final Sentence of Damnation ; but only both being Sins, they incurr'd the Guilt of Judgment, or Condemnation. But doth it therefore follow, that the Sin and Guilt is the same in both Cases ? Is he as Guilty of Damnation that Eats Swines Flesh Doubtingly, as he that Eats and Drinks Unworthily at the *Lord*'s Table? We read in *James* 3. 1, of a greater Condemnation ; the *Greek* Word is the same in both places, *viz.* James 3. 1. and 1 *Cor.* 11. 29. Seeing therefore there is a greater and lesser Damnation ; it will not follow, as *R. B.* would have it, that the Eating of Meats that are lawful, doubtfully, is as great a Sin, and deserves the same Condemnation that unworthy Eating at the *Lord*'s Table : One might argue after the like manner, that to make a Lye about a Trifle, brings as great Guilt and Condemnation, as downright Atheism, and denying the *Lord* that bought us.

Page 91. We find (faith *R. B.*) this Ceremony only mentioned in Scripture in four places, to wit, *Matthew*, *Mark*, and *Luke*, and by *Paul* to the *Corinthians---Matthew* and *Mark* give only an account of the Matter of Fact, without any Precept to do so afterwards; simply declaring that *Jesus* at that time did desire them to Eat of the *Bread*, and Drink of the *Cup*; to which *Luke* adds these Words, *do this in remembrance of me*.

Ans. That he calleth it a Ceremony, I know no Warrant he hath; the Scripture giveth it no such Name; they blame the use of the Word *Sacrament*, because it is not a Scripture Word; but to be sure Ceremony is no Scripture Word; they who are well Skilled in the *Greek* Language, say, that the *Greek* Word μυϛήριον, is well enough Translated Sacrament, as the vulgar Latin Translates it in that place, *hoc est magnum Sacramentum*. They further say; there ought to be no prejudice against it, because some *Heathen* Authors had formerly used it; for so had they used the Word Mystery, and had applied the same to the External Rites, and Symbols used by them in their Sacrifices to their Idols. When *Paul* would have himself and other Ministers of *Christ* to be accounted Stewards of the Mysteries of *God*, 1 *Cor.* 4. 1. They plead that by the Mysteries of *God* there, are to be meant, not only the Doctrins of the Christian Faith, but the Observation of these Institutions of *Christ*, of *Baptism* and the *Supper*; which none will deny who believe them to be his Institutions. But that he saith, *Matthew* and *Mark*, give only an account of the Matter of Fact, without any Precept to do so afterwards. *Ans.* Though the Precept is not expressed, it is implied; and *Luke* doth express it plainly, intimating they were commanded to do it afterwards. And if it were no where to be found, but in *Luke*; seeing it is acknowledged that *Luke* is of the same Authority, with the other Evangelists; it is sufficient, as well as that one place in *John* 6. concerning the Eating *Christ*'s Flesh, and Drinking his Blood, that is only expressive of that Mysterie, is sufficient to prove the Truth of it.

Page 92. Now this Act (faith he) was no singular thing, neither any solemn Institution of a Gospel Ordinance; because it was a constant Custom among the *Jews* (as *Paulus Ricius* observes at length in his Celestial Agriculture) that when they did Eat the Passover, the Master of the Family did take *Bread*, and bless it, and breaking of it gave it to the rest; and likewise taking *Wine*, did the same, &c.

Ans.

Anf. This Confequence will not follow; for it is as Idle and Groundlefs, as if one fhould argue, the *Jews* in the Time of the Law had their Religious Meetings, where Preaching and Prayer were ufed; therefore Religious Meetings, and Preaching, and Prayer are no Gofpel Inftitutions. But as his Confequence is not good, fo the Antecedent is not true, *viz.* That it was no fingular thing; for though it was not fingular in refpect of the Material Part; yet it was altogether fingular in refpect of its Formal Part. None of the Mafters of the Families among the *Jews* faid, Take, Eat, this is *Chrift*'s Body which is to be broken for you; and this Cup is the New Teftament in his Blood, &c. It was the great Love and Wifdom of *Chrift*, to eftablifh his Inftitutions under the Gofpel, relating to the external part of Religion, as near to the *Jewifh* Forms as poffible; excepting what might feem to favour their Superftitions, and other Shadowy Things that were to be Abolifhed. All the moral Part, as well as divers things of Inftituted Worfhip that were among the *Jews*, being commanded under the Gofpel. That of *Chrift*'s wafhing the Difciples Feet, which he infifteth on for feveral Pages, is fully Anfwered to in the firft Part. As alfo that of Anointing the Sick with Oyl; fo that no more needs be faid to it here.

As for thefe Objections that he raifeth about the Time of the natural Day, when this Inftitution fhould be practifed; as why not at Night, and what fort of *Bread*, whether Leavened, or Unleavened? and whether other Drink may not be ufed as well as *wine*? which he calls Difficulties, out of which it is impoffible, he faith, (p. 101.) to extricate themfelves, but by laying it afide; another of which Difficulties is to underftand, as he alledgeth, that thefe Words, Take, Blefs, and Break the *Bread* and give it to others, are to the Clergy, meaning the Paftors, but to the Laity only, meaning the People, Take, Eat, &c.

Anf. I do not find that he proveth in the leaft any fuch Difficulties; they may be all eafily extricated, much more than in many other Cafes, where far greater Difficulties occur. But this is too Rafh and Prepofterous; becaufe of fome feeming Difficulties, therefore to lay afide a Divine Inftitution, or to conclude it is no fuch thing. This is to cut the Knot, inftead of loofing it, and to Kill, inftead of Curing. At this rate, becaufe in *Paul*'s Epiftles, and in many other places of Scripture, there are things hard to be underftood and refolved, therefore all fuch places of Scripture are to be rejected: Who doth not fee the Impertinency of fuch Confequences? And the like may be faid in

Anf-

Answer to his Objection, from the great Contentions that have happened betwixt Papists and Protestants about the *Supper* (and betwixt the Protestants one with another) and the much Blood that hath been shed, occasioned by these Controversies. All which say nothing against the Institution it self, more than against *Christ* and his Gospel, about which more Blood has been spilt than about that. He should have better considered the distinction betwixt a *causa per se*, and *causa per accidens*, and the use of a thing, and the abuse of it.

SECT. VI.

Page 104. For would they take it as it lies, it would import no more than that *Jesus Christ* at that time did thereby signifie unto them, that his Body and Blood was to be offered for them, and desired them, *that whensoever they did eat or drink, they might do it in remembrance of him*, or with a regard to him, whose Blood was shed for them.

Ans. If this Supposition be true, as he would have it; that *whensoever they did eat or drink, they were to do it in remembrance of him*; then why hath he pleaded so much for the ceasing of it? Surely if they were to do it, whensoever they did Eat or Drink, they were to do it to the end of the World; because as long as the World continues, Eating and Drinking will continue. But we do not find that our Saviour's Words import any such Sense; he doth not say, *whensoever ye eat or drink, &c.* But as oft as ye eat *this* bread, and drink *this* cup; where the Word *this* Imports it to be another Eating than their common Eating, and the like is Imported by these Words; *let a man examine himself, and so let him eat, &c. whoso eateth* this *bread unworthily,* &c. 1 Cor. 11. 28, 27.

But to this Sense that he hath given, I find a Passage a little after p 111. that as I judge is a plain Contradiction to the former. He saith there the Apostles Words, *For as often as ye eat this bread, and drink this cup, ye do shew the Lords death till he come*, Imports no more a command, than to say, *As oft as thou goest to Rome, see the Capitol*, will infer a Command to me to go thither. Now if they were to obey this Institution, whensoever they did Eat or Drink; then surely they were to do it very often; and that by a Command which plainly contradicts this last Assertion of his; but the Words *As often as thou goest to Rome, see the Capitol*, implie neither a Command, nor any frequent

Pra-

Practice of going, therefore this Example is very improper and impertinent in this respect as well as in others.

Page 110, 111. As to that passage 1 *Cor.* 11. from 23. to 27. He saith, *There is no Command in this place, but only an account of matter of Fact.* He saith not, *I received of the Lord, that as he took Bread, so I should Command it to you to do so also*; there is nothing like this in the place.

Anf. Be it so, that there was no new Command given in the Case either to *Paul*, or by him to the *Corinthians*. It sufficed to *Paul* to give an account of the matter of Fact, as it was delivered to him from the *Lord* by Divine Revelation, as he plainly affirmed; That (saith he) *which I received of the Lord, that also I delivered unto you, that the Lord Jesus, the same night in which he was betrayed, &c.* Now, as all Divine Revelations are for some great end, we may safely argue, that since what the *Lord* did that night, was Revealed to him by the *Lord*, it was not an indifferent thing either to be Believed or Practised, since it had a Command in it, *This do in remembrance of me*: Here was a positive Command that *Christ* gave unto his Apostles, alledged both by *Paul*, 1 *Cor.* 11. 24. And also by *Luke* 22. 19. There was no need of renewing the same Commandments, as the Law of the Ten Commandments once given at *Mount Zinai* did oblige the twelve Tribes of *Israel*, without any other giving them; though what was then given them, was oft taught them, both by *Moses* and the succeeeding Prophets; so what *Christ* the great Law-giver under the New Testament, gave forth to be his Command, wherever that Command is made known to any People, Nation, or Country, it ought to be obeyed, without the requiring or expecting any new Sanction. And to shew a little further how improper his Example, of one saying *As often as thou goest to Rome, See the Capitol*, is to the present Case; If one that has the Command of another, should first say, *go to Rome*, and then add, *As often as thou goest to Rome, go to the Capitol* this would imply, a Command. Now *Christ* said first to his Disciples, *This do in remembrance of me*, as both *Luke* and *Paul* testifie; and then *Paul* adds further, v. 25. *As oft as ye drink it, this do in remembrance of me*; and v. 26. *for as often as ye eat this bread and drink this cup, ye do shew the Lord's death, till he come*, the Greek word καταγγέλλετε translated ye shew, may be translated, ye declare, or ye preach, for so is the same word translated, *Acts* 15. 26. *Acts* 13. 38. *Acts* 17. 13. which signifieth

fieth some Publick way of shewing it forth in Religious Meetings, that proveth it was not Mens private Eatings, which may oft happen when they are alone; and for this, and the like Reasons, some of the Antients, and particularly *Augustin*, called it *Verbum visibile*, the visible Word; which when joyned with the Word that is sounded in Mens Ears, has a double force upon the Minds of devout Believers: To which doth well agree that saying of *Chrysostome*, in his Homilies on *Matthew*, cited in the Title Page, *If thou hadst been without a Body, God had given thee naked and incorporeal Gifts; but because the Soul is planted in a Body, he giveth thee Intelligible things in Sensible things*. And it was well observed by the Antients, that all obsignatory Signs, have some words of *God* or *Christ* added unto them, to make them effectual, according to which *Augustin* said, *Accedat verbum ad rem, & fit Sacramentum*, i. e. *let the word be added to the sign, and it becomes a Sacrament*; and therefore we find in *Eph.* 5. 26. the washing of Water joyned with the Word —— *That he might sanctifie and cleanse it, with the washing of water by the word*. I know some will have the Water here to be meant, the inward Water, and the Word to be inward also; but such a Sense would be not only strained, but unintelligible, as to say with the washing of the Word by the Word, for they make the inward Water and Word to be the same thing here; but the Apostle distinguisheth them as two things, both which have the Efficacy by the inward working of the Holy Spirit, *Titus* 3. 5.

Page 111. He undertakes the Answering of the Argument for the Institution of the *Supper*, and its continuance until *Christ* come at the end of the World, from those Words, *Ye shew forth the Lord's death till he come*. To this he p. 112. Answers. *They take two of the chief parts of the Controversie here for granted without proof; First, that as often imports a Command, the contrary whereof is shewn, neither will they ever be able to prove it. 2ly. That this coming is understood of Christ's last Outward coming, and not of his Inward and Spiritual, that remains to be proved, whereas the Apostle might well understand it of his Inward coming and appearance.* —— And a little after he saith —— *Now those weak and carnal* Corinthians *might be permitted the use of this, to shew forth, or remember Christ's Death, till he come to arise in them. For, though such need those Outward things to put them in mind of Christ's Death, yet such as are dead with Christ, and not only dead with Christ, but buried, and so risen with him, need not such Signs to remember him.* Ans.

Anf. That *as often*, together with the foregoing words, import a Command, I have already proved, and it was rashly said in him, that he had shewn the contrary, and that they will never be able to prove it. And whereas some argue, had it been a Command, some certain times would have been mentioned, how oft in a Week, Month, or Year it should have been Practised. To this it is Answered; that it followeth not more than to argue that, because it is not mentioned how often in a Week, Month, or Year, Publick Prayer is to be used; that therefore they are not Institutions of *Christ*; for as Publick Preaching and Prayer is to be used as frequently as can stand with the Ability and Conditions of both Preachers and Hearers; so this Practice as frequently is to be used; which, as the time of those, is to be left to the Discretion of the Persons, as *God* shall inwardly Guide them, and outwardly afford them the Convenience; so is the Time of this to be left to the like Discretion, Guidance, and Convenience; which as it seemed to be the Practice of the Church in the Days of the Apostles; each Lord's-day, being the first Day of the Week, so it is clear from *Justin Martyr*, and other ancient Writers; that it was the constant Practice of the Christians, Solemnly to Celebrate the same every Lord's-day; besides what other times they might have done it.

As to the second, which he calls together with the other, the chief thing in Controversie, it is indeed so, even the chief thing; and therefore if this be effectually proved against them, that those Words, *until he come again*, are understood of *Christ*'s last outward coming, the Cause is gained. But first, let us examine what Proof he brings, that they are not to be understood of *Christ*'s last outward coming. First, he saith, the Apostle might well understand it of his inward coming and appearance; but what Proof doth he give of this? None at all, but his simple Affirmation.

Secondly, He saith, these Weak and Carnal *Corinthians* might be permitted the use of this, to shew forth, or remember *Christ*'s Death till he should arise in them. But what Proof gives he of this, that this was, or might be a Permission? for no such Permission is any where expressed in the Scriptures; the things that simply were permitted, as Circumcision, were used but by a few, and not long; *Paul* severely opposed them after some time; but so he never did either *Water-Baptism*, or the *Supper*. Thirdly, That he said, *though such need these out-*

K *ward*

ward things to put them in mind of Chrift's *Death*; why then, feeing there are now in all Churches and Chriftian Societies, fome that are as weak as thofe *Corinthians* were, do not they allow the ufe of them to fuch as need them? *Fourthly*, That he faith, fuch as are Dead and Buried with *Chrift*, and Rifen again with him, need not fuch things to remember him. *Anfwer*, Here, as elfewhere, his Argument is faulty, by arguing; that becaufe fuch things are not abfolutely neceffary, therefore they are not ufeful, or neceffary in any refpect. Befides, as I have above fhewn, his Argument has the fame force againft the ufe of the Holy Scriptures, and all Books, all Preaching of the beft Men, and all External Parts of Worfhip, *viz.* They that are Dead and Buried with *Chrift*, and Rifen with him, need none of thefe outward things. But the beft Men, and fuch are the moft humble, will and cannot but acknowledge, that all outward Helps and Means that *God* hath afforded them, are very ufeful to them, and help to ftir up the pure Mind in them. Nor are any fo Rifen with *Chrift*, as the Raifed Saints fhall be at the Refurrection; therefore till then, they may be helped with outward Means of *God*'s appointing. It is very Unwifely, as well as Irreverently Argued; we need not thofe things, therefore they are not commanded. The contrary is the better Argument; they are commanded, therefore they are needful, at leaft in fome refpect; *God* better knoweth what we need, than we do our felves; and therefore in his great Love and Wifdom, hath provided outward Helps for us, as well as inward. But feeing they will needs underftand the Words, *until he come*; not to mean *Chrift*'s laft outward coming, but his inward; then with the fame Pretext, they may as well underftand his Death, of an inward Death of *Chrift* in them; and the fhewing his Death of an inward fhewing; and then all Remembrance of *Chrift*'s Death, as he Dyed outwardly may be forgotten. But if by the *Lord*'s Death, is underftood his outward Death, by as good reafon, by his coming is underftood his outward coming.

SECT.

SECT. VII.

Having thus shewn the Invalidity of his Proofs, that by the *Lord*'s coming, is understood his inward coming into their Hearts, and not his outward coming, I shall give some clear Reasons, why it must be understood his outward coming at the general Judgment. The first Reason is; because the Reason of the Command continuing to his last outward coming, the Command doth also continue; for so long doth any Command continue in Force, as the Reason of it continueth; but the Reason of the Command, *Do this in remembrance of me,* &c. doth continue to *Christ*'s last outward coming; which Reason is this; that by that Practice they might remember the *Lord*'s Death; and not only remember it, but shew it forth, Publickly Declare and Profess, it, and the inestimable Benefits they have by it. Now put the case, that any had so good and living Remembrance of it; that they needed not the outward things to put them in remembrance thereof; yet that is not enough to Answer the Reason and End of the Command, which is by this outward Practice to shew it forth, and declare it by a publick Profession, that they owe Remission of Sin, and Salvation to the Crucified *Jesus*, and that they are not ashamed to own and confess him their Saviour, their King, their Priest and Prophet, and in Token thereof they give Testimony of their Obedience to these his peculiar positive Laws and Institutions of *Water-Baptism*, and the *Supper*; for if these be rejected, by the same Method Men may reject all other his positive Institutions, relating to External Practice of Religion, and so turn the Christian Religion into meer Deism, and Pagan Morality. The second Reason is, that the end of this Institution, being a solemn Commemoration of *Christ*'s Death and Sacrifice which he offered up to *God* for our Sins above sixteen hundred Years ago, and of the great Spiritual Blessings we have thereby; there is the same Cause and End for it to continue to our Day, and to the end of the World, as when it was first appointed. Had it been indeed only a Prenunciative Sign of some things to come, or of the hidden invisible Substance, as *W. Penn* terms it, meaning thereby the Spirit of *Christ* within, at the coming of the Spirit within into their Hearts; the Sign might have ceased, as the Prenunciative Signs of *Christ*'s outward coming in the Flesh were to cease after his outward coming, and accordingly did cease. But the Signs of *Water-Baptism*, and the *Supper*, as commanded by *Christ*, and Practised by the Apostles; were not such Prenunciative Signs of the coming of his Spirit within them, but were chiefly Commemorative Signs of him as he had come; for both of them were appointed by him when he was come, and the Institution of *Baptism* was appointed by him after his Death and Resurrection, the Institution of the *Supper*, so near to his Death, that it was in the very Night when he was Betrayed, and at which time he had the great Sense and Weight of his Sufferings upon him, and as then in great part begun; and because the use of those Signs of *Bread* and *Wine*, the *Bread* being broken, and the *Wine* poured out, was a Solemn Commemoration of his having *given his Body to be broken for them, and his Blood to be shed for them*; therefore he said, *Take, Eat, this is my Body that is broken for you*; he did not say, this is my Spirit, or this is the inward visible hid Substance that ye shall afterwards receive; *but this is my Body; Take, Eat*; and though they were not to eat his Body with the Carnal Mouth, but only the *Bread* which signified it; yet by Faith they were to eat his Body, that is to say, they were to partake of a Mystical Union with his Body, and to have their Right and Interest in him confirmed to them by that Symbol, by means whereof they were to receive plentifully of his Grace and Spirit, as the Consequent and Effect of that Union with him. Therefore they were not so to mind the Effect, as to neglect the great Cause of that Effect; which great cause was *his giving his Body to be broken for them, and his Blood to be shed*; for to mind only the Effect, and neglect the Cause, were like the Hogs that greedily run after the Acorns, or Nuts; but are unmindful of the Tree that beareth them. But as the Spiritual Eyes of Believers, are to be to the Graces and Gifts of *Christ*; so especially, and chiefly to him, from and by whom they have them, and their Faith and Love ought chiefly to act upon him, and upon *God* the Father, in and through him, as also upon the Holy Spirit, as principally residing in him, from and by whom we derive our several Measures of the same. The Third Reason is this; when *Christ* gave the Cup, he said; *this Cup is the new Testament in my Blood, shed for the remission of the sins of many*. Now how is that Cup the New Testament? surely no other ways but as an Obsignatory Sign of the New Testament, obsignating to Believers, *remission of Sins by his Blood outwardly shed*; which New Testament hath in it the Force and Essence of the Covenant of Grace, which *God* maketh with Believers, through *Christ* the Mediator of it; and as *Christ* hath confirmed this Covenant of Grace and Testament with his Blood that was Shed once for us; so he hath given to Believers this

obsig-

obsignating Pledge of it, by way of Investiture; as when a Man has an Estate of Land conveyed to him, and gets the Investiture of it, it is by some outward Sign, as here in *England* in some Places, by delivering to him Twig and Turf; and as Kings were Invested with their Kingly Power, by having Oyl poured on them; and as *Aaron* was Invested into the Office of Priesthood. And indeed all Covenants that ever *God* made with any People, have always been by some outward obsignatory things, as in his Covenant he made with *Noah*, he gave the Bow in the Cloud for the Token of that Covenant; in the Covenant with *Abraham*, he gave the Sign of Circumcision, which by a Metonymy is called *God*'s Covenant in Scripture. Also the Sacrifices under the Law, were Signs obsignatory of *God*'s Covenant with them who offered those Sacrifices. And in all the Covenants that we read of in Scripture, that any of the Fathers made with the Neighbouring Princes, or Inhabitants, there were obsignatory Signs and Pledges; so that who rightly understand the Nature of a Covenant, Transacted after any publick manner, must acknowledge it cannot be without some obsignatory Pledge, or Sign outwardly to be seen, given by the one Party to the other; insomuch that it seems to be a general Instinct in Mankind, or at least the Equivalent of it, an universal Custom received and practised even among *Heathens*, as to my certain knowledge it is among the *American* Heathens; who in all their Covenants make use of Signs for the greater Security and Confirmation. Thus in the 50th *Psalm*, it is said, *gather my Saints together, who have made a covenant with me by sacrifice*, v. 5. And if any should be so Stiff and Pertinacious, as to deny that outward Signs are necessary to the Confirmation of Covenants universally; yet the Case is plain here, as to the *Supper*; for *Christ* himself hath said it, *this Cup is the new Testament in my Blood*, &c. Which must have this meaning; *that the Cup was Christ's Testament, as Circumcision was God's covenant with Abraham and his seed*; for so it was called in Scripture; that is to say, *the Cup is a sign of Christ's Testament, and of the covenant of grace that God hath made with believers, through Christ the Mediator of it*. But if any object, this would seem to make the outward *Baptism*, and *Supper*, of so great necessity, as that it cannot be said, that the Covenant is duly confirmed without them, betwixt *God* and Believers. *Ans.* It sheweth inded a great necessity of them, as in respect of any People being in Covenant with *God*, in a visible way of a Church, and as Members of a visible Church or Society, well and duly constituted; for all the Members of

a vi-a visible Church, as they are in Covenant with *God* inwardly by the Faith and Obedience of their Hearts, so they are in Covenant with him outwardly by the Confession of their Mouths, and other External Acts of Religion, whereby they declare their professed Subjection to him, and to his Laws. Hence we find in Scripture, that not only Faith is required in order to Salvation, but Confession also; and that Confession is not only with the Mouth, but by External Works of the Body, proceeding from a living Principle of Faith in the Heart, among which Works are the External Practices of outward *Baptism*, and the *Supper*, where they can be duly had, whereby they declare their Subjection to the positive Laws and Institutions of *Christ*, and thereby distinguish themselves from either *Jews* or *Pagans*, who may be Moral Men, and Profess Faith and Religion towards *God*, as a Creator, and yet be professed Enemies to the Christian Faith, such as many *Jews* and *Heathens* were in the Apostles Days, and are in our Days. And therefore the outward *Baptism*, and the *Supper* have been not unfitly called and esteemed *Badges of Christianity*, peculiarly distinguishing Christians from *Jews* and *Pagans*; though not the only Badges, but when they are accompanied with a good Conversation of Sobriety, Justice, and Piety, they do make the distinction betwixt true Christians, and *Jews*, and *Heathens*, much more apparent; for if these External Practices, Instituted by *Christ*, be laid aside, whereby shall it outwardly appear that Men and Women are Christians? If it be said, by the Sobriety, Justice, and Piety of their Conversation; But these are no positive distinguishing Marks of Christianity, because Men and Women that are no Christians, may have as much of the out-side of Sobriety, Justice, and Piety towards *God*, as many true Christians have. If it be again said, their frequent Prayer to *God*, in the Name of *Christ*, and calling on the Name of the *Lord Jesus Christ* in Prayer, is a Badge of their Christianity. I answer in part it is so, but not in full, or in the whole; for he that not only Prayeth to *God* in the Name of *Christ*, and confesseth him in Words, but also sheweth his Obedience and Subjection to all the Commands of *Christ*, the least as well as the greatest, whereof the outward *Baptism*, and the *Supper* are some, is the most Accomplished Christian, and beareth the most compleat Badge of Christianity. And though Men's Ignorance in their not knowing them, or not being persuaded concerning them, that they are the Commands of *Christ*, being darkned by the Prejudice of Education, or fasly persuaded by Seducers and false Teachers, doth in part excuse them, or

at

at least where Sincerity is, as to the main gives ground of Hope, that *God* will forgive them the Omission of these Practices; yet where Obedience is not given to every Command of *Christ*, even the least as well as the greatest, though the Omission be through Ignorance, or false Persuasion, yet it is a Sin, and renders the Persons found in that Omission defective and incomplete Christians.

SECT. VIII.

THE *4th*. Reason is this, These outward practices of *Baptism* and the *Supper*, are not only visible Signs and Pledges of our being in Covenant with *God* thro' *Christ*, and that as he is our *God*, so we are his People; but they are also the visible Signs and Pledges that we are in the Unity and Communion of the Church, as Children of one Family, begot of one Father, having one Faith and Hope, one *Lord*, and being Members of one Body. And though the Communion of Believers consists chiefly in the Spirit, and the inward Graces thereof; yet, as they are a visible Body and Society, they are to have some outward and visible Signs and Pledges of the same, that carry some distinguishing Character, to distinguish them, not only from professed Infidels, but also from loose and scandalous Persons, professing the Christian Faith with them: Therefore as in the *Jewish* Church, *God* had appointed, that whoever did not obey the Mosaical Precepts, were to be excluded the Congregation, and debarred from the external Privileges that they had as a Church, even so *Christ* has appointed, that whosoever professing him in Words, deny him in Works, and walk disorderly and offensively, as well as who err concerning the Faith, so as not to hold the Head, that they ought to be rejected and disowned; in token whereof, they are to be debarred from the external Signs of the Saints Communion with *God* and *Christ*, and one with another. Otherwise, what can be meant by *rejecting, casting out, and purging out*, in the Scriptures of the New Testament? Also by the word *separating, and withdrawing*, so as to have no Fellowship with them? Surely it was more than a verbal denyal of them, or giving forth a Paper against them. Doth not *Paul* tell us what it was, when he saith 1 *Cor.* 5. 11. *If any man that is called a brother be a fornicator, &c. with such an one no not to eat.* This *not to eat* cannot be meant the common Eating, but such as that 1 *Cor.* 10. 21. to wit, *at the Lord's Table.* And therefore the *Lord* did see it meet, that as the Outward *Baptism* should be a Sign declarative of the Persons Baptized taking or putting on the Profession of a Christian, so the Eating at the *Lord*'s Table should be a Sign, that they did remain Faithful under that Profession, and did continue in the Unity and Communion of the Church, as *Paul*'s words declare, *we being many are one bread, and are all made partakers of that one bread, &c.* Even as under the Law, the receiving of Circumcision was the Sign or Badge of their being Members of the *Jewish* Church, and their Eating of the Passover, and of the Sacrifices, (such as were allowed to them to Eat) was a Sign of their being still owned as such; and if any by their offensiveness and disobedience did-occasion the Church to debarr them from the external Privileges of that Church, when upon their Repentance and Reconciliation, they were again received, they needed no second Circumcision; so nor do professed Christians, having committed any thing that occasion their casting out, being again received by Repentance, need a second Baptism. Now if *Baptism* had been the alone obsignating token of the Covenant, and Badge of Christian Communion, how should Persons be received into Communion, without a new *Baptism*? but to have a new *Baptism*, is as improper as for a Woman after some just offence against her Husband, that he has put her from him, if upon her Repentance he receive her again, to need a second Marriage with the same Husband; but tho' she need no second Marriage, yet that her Husband give her some token and pledge of his Favour, and Acceptance is very suitable. And now seeing these external Practices have so many necessary uses in the Church, so that the Church cannot, in all respects, be duly constituted, and have all things in order without them, it is evident, that as long as the Church was to continue on Earth, in its due Constitution, so long should these external Practices remain; and seeing *Christ* enjoyned this of breaking Bread to remain to his coming, it is evident, that it is his last outward coming.

The Fifth Reason is, that *Christ's* Inward coming was then in and among the Disciples when he did Institute these Outward Practices. The Church was never without the Inward Presence of *Christ*, and of *God*, and of the *Holy Spirit*: It is true, that *Christ* promised his Inward Presence to be with them and in them; but this was not so to be understood, as if the Faithful had him not present formerly, in all Ages, as well before, as after his Outward coming; for without the Inward Presence of *God*, and *Christ*, and the *Holy Spirit*,

Spirit, there can be no true Faith nor Holiness. We find that the Faithful are called Saints, as well in the Old Testament, as in the New, and therefore they had as true Inward enjoyments of *God* then as since, the difference at most is but in degree, betwixt the Divine Enjoyments of the Faithful, before *Christ* came in the Flesh, and since as to the general. And if it be said, that though *Christ* was Inwardly come to some, yet not to all in the Apostles times, so as to Answer to the full extent of the fulfilling of the Promise of his Inward coming; It may be answered, nor is he so come now; for as *Christ* said, the Poor ye have always with you; so until the end of the World there will be in the Church Babes and little Children as well as young Men, and Fathers; and therefore on the account of such by *R. B.*'s Confession, that are weak, as some of the *Corinthians* were, that needed those Outward things to put them in Remembrance of *Christ*'s Death, they are still to be continued, even to *Christ*'s last Outward coming; but there are too many among the Quakers that think there is no need to Remember *Christ*'s Death, as he dyed at *Jerusalem*, abusing and perverting *Paul*'s words, *henceforth we know Christ no more after the flesh*, and so there is no need or use of Remembring *Christ*'s Death; that they say is but History, but *Christ* within is the Mystery, whereas *Christ* within is not the whole Mystery, but in part, and the lesser part too; the whole Mystery of *Christ* is *Christ* both Outwardly come in the Flesh, and Inwardly come by his Spirit into the Hearts of the Faithful.

The Sixth Reason is, that to understand by the coming of *Christ* in these words —— *untill he come*, 1 Cor. 11. His Inward coming, and not his coming Without us at the day of Judgment, by the same pretext and method of Interpretation, All the other Scriptures every where that mention his coming throughout the whole Bible, and especially throughout the New Testament, shall be understood only of his Inward coming: And thus we shall have not one proof left us in all the Bible, to prove that there is any other coming of *Christ* to be expected, than his Inward coming in Mens Hearts. And accordingly indeed we find, that too many of the Quakers have by this manner of perverting this place of Scripture, been led to understand all these other places of Scripture in the New Testament that mention his coming since he came in the Flesh, to be only understood of his Inward coming in Mens Hearts, and on this account have denyed any other coming of *Christ* to be expected, but only his Inward

L coming

coming, being perſuaded into this Falſe and Antichriſtian Belief, by ſome of their great Teachers, witneſs what *William Baily*, a great Teacher among them, hath plainly declared in this matter, p. 306. of the Collection publiſhed by the 2d. days Meeting of the People called Quakers, at *Grace-Church-Street. I never read in all the Scripture*, ſaith he, (*as I can remember*) *of a 3d. coming of Chriſt, perſonally in his own ſingle perſon, or of a perſonal Reign beſides what ſhall be in his Saints. But I have read of his coming the 2d. time, without Sin unto Salvation*, &c. *which the Apoſtles in their days did witneſs.* Witneſs alſo *Rich. Hubberthorn*, another great Teacher, in his Collection publiſhed after his death alſo by the 2d. days Meeting, p. 56. in anſwer to his Opponent. —— *How many Souls haſt thou led into that Pit of Darkneſs and Blindneſs, as to believe that Chriſt is yet to come in Perſon? Now the Scripture which thou bringeſt proves no ſuch thing,* Matth. 24. 27. And a 3d. witneſs is *G. Whitehead* in his *Nature of Chriſtianity* againſt *R. Gordon*, who p. 29. ſaith, *Doſt thou look for Chriſt, as the Son of* Mary, *to appear Outwardly in a bodily Exiſtence to ſave thee, according to thy words,* p. 30. *If thou doſt, thou may'ſt look until thy Eyes drop out before thou wilt ſee ſuch an Appearance of him.* And p. 41. (Where 'doth the Scripture ſay, he is Outwardly and Bodily Glorified at *God's* 'right Hand? Do theſe words expreſs the Glory he had with the Fa- 'ther before the World began, in which he is now Glorified?) This and the two foregoing Quotations are to be found more large in my Two Narratives of the Proceedings at *Turners-Hall*; all which ſufficiently prove that they believed no Outward coming of *Chriſt*, as a thing to come; therefore it is no wonder that they meant only *Chriſt's* coming Inwardly into Mens Hearts by theſe words, *ye ſhew forth the Lord's death until he come*; for from the ſame Unbelief they have conſtrued all the other places that mention *Chriſt's* coming after his Reſurrection, of his Inward coming, and all this in prejudice of his Outward coming, which theſe Men did not believe, which places of Scripture are many, as *Matth.* 24. 27. This very place *G. W.* denyeth to be meant of his Outward coming at the Day of Judgment, as alſo 1 *Theſſ.* 4. 15. In his Book called *Light and Life*, in Anſwer to *W. Burnet*; and *Heb.* 9. 28. Now by the ſame Method whereby they deny any of theſe four places now mentioned, to be underſtood of any other coming of *Chriſt* than his Inward coming, they muſt deny all other places that mention his coming after his Reſurrection, to be meant of his Outward coming in the true Nature of Man, becauſe they have declared

clared they own no such thing, as *Christ's* being in Heaven without us in a Personal and Bodily Existence; and that which is not in Being, they cannot believe will come.

But no such Error I charge as this on *R. B.* who I know did own that *Christ* had the true Being and Nature of Man in Heaven, and that he would come and appear without us in that Nature to judge the World in Righteousness. But to prosecute the Argument, that by the words ---- *until he come* must be understood his Outward coming; it has the more force against *R. B.* because he believed that *Christ* was Outwardly to come, and that there were sufficient proofs of Scripture for it, as indeed many there are besides those already named, as *Acts* 1.11. 1 *Cor.* 4. 5. *Joh.* 14. 3. *Mark* 8. 38. *Luke* 12. 37, 43. 1 *Cor.* 1 5. 23, 24. *Jude* 14. *Rev.* 17. 1 *Cor.* 1. 7. 1 *Thess.* 2. 19. 1 *Thess.* 3. 13. 1. *Thess.* 5. 23. 2 *Thess.* 2. 1. 2 *Pet.* 3. 12. 1 *Pet.* 5. 4. 1 *Joh.* 2. 28. 1 *Joh.* 3. 2. Now seing *R. B.* did believe that all, or Many of these places were to be understood of his Outward coming, how could he have convinced his unbelieving Brethren, that any of these places were to be understood of his Outward coming more than that, 1 *Cor.* 11. 26. ---- *till he come,* seeing from the reasons above given, as much evidence appeareth, that by his coming, 1 *Cor.* 11. 26. is meant his Outward coming, as from any other places above cited, or any that can be brought, his Outward coming can be proved? And so indiscreetly Zealous have some of their great Teachers been for *Christ's* Inward coming (which is a Truth very great and necessary to be believed rightly and duly understood, but ought not to be proved by perversions of Scripture that mean not so, whereas sufficient proofs can be brought for it, without all such perversions,) that divers of the Prophecies of the Old Testament, concerning *Christ's* coming in the Flesh, they have turned to *Christ's* Birth within them, as that in *Isaiah*; ----- *Unto us a Child is born, a Son is given:* And that in *Isaiah* 53. concerning his Death and Burial without us in his real Body of Flesh, *He made his grave with the wicked,* &c. *Rich. Hubberthorn* turns it to *Christ's* being buried in the wicked, contrary both to the true translation, as well as to the true sense of that place. And thus by this presumptuous Liberty they take, to expound the Scriptures falsely, contrary to all reason and common Sense, they seek to disarm the Christians from bringing proofs out of the Old Testament against the *Jews,* to prove that the promised Messiah is already come in the Flesh, or that he hath suffered in the Flesh. And though I was so far blinded by them, that

I did

I did underſtand 1 *Cor.* 11. 26.——*till he come,* of his Inward coming; yet I had always a firm Belief, both of *Chriſt's* being in Heaven in the glorified Nature of Man, and that he would come in that glorified Nature of Man to judge the World. And now I plainly ſee, that his coming, 1 *Cor.* 11. 26. is as really his Outward coming, as any where elſe in all the Scripture; and I hope I have ſufficiently proved it to all impartial and intelligent Perſons, who ſhall read my Reaſons I have brought to prove the ſame.

Page 113. His Quotation of the Syriack tranſlation doth no ways favour his Senſe, as that the Eating 1 *Cor.* 11. 26. was only by Indulgence, and not by Command. The Quotation is this. *In that concerning which I am about to Command you (or Inſtruct you) I Commend you not, becauſe ye have not gone forward, but are deſcended into that, which is leſs, or of leſs Conſequente.* From this he infers, that *Paul* judged the Bread and Wine to be beggerly Elements: But the Syriack tranſlation ſaith no ſuch thing; he might well have blamed them, that they were not gone forward in the Life of Chriſtianity, but rather backward, becauſe of the corrupt and irregular manner of their practiſing that Inſtitution, that ſome were drunk; ſurely this was to go back, but this is no proof againſt the regular Practice it ſelf. And what he further quotes of the ſame Syriack Verſion, is as improper and invalid to his purpoſe, v. 20. *When then ye meet together, ye do not do it, as it is juſt ye ſhould do in the day of the Lord, ye eat and drink;* thereby ſhewing to them, to meet together to Eat and Drink outward Bread and Wine, was not the Labour and Work of that Day of the *Lord.* But nothing appeareth from this, that he blamed the regular Practice of it, but their undue and corrupt manner of doing it; ſo that their doing of it, as they did it, was not the Work of the Day: And therefore he might well ſay, as it is v. 20. of 1 *Cor.* 11. *When ye come together therefore into one place, this is not to eat the Lord's Supper, becauſe they had turned it into a prophanation*; But *R. B.*'s obſervation on theſe Words, p. 109. is of no force at all to prove his purpoſe: *He ſaith not, this is not the right manner to eat, but this is not to eat the Lord's Supper,* becauſe (ſaith he) the Supper of the *Lord* is Spiritual, and a Myſtery. *Anſ.* But the right manner of a thing in many caſes is ſo eſſential to the thing, that the want of the right manner deſtroys the thing it ſelf. As the right manner of a Circle is to have all the ſtraight Lines drawn from the Center to the Circumference equal, and if this be wanting, the Figure is not a Circle. Yea, If the right

man-

manner of Prayer be wanting, so that it be directed to *God*, yet not in true words, it is not true Prayer, and if not in truth and sincerity of Heart, it is not true Prayer. His other Arguments from *Rom.* 14.7. *Coloss.* 2. 16. *Heb.* 9. 10. are all answered above sufficiently, Part 1. Sect. 6.

SECT. IX.

Page 121. *His last Argument is general against both the Outward Baptism, and the Supper. It remains* (saith he) *for our Adversaries to shew us how they come by Power and Authority to Administer them.* ——. *Their Power must be derived from the* Apostles, *either mediately, or immediately; but they have no mediate Power, because of the Interruption made by the Apostacy: And for an immediate Power or Command by the Sprit of God to Administer these things, none of our Adversaries pretend to it.*

Ans. 1. The Argument is unduly worded in the former part of it; for Men may have a Power that is neither from the Apostles mediately nor immediately; not mediately, as he thinks he has proved, nor yet immediately from the Apostles, because not their immediate Successors. But, why may they not have a Power mediately from *Christ*, after some true manner, and yet in some sort immediate also? If we consider the several significations of the Words mediate and immediate, none of which are Scripture words, any more, or scarce so much, as other words they reject, because not Scripture words; and because of the ambiguous and doubtful signification of the Words mediate and immediate; they may be omitted, and other Words used to as good, or better effect. But if we may be allowed to use the words mediate and immediate; one Sense of the word *immediate* is a Call from *Christ's* Person, speaking with an audible Voice to the outward Ear; such as the twelve Apostles had, and *Paul* also. This I know none now pretends to. Another Sense of the word immediate is, a Call by the Holy Spirit in the Hearts of them who are so Called, in the same way and manner, as the Prophets were both taught their Prophecies, and called to deliver them, and commit them to Writing, which was by a Prophetick Spirit that did Infallibly guide them, in every Sentence and Word of their Message, without the least possibility of Error or Mistake; and as so Taught and Called, without the need or use of any outward means whatsoever. If some of the Teachers among the Quakers have pretended to any such Inward Teaching or Calling, as

it

it can be easily proved they have, it can be as easily proved, that they have not been so taught nor called, because in too many things, wherein they have pretended to such Teaching and Calling, they have Bewrayed themselves miserably, and laid themselves open to the Judgment of the weaker sort of Sincere Christians, who have been able to prove, that in too many things they have delivered as Divine Revelations, they have contradicted the Holy Scriptures, and so have grosly Erred. A Third sort of immediate Teaching and Calling, is by taking the Etymologie of the Word immediate, to signifie not without all Means, but in and with the Means; as when it is gene rally acknowledged, that there is an immediate Supernatural Divine Concurrence of the Spirit of *God*, that assisteth the Faithful in all truly holy Actions; yea, in all holy Thoughts and Desires, Words and Works; yet not without the use of outward Means, but in the due and frequent use of them; as in Reading, Hearing, and Meditating upon what hath been Read, or Heard. Now this sort of inward Teaching and Calling by the Spirit, as it is not without means altogether; so is it not without all possibility of Erring, or Mistake; for though no Error can proceed from the Spirit of *God*, nor can the Spirit Err; yet a Man that has the Spirit of *God* working in his Heart, both to illuminate his Understanding, and move and incline his Will to good Things, may through Humane Weakness and Inadvertency, or by some Prejudice of Education, or wrong Information of his Teachers, misapply, and misunderstand the Spirits inward Illuminations and Motions, which he is the more likely to do, if he do not duly and diligently apply his Mind, as to the Spirits inward Illumination, so to the Directions and Instructions, given to us in the Holy Scriptures, to examine and find the agreement of the inward with the outward; for certainly if the Persuasions that any Man hath, contradict the plain Directions and Institutions given in the Holy Scriptures, they are not of the Spirit of *God*, whatever appearance they may seem to have of Power or Evidence; the joynt concurrence of the Spirit of Truth within, and the instrumental and subordinate help of the Scripture without, given us to help our weakness, may be compared to the natural Light of the Sun, or Candle that we read with (in some sort) though this, and all other Similitudes fall short of a full Illustration; for as we cannot Read without the Light, though the Book lie open before us; so when the Light Shines, yet it will not

teach

teach us what is in the Book, unless we look on it, and also be taught to Read in it. Even so the Light of the Holy Spirit, shining upon the Ideas, and Perceptions of our Minds, as conveyed to us by what we have heard or read out of the Holy Scriptures, opens to us the true hidden Sense and Truth of them, with Life and Power, and great inward Clearness and Evidence, Joy and Satisfaction ; and thus if we find that the Spirits Illumination, worketh in our Hearts and Minds an Assent to the Truth of what is Recorded in the Holy Scriptures ; we can with all readiness receive it. But if what we suppose to be a Divine Illumination, discord from the Truth of the Scriptures ; we ought to reject it, and by no means to receive it, for it is not Divine, but Humane ; or which is worse, Diabolical. Now according to this last Sense of the Word immediate, *i.e.* inward Teaching, and Call of the Spirit, in the use of outward Means and Helps, and especially the Holy Scriptures, I see not, but it may be granted that Men may be found, and are to be found, that have a true immediate Call from the Spirit of *Christ* in their Hearts, both to Preach, and Administer these Divine Institutions of the outward *Baptism* and *Supper* ; and all this well consisting with the mediate orderly Call, where there is a Constitute Church, though not every way so rightly and duly Constitute, as was in the Apostles Days, and in the purest Times succeeding the Apostles. There is ground to believe, that *God* raised up many such in the beginning of the Reformation from Popery ; and though since that beginning, too many Particulars have rather gone backward than forward ; yet the Success of the Ministry, and excellent Books that have come forth, time after time, of many Worthy Persons, however in some things mistaken, and the truly Christian Lives and Conversations of many, through all the Protestant Churches, though in comparison of the great multitude that are Prophane and Scandalous, they are but a few, may be a good Ground of Evidence, that *God* is truly among them, and doth own the Remnant that are Sincere, and their Ministry ; to whom an Allusion may be made of what was said to the Church of *Sardis*, (the *Greek* Word *Sardis*, is in the Plural Number) thou hast a few Names in *Sardis*, who have not Defiled their Garments ; they shall walk with me in White, for they are Worthy. I know there are some, who do more than make an Allusion in the Case, and think that by the Church of *Sardis*, is really meant the collective Body of the Protestant Churches, throughout the several Parts of the World ; which I will not here be positive, either to affirm, or deny, but either by way of Allusion, or by Hypothesis, let us conceive that the Collective Body of the Protestant Churches, answers to *Sardis*, and not this or that particular spot or part of the Earth, or this or that particular Country, Province, or City, but the Collective Body of the whole, that by the Harmony of their Confessions already extant, may be allowed to hold the Fundamentals of the Christian Faith, however many are under great mistakes in other things. Now we do not find this Church of *Sardis* blamed for Idolatry or suffering it, as some of the other Seven Churches we find so blamed, and particularly that of *Pergamus* and *Thyatira*, that may allude to the Dark and Idolatrous Times of Popery, for divers Ages foregoing. The great things of the *Sardis* Church that are blamed are, that her Works were not perfect before *God*; that she had more a Name of Life, than the possession of it, which seems to paint out to the Life, the Collective Body of the Protestant Churches, who yet have a few Names, who have not defiled their Garments, and who are worthy; which few Names are not confined to this or that particular Denomination, but scattered and dispersed through the whole, as so many Grains of pure Silver or Gold thro' a great mass or Lump of Oar, where is much more Dross and Refuse.

And because things receive their denomination from the better part frequently, therefore I judge that the Protestant Churches are, with a respect to, and on the account of these few Names that have kept their Garments clean, to be reckoned a true Church, and is so reputed of *God*. And therefore it were very advisable, that all that sincerely Believe in *God*, and in *Christ*, and love *God* and *Christ*, and agree in Fundamentals, as they generally do, that they would Love one another, and Repute one another as Brethren, walk together, and worship *God* together in Spirit and in Truth; the Stronger condescending to the Weaker, and becoming all things to all Men, and in every thing that is not manifestly sinful, yielding one to another, endeavouring to be of one Heart and Soul in true Christian Love and Affection, however differing in some lesser matters, both as to Judgment and Practice. This I hope *God* in his own time will bring to pass; and for this, as many (I believe) sincerely pray, so do I cordially joyn my earnest Supplications with them. And let this suffice at present for an Answer to that last Argument, about the Call, as whether mediate or immediate.

It

SECT. X.

IT is not to be doubted, but many in the Proteſtant Churches can give as great evidence, and far greater, of their true Inward Call to the work of the Miniſtry, than many, or moſt of the Teachers among the People call'd Quakers; and that not only by the conformity of their Doctrine and Converſation to the Holy Scriptures, but the real ſucceſs and good effect of their Miniſtry by the Bleſſing of *God* upon their Labours: And if the noiſe of boldly claiming to themſelves the only Privilege of being the Church of *Chriſt*, and their Teachers and Miniſters the only Miniſters of *Chriſt*, having only the Inward Call, and furniſhing of the Spirit, be laid aſide, and the Queſtion fairly and calmly ſtated, it will not bear great Diſpute to make it appear which of the two ſorts have the beſt Marks of the true Church and Miniſtry. Would the Quakers leſs value themſelves, for ſome ſingular things, which at beſt are but as the Cummin and the Mint, and ſome of them not ſo much, they might eaſily find themſelves equalled, and far excelled in great part by many others in the greater things of true Divine Knowledge, Piety and Virtue. Only, for a Concluſion, let this be added; that ſuppoſe preſent Adminiſtrators could not be readily found, ſo qualified, as to ſilence all the ſcrupuloſities of Objectors, this will not prove that *Baptiſm* and the *Supper* are not the Inſtitutions of *Chriſt*, as it will not prove that Preaching the Goſpel is not a Divine Inſtitution, becauſe in many parts of the World true Preaching has been wanting, and yet is; yea, according to the Quakers narrow and ſcanty Charity, true Preaching was generally loſt in the World, untill the Quakers were raiſed up about the year 1648. Doth it therefore follow, that it was no Inſtitution of *Chriſt* to the Apoſtles, and their Succeſſors to Preach the Goſpel? And here let it be noticed, that I put a diſtinction betwixt a Power given to a Man to uſe the Gifts that *God* has given him, in teaching others leſs knowing, and a Paſtoral Gift, of not only Teaching, but Adminiſtring theſe Divine Inſtitutions of *Baptiſm* and the *Supper*, and doing divers other things relating to the Diſcipline, Order, and Government of the People, over whom, by *God*'s appointment, and the Peoples conſent, he is ſet to be their Paſtor and Watchman.

Here Note Reader, that what is ſaid in this ſmall Treatiſe, in Anſwer to the Arguments of the principal Teachers of the Quakers a-above named, will also serve for an Answer to *W. Dell*'s Book, against *Water-Baptism*; for there is nothing Material in his Book, but what is in their Books, upon that Subject, though they borrowed his Arguments, and have so great a liking to his Book, that they have Printed it often, again, and again; and indeed, as they borrowed from him, so the most of his Arguments he seems to have borrowed from *Socinus*, who hath used the same Arguments for the most part, long before *W. Dell*, or the *Quakers* appeared in the World. Only please Reader to take notice of that great piece of Ignorance in *W. Dell*, to affirm so bold an Untruth; that *Zacharias*, *John* the Baptist's Father was High Priest. The more particular Questions about *Baptism*, relating either to the proper Subjects of it, or manner of it, are not needful to be handled here, the design of this Treatise being to Convince such of the *Quakers* as are willing to read it, that *Baptism*, and the *Supper* are Divine Institutions; till they own this, it would be Preposterous to persuade them about those other. Were the People, called *Quakers*, convinced of this great Truth; that the outward *Baptism* by *Water*, and the *Supper*, are Divine Institutions, and ought to be practised by them, as becoming true Christians, there are some thousands of them who are at Age, and have Children at Age, who never had any manner of outward *Baptism*; if these have true Faith in *Jesus Christ*, and can sincerely say, as the Eunuch did, *Acts* 8. 37. *I believe that Jesus Christ is the Son of God, and do renounce all those Errors that are contrary to the true Faith in the Fundamental Doctrins thereof*; there is no question but they may be *Baptized*, they are proper enough Subjects of it; and when they are thus well Prepared and Qualified to Receive it, it may be hoped that they will be Directed and Guided by the *Lord*, where, and how to find the Persons that may be fit to Administer it unto them. Such among them who scruple, or question the manner of *Baptism* by Sprinkling, may receive it by Dipping; for all *Christendom* own that that Form may be used Lawfully; and that Adult Persons having Faith in the *Lord Jesus*, after their giving the Confession of the same, may, and ought to be *Baptized*. And such among them who might scruple to receive it from Persons of another Denomination, might find some of their own Way to Administer it unto them. For it were strange, to suppose, that among so many hundreds of Men, professing to have an immediate, or inward Call to that part of the Ministry by Preaching, and Prayer, there should not be some found among them, who might

might apprehend that they are as immediately call'd to the other part of the Miniſtry, of *Baptiſm*, and the *Supper*, after they are truly convinced that they are Goſpel Inſtitutions. There is ſome Ground of Hope, that many among them will be brought to ſome good Conſideration, and better Underſtanding, ſo as to ſee the great hurt and loſs that it has been unto them, to reject thoſe things, and alſo to come to that good and ſolid Diſcretion and Judgment of the great Profit and Advantage it would be to them, to receive the Practice of them among them, for their Spiritual Good and Honour of their Chriſtian Profeſſion (thereby declaring, as well as by their Chriſtian Lives and Converſations, that they are the Diſciples of *Chriſt*, by this Teſtimony of their Love to him; that they keep theſe his Commandments, as well as the others that he has enjoyned; remembring that he that breaketh the leaſt of his Commandments, and teacheth Men to do ſo, ſhall be leaſt in the Kingdom of Heaven) and alſo for the removing the great Scandal and Offence of many Tender People, who are greatly ſtumbled at their Way, in not only omitting, but ſpeaking Reproachfully againſt thoſe Sacred Inſtitutions. It will be no occaſion of Diſhonour to them, nor Argument of their declining, or going backward from the Truth, to own and receive the Practice of theſe things, that they have needleſly, and for want of due Conſideration, dropt, and loſt; more than it would be to a Man that had dropt ſome piece of Money, or Jewel, to return, and ſtoop to take it up again. That which addeth to my Ground of Hope in this thing, is, that ſome among them have privately acknowledged, that they are ſenſible of the Hurt and Diſadvantage that they have been at, as a Body of People, for laying thoſe Practices aſide.

SECT. XI.

Having finiſhed my Anſwers to the Arguments of the four Perſons, above named, againſt the outward *Baptiſm*, and the *Supper*, I think fit to take notice of the Arguments of *George Fox*, (the greateſt Perſon among the *Quakers*, when living, and whoſe Words are ſtill as Oracles unto them) againſt theſe Divine Inſtitutions; to which indeed little more Anſwer is needful, than what is given to thoſe other, for his Arguments are Included in theirs, and ſo may the Anſwers be in the Anſwers to them. His Argument againſt the outward *Baptiſm*, I find to be but one, in a Book of his, called, *Something in Anſwer to the Old Common-Prayer-Book, Printed at London*, 1660 p. 18.

p. 18. *And doth not that in* Mattth. 28. *say, Baptize into the Name; and is n.t that more than in the Name?* This the Reader will find Anfwered above, in Reply to fome of their Arguments; *but to Baptize into the Name,* Acts 8. they grant not to be the inward *Baptifm*; and therefore, nor is that *Matth.* 28. the Particles *in,* and *into,* being frequently the fame in Signification, both in *Englifh.* and *Greek,* yea, and in *Hebrew* alfo, and *Latin,* and generally in other Languages.

His Arguments againft the outward *Supper,* are as followeth, p. 26. *They that received the Bread and Wine in remembrance of Chrift, fhewing his Death till he come, which the Apoftle had received of the Lord, and delivered to the* Corinthians, *which they were to examine, and Eat, and Drink in remembrance of Chrift's Death, till he come.* This was in, 1 Cor. *Then he wrote again to the* Corinthians, *and bids them examine themfelves, and prove their own felves; knew they not that Chrift was in them, except they were Reprobates?* So they may fee that this was not a ftanding Form; *but as often as they did it, they did it in remembrance of Chrift, till he come; and then examine your felves, prove your felves, If Chrift be not in you, except ye be Reprobates; fo if you have him within, what need you to have that which puts in remembrance of him? And fo if ye be rifen with Chrift; feek thofe things that are above; for now Bread and Wine is below, which is the remembrance of his Death, fo that part dies with him; which muft have a Sign to put in remembrance of him. For the Apoftles forgot, who faid, that they thought that that Man fhould deliver Ifrael.*

Anf. The fubftance of this is replyed unto above; only I thought fit to take notice, how impertinent and idle his Argument is, from his comparing the firft Epiftle to the *Corinthians,* with a paffage in his fecond Epiftle to them; as if in his firft Epiftle *Paul* had delivered the Command or Practice of it unto them, becaufe *Chrift* was not then come in them; but when he wrote again, he was come in them. Which reafoning of G. F. is built on a moft falfe Foundation; for *Paul* did believe that *Chrift* was as truly come in the *Corinthians,* at his firft writing, as at his fecond; for as he faid unto them in his fecond Epiftle, *know ye not that Jefus Chrift is in you,* &c. 2 Cor. 13. 5. So he faid in his firft Epiftle, 1 Cor. 6. 19. *Know ye not that your body is the Temple of the Holy Ghoft, which is in you, which ye have of God,* &c. And furely, when they had the Holy Ghoft in them, they had *Chrift* in them; from which it appears, that this Argument of G. F. is exceeding impertinent, and built on a grofs and manifeft untruth. But it

was

was the way of *G. F.* What he neither did nor could prove from Scripture, he would boldly perſuade by his Authority and Stamp, with ſaying, *This is the word of the Lord unto you,* and then it was no more to be queſtioned; and if any did, they were reckoned bad Spirits, like *Corah,* &c. Alſo his ſaying, Bread and Wine is from below, and they who have *Chriſt* in them need not the Sign; all this is anſwered above; and had he not been very weak in his underſtanding and inconſiderate, he might have eaſily obſerved, that this way of his Reaſoning was equally againſt all Outward Miniſtry, Words, and Writings, which are not *Chriſt,* more than Bread and Wine. And are not his many Papers, about Orders, and Womens Dreſſes, from below, ſeeing they are viſible things, and therefore by his Argument, they ſhould be rejected?

There is yet one Argument behind, which I have found in a Manuſcript having *Humphry Norton*'s Name to it, a Preacher of great Name formerly among the Quakers, and in extraordinary repute with *Edward Burrough,* and *Francis Howgil,* as appeareth by their Epiſtles of Recommendation concerning him, they both ſent with him to Friends in *Ireland,* contained in the ſaid Manuſcript; unto you all (ſaith *Edward Burrough*) I do him recommend, as a faithful Labourer, to be received by you in the Name of him that ſends him, in tender pity for you all, and the Bleſſing of the *Lord* upon his Faithfulneſs I doubt not, *&c.* Dated *London* 19. 3d. mo. 1656. And ſaith *Fr. Howgil,* receive *Humphry Norton* in the *Lord,* whom the *Lord* hath moved to come unto you, who is a Brother, and Faithful in the *Lord*'s Work, and be Subject unto him in the *Lord,* all unto him; for I much deſired that he might come unto you, and ſo the *Lord* hath ordered it; and as you receive him, you receive me, *F. Howgil.*

This Man, *Humphry Norton,* after his Arrival in *Ireland,* in the year 1656, writ, and ſpread about ſeveral Papers among the People, call'd Baptiſts, and others; of which I have ſeen divers contained in a Manuſcript, all Writ by one Hand, and having his Name to them.

His Argument againſt *Baptiſm,* is in the following Words. Q. 15. And now ye Baptiſts, ſeeing that *Chriſt* is come, and hath *Baptized* us, and all Men come unto him, tell me, whether there be *any Baptiſm but one;* ſeeing the Apoſtle ſaith, *one Lord, one Faith, one Baptiſm,* Eph. 4.5,6. And whether *Baptiſm* be not a Doctrin, yea, or nay? If you ſay an Ordinance, whether it be not Aboliſhed; yea, or nay; ſeeing the Scripture ſaith, *having aboliſhed in his Fleſh the Enmity, even the Law of Commandments contained in Ordinances; for to make in himself of Twain, one new Man; so making Peace*, Eph. 2. 15.

Ans. That concerning one *Baptism*, is fully Answered above: To the latter concerning Ordinances, the Word in the Greek ἐν δόγμασι is not properly Translated Ordinances, but rather Opinions, or Persuasions. But let it be Translated Ordinances; how doth this prove, that therefore *water-Baptism* is Abolished, unless the Argument be built upon this Supposition; that all Ordinances are Abolished, and consequently *Baptism* with *water*, and at the same rate, Preaching and Prayer must be Abolished, which are no less Ordinances.

And in the same Parcel of Queries, the fifth Querie is; now Answer in plain Words; From whence must this *Christ* ye wait for come, and in what Generation, and of what Family, and out of what Country, and of whom must he be Born? that they may no longer be deceived by you, who have kept them gazing after a false *Christ*; well may it be called Gazing; but leave it, and mind these in white Apparel, which Reproves you for it, *Acts* 1. 10, 11.

This *Humphry Norton*, after some Years went into New *England*, and after his Return, Prints a Book at *London* (which I find Quoted in another Printed Book) having the like, or the same Queries for Substance; the Words are these. *Is not Christ God, and is not God a Spirit? you look for a Christ without you; from what Coast or Country shall he come? What Country-man is he? You stand Gazing up in the Clouds after a Man, but we stand by in white chiding of you.* Reader, are not these dreadful Words, enough to make all Christian Ears to tingle? it is no wonder that they have so generally Construed these Words; *ye shew forth his Death until he come*, to be only his inward coming; when the chiefest Teachers among them had no Faith of his outward coming to Judge the World. And it is but too likely, that *E. Burrough*, and *F. Howgil*, were as great Unbelievers as he in that great Fundamental Article of the Christian Religion; and if they were not, they were miserably deceived, and did miserably deceive themselves by their supposed Gift of Discerning; to give such high Recommendations and Praises of a Man, that deserved not to be numbred among the lowest Rank of Christians, who hath dared thus openly, like one of the *Heathen* Opposers, to Scoff at our Blessed *Lord*'s coming without us to Judgment; but never any Christian gave him occasion for such a Scoffing manner of Questioning, it being universally believed by all Christians, that our *Lord* will come from Heaven in the same Body wherein he Ascended, ed, and is not to be Born again of a Woman. Again, In another Paper that hath his Name to it, there are these Words; *and whereas he Accused us for denying Chrift's Merits; I say, that which can be Merited, is of Self; and that which is of Chrift is freely given.* But such a word is *not in Scripture, as* Chrift's *Merits, but is fetch'd from the whore a at* Rome *by them.* Behold the Man, whom *E. Burrough's* called a Faithful Labourer, and *F. Howgil* called a Brother Faithful in the *Lord's* Work, to whom he would have all the *Quakers* in *Ireland* to be Subject! How can they who follow such blind Guides, but fall into the Ditch with them? Is there any greater, or so great Blindness to be found in the Blindeft, and moft Ignorant of the Papifts?

In a Book of mine, called, *Truth's Defence,* p. 140. I find an other Argument I have used against the *Supper*; the Effect of which is contained in these following Words; *what Chrift did at that time, and bid his Difciples do until he come, is no Gofpel Ordinance, becaufe it was done in the Night, or Evening of the old Covenant Difpenfation, and confequently was to come to an end with it. Anf.* I freely acknowledge this Argument is Weak and Unfound, and the way to Anfwer it, is by denying the Confequence to be True and Juft; for moftly what *Chrift* Taught was in the Evening, or latter part of the old Covenant; but it doth not therefore follow that it was to end with it. As also where I have said in my Book, called, *Presbyterian and Independent Churches,* &c. P. 185. *That which ye now use is neither Subftantial Dinner nor Supper, being only a Crumb of Bread,* &c. I acknowledge, was unadvifedly faid, and as weakly Argued; for the end of that outward Inftitution, was not any outward Subftantial *Dinner* or *Supper,* as neither was that of the Paschal Lamb. And also where, p. 184. of the fame, I have argued, that the use of the outward Signs of *Baptifm* and the *Supper,* did fuit moft with the Ages and State of Children, for they fuit well enough with the moft grown Chriftians, while remaining in the Mortal Body.

SECT. XII.

AND thus I have Anfwered to all the Arguments brought againft the outward *Baptifm* and the *Supper,* by their feveral Writers, and chief Teachers that I have found in their Books; not omitting any to my beft Remembrance, of any Note; where though I have brought in *G. Fox* among the laft, becaufe I had not found the particular Book

where

where his Arguments were, until I had finished my Answer to the other four preceeding; yet he was the first among the *Quakers*, that led them, as into divers other great Errors, so into this of rejecting the outward *Baptism*, and the *Supper*, grounding all upon a pretended Divine Inspiration; and as by that Pretence he did throw down the Institutions of *Christ*, leading many thousands into the Ditch with him; So by the same pretended Authority, he set up outward Orders and Ordinances of his own, particularly that of Women's Meetings, giving them Rule and Government in the Church, and appointing all Marriages to come before the Women's Meetings, before they could pass, or be allowed by the Community; which hath no Footstep, or Warrant from the Holy Scripture. And when it could not be proved from Scripture, though Essayed by him and others, miserably straining the Scriptures, contrary to their true Sense; the Result was, that it was commanded by *G. Fox*, and whoever did not Obey, were judged by him and his Followers, Apostates, and Enemies to Truth.

In the next place, I shall bring some clear Proofs from Scripture; shewing that outward *Baptism* and the *Supper*, are the Institutions of *Christ* under the Gospel. And first, as to *Baptism* with *water*. That is an Institution of *Christ*, which he did command his Apostles, and their Successors, to Practise to the end of the World.

But he commanded them to Practise *Baptism* with *water*, &c. Therefore,

That he commanded them to Practise *Baptism* with *water*, is proved from *Matth.* 28. 19. And from what is above Discoursed in Answer to their Objections, it is apparent that *Water-Baptism* is there meant.

And that the Apostles, and all the Churches of *Christ* did understand that *Water-Baptism* was an Institution of *Christ*, is clear from the universal Practice of Believers in the Apostles Days; so that it cannot be instanced where any came under the Profession of Faith in *Christ*; but they received *Baptism* with *water*, either by the Apostles, or other Ministers of *Christ*.

Again, That which is declared in Scripture to be a means of Grace and Salvation, and which hath Gospel Promises annexed to it, is a Divine Institution.

But so is *Baptism* with *water*, as the following Scriptures prove, *Mark* 16. 16. *Acts* 2. 38. *Acts* 22. 16. *Rom.* 6. 3. *Gal.* 3. 27. *Col.* 2. 12. 1 *Pet.* 3. 21. And though these *Quakers* will not allow that the

Scrip-

Scriptures above-mentioned, are to be understood of *Baptism* with *Water*; yet by what is above Discoursed, in Answer to their Objections, it is evident, that they are to be understood of *Baptism* with *Water*, the Sign being accompanied with the thing signified, in all that duly received it.

Again, That which is made a Ground of Unity among the Faithful, together with Faith and Hope, and Calling, is a Divine Institution; but one *Baptism*, as well as one Faith, one Hope, one Calling, is made a Ground of Unity among the Faithful, *Eph.* 4. 5.

And that the *one Baptism* there, is the *Baptism* with *Water* (the thing signified going along with the Sign) is above proved in the Answer to the foregoing Objections. And thus much briefly, for Proof of *Water-Baptism*, its being an Institution of *Christ* under the Gospel, to continue to the end of the World; because he promised to be with his Ministers to the end of the World, in their doing what he commanded them.

Next, That the *Supper* by breaking of *Bread*, and the use of the *Cup* is an Institution of *Christ*, until his last coming, is proved by the like Arguments, that *Water-Baptism* is proved to be an Institution of *Christ*; for first it was commanded by *Christ*; *Do this in remembrance of me*; *as oft as you Eat this Bread, and Drink this Cup, ye shew forth the Lord's Death till he come.* And that this is his outward coming to Judge the World, is above proved.

Secondly, it is a Means of Grace; *the Bread which we break is it not the Communion of the Lord's Body? The Cup which we bless is it not the Communion of his Blood?* That is, are they not, both Signs and Means exhibiting to us the Communion of his Body and Blood, and the Spiritual Blessings that come to Believers thereby? For indeed all the Signs that ever *God* appointed to his People, were Means of Grace, and not bare Signs or Symbols.

Thirdly, the *Bread* and *Wine* in the *Supper*, is made a ground of Unity among the Faithful, as well as *Baptism*; *we being many are one Bread, and all are made partakers of that one Bread.* The Objections made against the Sense of these and the like Scriptures, are above fully Answered; so that I see no occasion to say any more at present, by way of Argument on this Subject.

N

An APPENDIX.

Containing some Observations upon some Passages, in a Book of **W. Penn,** *call'd,* A Caveat against Popery; *and on some Passages of a Book of* **John Pennington,** *call'd,* The Fig-Leaf Covering Discovered.

IN a Book of *W. Penn*, called, *A Seasonable Caveat against Popery*, Printed in the Year 1670. I find the following Passage, p. 18. *But if there be some Virtue signified by the Wine, more than by the Bread, it is horrid Sacriledge to Rob the Sign, much more the thing signified. It is a Supper, and at Supper there should be to Drink, as well as to Eat; there can be no Body without Blood, and the Drinking of his Blood, shews a Shedding of his Blood for the World, and a Participation of it. Besides the Sign is incompleat, and the end of that Sacrament, or Sign, not fully Answered, but plainly maimed, and what God hath put together, they have put asunder; so that the Falseness and Inscriptural Practice of these Men are very manifest.*

Obs. Reader: Wouldest thou not think by these Words, that *W. Penn* was in good earnest, Pleading for the Sacrament (as he calls it) or Sign of the Supper? And hadst thou not known that *W. Penn* was the Author of that Book; would'st thou not have concluded, whoever was the Author was rightly Principl'd for the *Supper*, compleatly Administred under both Signs, by the Arguments he brings for it? as first, If there be some Virtue signified by the *Wine*, more than by the *Bread*, it is horrid Sacriledge to Rob the Sign, *&c.* The Antecedent is true, by *W. Penn*, otherwise his Argument is vain; and therefore the Consequence must be true, which is this; It is horrid Sacriledge to Rob the Sign. Now if it be horrid Sacriledge in the Popish Priests and Teachers, to Rob the Sign of *Wine* in the *Supper*; is it not as horrid, or rather more horrid Sacriledge in *W. Penn*, and the rest of the Teachers of the *Quakers* to have Robb'd both the Signs, the *Bread* as well as the *Wine* ? and under the Guilt of this Robbery and Sacriledge they still continue, I wish they may Repent of it, that they may find Mercy and Forgiveness. His second Argument is this. *It is a Supper, and at Supper there should be to Drink, as well as to Eat.* But how is it a *Supper*, when there

An Appendix.

is neither to Eat nor to Drink: If the Popish Teachers have maimed the *Supper*, which he blames them for; how much more is he and his Brethren Blameworthy, who have quite Abolished it? His third Argument for the Cup is, the Drinking of his Blood, shews a Shedding of his Blood; but how doth it shew it among the *Quakers*, who have totally Abolished the *Bread* as well as the *Cup*? His fourth Argument is, *the Sign is incompleat, and the end of that Sacrament or Sign, not fully Answered.* But how is the end of that Sacrament, or Sign any wise Answered among the *Quakers*, who have Abolished both Signs? His fifth Argument is, *what God hath put together, they have put asunder*; so that the Falsness and Inscriptural Practice of these Men is very manifest. Now to Prosecute and Retort his Argument upon himself; If it be a hainous Sin to put asunder what *God* hath put together; is it not as hainous, or rather more, to put away, or Abolish both things which *God* hath put together? If they do Evil that separate Man and Wife, whom *God* hath joyned, or put together; do not they worse who kill them both?

If it be said, *W. Penn*'s Arguments are only on Supposition, and used against the Papists, *ad hominem.* I Answer, first, This doth not appear by his Words, which are Positive. Secondly, If here he only Argues on Supposition, and *ad hominem*; how shall we know when he Argueth Positively, and is in good earnest? Thirdly, His Arguments seem to me and, I think they will seem to many others, not only Positive, but more valid and strong, than any Arguments he hath brought against them.

Again, In the same Book, p. 20. concerning the Sacrifice of the Altar, he saith ——notwithstanding the Scripture expressly tells us, *that we have our High Priest, that needs not Sacrifice once a year, but who hath offered one Sacrifice, and that by the will of God we are Sanctified, through the Offering of the Body of Jesus Christ, once for all, and that by one Offering he perfected them that are Sanctified,* Heb. 10. 10, 11, 14. *Yet do they daily Sacrifice him afresh,* As if his first were insufficient, or their daily Sins required a new one.

Obj. Do not these Arguments of *W. Penn*, against *Christ*, his being daily Offered up a Sacrifice in the Mass, prove as effectually, *W. Penn*, and *G. Whitehead*'s Doctrin to be false, in their Defence of *W. Smith*, who said, in p. 64. of his Primmer, second Part; *we believe that Christ in us doth offer up himself a living Sacrifice unto God for us; by which the Wrath and Justice of God is appeased towards us.* This *W. Penn* Confirms

An Appendix.

in his *Rejoynder to* J. Faldo, p. 285. *saying, that Chrift offers himfelf in his Children, in the nature of a Mediating Sacrifice; and that Chrift is a Mediator, and an Attoner in the Confciences of his People, at what time they fhall fall under any Mifcarriage, if they unfeignedly Repent;* according to 1 John 2. 1, 2. and *G. Whitehead* is very large in the Defence and Confirmation of it, in his Book, called, *The Light and Life of Chrift within*, p. 44. And Quotes at leaft feven feveral places of Scripture to prove it, *viz. That Chrift in them doth offer up himfelf a Sacrifice unto God for them, by which the Wrath and Juftice of God is appeafed towards them*. All which Scriptures, and many more, refpecting the Sacrifice of *Chrift* without us, and his Blood outwardly Shed, they have moft grofly Perverted and Mifapplyed to a fuppofed Daily Offering of *Chrift* by way of Sacrifice in them to Appeafe the Wrath and Juftice of *God*. Now let *W. Penn* Anfwer to his own Arguments which he had ufed againft the Sacrifice of *Chrift* in the Mafs; for any that are not wilfully blind may fee, they are of equal force againft his fuppofed and invented Sacrifice of *Chrift*, daily offered in every *Quaker* when they Sin, to Appeafe the Wrath and Juftice of *God*.

And here I think fit to repeat fome Queftions I Propofed to *W. Penn*, by way of Argument, againft this falfe Notion of his, (and of *G. Whitehead*, which they Originally received from *G. Fox*, and he it is very probable from Familifts and Ranters, who had the fame Notion, as I can eafily prove) that *Chrift* offers up himfelf in them, to Appeafe the Wrath and Juftice of *God*, in the Nature of a Mediating Sacrifice. (Note Reader, thefe Words befpeak their Senfe to be a Sacrifice, really and ftrictly fo taken; yea, the Sacrifice within, to be the only real and ftrict Sacrifice; for the other without, of *Chrift*'s Body and Blood without the Gates of *Jerufalem*, was the Type, the Hiftory. The Lamb without, fhews forth the Lamb within, faid *W. Penn*, one outward thing cannot be the proper Figure, or Reprefentation of another outward thing). Thefe Queftions are in my Book, called, *Grofs Error and Hypocrifie Detected* in *G. Whitehead*, and fome of his Brethren, p. 20. And I have juft caufe to propofe them again, to his and his Brethrens Confideration; becaufe I have not to this Day received any Anfwer to them, either from *W. Penn*, or *George Whitehead*, nor from *Tho. Elwood*, who hath Writ a pretended Anfwer to this very Book, called, *Grofs Error*; &c. who hath paffed by, not only thefe Queries containing fo many Arguments as there are Queries; but the other chief things in that Book; and yet he and his Brethren Glory, how they have Anfwered.

An Appendix.

fwered all my Books, when in effect they have Anfwered none of them to purpofe, and fome of them not at all; as my fecond Narrative of the Proceedings of the Meeting at *Turner's-Hall*, that has been above a Year in Print; (as no more have they Anfwered to *Satan Difrob'd*; done by the Author of the *Snake in the Grafs*; being a Reply to *Tho. Elwood*'s pretended Anfwer to my firft Narrative, which faved me the Labour of Replying to it.) And indeed, the Book, called, *Grofs Error*, &c. has been in Print near three Years, and yet no Anfwer has been given to thefe Queries; which are as follow. 1. If Satisfaction be totally Excluded (as *W. Penn* hath Argued againft the Satisfaction of the Man *Chrift Jefus* without us; and by his Death and Sufferings on the Crofs, *Reafon againft Railing*, p. 91. becaufe a Sin, or Debt cannot be both Paid and Forgiven; what need is there of a Mediating Sacrifice of *Chrift* within Men, more than without them? 2. Seeing it is the Nature of all Sacrifices for Sin, that they be Slain, and their Blood Shed; how is *Chrift* Slain in his Children, and when? For we Read in Scripture, that *Chrift* lived in the Faithful, as he did in *Paul*; but not that he is Slain in them. 3. If any Slay the Life of *Chrift* in them by their Sins; doth not that hinder the Life to be a Sacrifice by *G. Whitehead*'s Argument; that the Killing of *Chrift* outwardly, being the Act of Wicked Men, could be no Meritorious Act? 4. Where doth the Scripture fay, *Chrift* offers himfelf up in his Children a Sacrifice for Sin? 5. Is not this to make many Sacrifices, or at leaft to fay, that *Chrift* offers himfelf often, yea, Millions of times, contrary to Scripture, that faith, *Chrift* offered up himfelf once? 6. Why could no Beaft under the Law, that had a Blemifh, be offered; but to fignifie that *Chrift* was to offer up himfelf in no other Body, but that which was without all Sin? 7. Why was it Prophecied of *Chrift*; a Body haft thou prepared me, why not Bodies many, if he offer up himfelf in the Bodies of all the Saints? 8. Is not this to make the Sacrifice of *Chrift* of lefs Value and Efficacie in his own Body, than his Sacrifice in *W. Penn*'s Body? becaufe the Sacrifice of *Chrift*, in that Body that was offered at *Jerufalem*, was the Type, this in *W. Penn*'s Body, the Anti-type; That the Hiftory, This the Myftery. 9. Doth not this ftrengthen the Papifts in their falfe Faith; that *Chrift* is daily offered in the Mafs, an unbloody Sacrifice? I defire that *W. Penn*, and *G. Whitehead*, will give a pofitive Anfwer to thefe Queries; and fhew, wherein my Arguments againft their Notion of *Chrift*'s being offered a Sacrifice in Men, are not fo ftrong againft them, as *W. Penn*'s Arguments

ments are against the Papist's Notion; that *Christ* is offered up daily in the Mass.

I. Note, Reader, Whereas my Adversaries, *Tho. Elwood*, and *J. Pennington*, in their Books against me, have brought several Quotations out of some of my former Books, particularly *The Way cast up*, p. 99. and *The Way to the City of God*, p. 125. on purpose to prove that I was of the same Mind and Persuasion with *W. Penn*, and *George Whitehead*, concerning *Christ* being a real Sacrifice for Sin in Men, to Appease the Wrath and Justice of *God*; and his being the Seed of the Woman in them, having Flesh and Blood, *&c.* to be understood without any Metaphor, or Allegory, or other Figurative Speech, is what I altogether deny, can be inferred from my Words; for as I have shewed in my Book of *Immed. Revel.* p. 14. 15, 16. (which *John Pennington* hath perversly applyed in his Book, called, *The Figg-Leaf Covering*, p. 5, 4.) *The Spiritual Discerning of the Saints (in Scripture) is held forth under the Names of all the five Senses;*——*In like manner the things of God themselves, are held forth in Scripture, under the Names of sensible things, and which are most Taking, Pleasant and Refreshing unto the Senses; as Light, Fire, Water, Oyl, Wine, Oyntment, Honey, Marrow and Fatness, Bread, Manna, and many other such like Names, which I expresly grant are Metaphors*; yet that hinders not (said I) *but that the Spiritual Mysteries Represented under them, and signified by them, are real and substantial things*; to wit, God's *Power and Virtue, Spirit, Light, and Life, and the wondrous sweet and precious workings and Influences thereof* (which I expresly mention, p. 14.). *and indeed these outward things are but Figures of the Inward and Spiritual, which as far exceed and transcend them, in Life, Glory, Beauty, and Excellency, as a living Body doth the Shadow.* Now all this I still firmly hold and believe as much as formerly, when I Writ those Words; for indeed, because we have not proper Words, whereby to signifie Spiritual and Divine Enjoyments and Refreshments in the Souls of the Faithful; therefore Words are borrowed, and transferred from their common Signification, to a Metaphorical, and Allegorical; whereby to signifie the Spiritual Enjoyments and Refreshments of the Saints, from what they Witness and Experience of the Power, Vertue, Light, Life, and Love of *God* and *Christ* in them. So that I still say, the outward Light of Sun, Moon, Star, or Candle, is but a Shadow, or Figure, compared with the Divine Light of *God* and *Christ* within; the outward Bread, Wine, Flesh, though ever so excellent that the outward

Man

An Appendix.

Man tafts of, is but a Figure and Shadow; being compared with that inward Bread of Life, inward Wine and Flesh, Oyl, and Honey, that is inwardly tafted and received by the inward Man. But behold the wretched perverfion that my Prejudiced Adverfary, *John Pennington*, puts upon my found Words, and the wretched Conclufion that he draws from thence; as if therefore I did hold then, that the outward Death of *Chrift* was but a Shadow, or Sign of the inward Death of *Chrift* in Men, and his outward Sacrifice and Blood outwardly Shed, was but a Figure and Shadow of his being a Sacrifice within Men, and his Blood inwardly Shed; which as it hath no Shadow of Confequence from any Words, fo it never came into my Thoughts, fo to imagine; for in that place of my Book, of *Immed. Rev.* above quoted by him, I did not compare *Chrift*'s Death without, and his Death within, or his Blood without, to his Blood within; making That the Shadow and Figure, and This the Subftance, as they do: But I was comparing the outward Meats and Drinks, as Bread, Flesh, Wine, Marrow and Fatnefs, with the Divine Enjoyments of the Saints, which borrow the Names of thefe outward things, and whereof they are but Figures and Shadows.

II. And when I faid in fome of my former Books, that *Chrift* was the Seed of the Woman, that bruifed the Serpents Head in the Faithful in all Ages; I did not mean that *Chrift*, as he was born of the Virgin *Mary*, was a Figure, or Allegory of *Chrift's* Birth, or Formation in the Saints. But on the contrary, *Chrift* inwardly Formed, is the Allegory and Metaphor; yet fo that *Chrift* inwardly enjoyed in the Saints, is a real Divine Subftantial Enjoyment and Participation of *Chrift*, his Life, Grace and Virtue, in meafure which they receive out of the Fulnefs of the Glorified Man *Chrift Jefus* in Heaven; for though to Call *Chrift* inwardly the Seed Born, or Crucified, is Metaphorical; yet the inward Life of *Chrift* is Real and Subftantial that the Saints Enjoy; and being a Meafure out of the Fulnefs that is in the Glorified Man *Chrift Jefus* in Heaven, it is of the fame Nature therewith; and it is one and the fame Mediatory Spirit, and Life of *Chrift* in him; the Head dwelling in Fulnefs, and in them in Meafure, as *Paul* faid, *to every one of us is Grace given, according to the Meafure of the Gift of Chrift.*

And whereas he quotes me in his 55th p. faying, *This is the promifed Seed which God promifed to our Parents after the Fall, and actually gave unto them, even the Seed of the Woman, that fhould bruife the Head of the Ser-*

An Appendix.

Serpent. But doth this prove, that *Chrift* being inwardly Formed in the Saints, was more properly (and without all Allegory Metaphor, or Synecdoche) the Seed of the Woman, than as he was Born of the Virgin? I say nay; though he would ftrain my Words to this, to bring me into the fame Ditch with him and his Brethren; who make *Chrift* without, the Type and Hiftory, and *Chrift* within, the Subftance and Myftery.

That the promifed Seed was actually given to Believers, immediately after the Fall, hath this plain Orthodox Senfe. That the Power of *Chrift*'s Godhead or the Eternal Word that was in the beginning, and which was in the Fulnefs of Time, to take Flefh and Blood, like unto the Children, did actually break the Power of Sin and Satan in the Faithful; and this Power was the real Power of the Seed of the Woman that was Born of the Virgin *Mary*; and what that Power effected and wrought in the Faithful, in the Ages before *Chrift* came into the Flefh, it was with Refpect to his coming in the Flefh, and to what he was to do and fuffer in his Body of Flefh for their Sins. And what I faid, as Quoted by him, page 35. out of my Book, *Way to the City of God*, page 125. *Even from the beginning, yea, upon Man's Fall,* God *was in* Chrift *Reconciling the World to himfelf, and* Chrift *was manifeft in the Holy Seed inwardly, and ftood in the way to ward off the Wrath of* God, *from the Sinners and Unholy, that it might not come upon them to the uttermoft, during the Day of their Vifitation.* All this, or what ever elfe of that fort, I have faid, in any of my Books, hath a fafe and found Senfe, rightly underftood; though this Prejudiced Adverfary, feeks by his own Perverfion to turn them to the contrary: The Word *Reconciling, Redeeming,* hath a two-fold Signification; the one is to fatisfie Divine Juftice, and pay the Debt of our Sins; this was only done by *Chrift,* as he Suffered for us in the Flefh; the other is to Operate, and Work in us, in order to flay the Hatred and Enmity that is in us, while Unconverted; that being Converted, we may enjoy that inward Peace of *Chrift,* that he hath Purchafed for us by his Death and Sufferings, Now that the Light, Word, and Spirit, gently Operates and Works in Men, to turn and incline them to Love *God,* to Fear him, and Obey him, to Believe and Truft in him; that is, to Reconcile Men to *God,* and to ward, or keep off the Wrath of *God* from them: And thus, *God was in Chrift, Reconciling the World to him in all Ages.* But this is not by way of *Satisfaction to Divine Juftice for Men's Sins*; but by way of *Application,* and *Operation*; inwardly Inviting, Perfuading, and as it were Intreating Men to be Reconciled

unto

An Appendix.

unto *God* ; that so the Wrath of *God* that hangs over their Heads, may not fall upon them ; for while *God* by *Christ*, thus inwardly visits the Souls of Men, inviting and perswading them to turn and live; saying, *why will ye Dye ?* the Wrath is suspended, and delayed to be Executed upon them; yet it is not removed, but abides upon them, until they Repent and Believe, as the Scripture testifieth ; *he that believeth not, the Wrath of God abideth on him*. And though this inward Appearance, and Operation in *Christ* in Men's Hearts, stayeth the Execution of Divine Wrath and Justice; yet that inward Appearance, is not the Procuring and Meritorious Cause of Men's Reconciliation with *God*; but the Means whereby, what *Christ* by his Death and Sufferings hath Purchased, is applyed ; for though *Christ* made Peace for us by his Blood outwardly Shed ; yet that Peace cannot be, nor is obtained, or received by any, but as the Soul is inwardly Changed and Converted, and so Reconciled unto *God*.

III. And the like twofold Signification, hath the Word to *Attone* ; for as it signifieth to Attone, or Reconcile *God* and us, that wholly is procured by *Christ*'s Obedience unto Death, and Sacrifice that he offered up for Men on the Cross ; but as it signifieth the effectual Application of that great Attonement, made by *Christ* for Men at his Death ; that is wrought by his Spirit, and inward Appearance in their Hearts. And I might well say, at Man's Fall, *the Seed of the Woman was given, not only to bruise the Serpent's Head, but also to be a Lamb or Sacrifice, to Attone and Pacify the Wrath of God towards Men* ; as he Quotes me in my Book, *Way to the City*, p. 125. For taking *Attoning* in the first Sense, the Virtue, Merit, and Efficacy of *Christ*'s Sacrifice on the Cross, did as really extend to the Faithful for Remission of Sin, and bringing into Reconciliation and Peace with *God*, from *Adam*'s Fall, as it now doth ; which this Prejudiced Author seems wholly ignorant of, as well as his Brethren : Again taking it in the second Sense ; for the effectual Application of the Attonment made by *Christ*'s Death, through his Meek and Lamb-like Appearance by his Spirit and Life in Men's Hearts, it has a Truth in it : And *Christ* may be said to be the Lamb of *God* that taketh away the Sins of the World ; both by his outward Appearance in the Flesh, as he Dyed for us, to Procure and Purchase the Pardon of our Sins, and our Justification before *God* ; and also by his inward Appearance, to Renew and Sanctifie us ; for as by our Justification the Guilt of Sin is taken away ; so by our Sanctification is the Filth of it removed : Both which is the Work of *Christ*, the Lamb

An Appendix.

of *God* respecting both his outward and inward Appearance; in his outward, being a Sin-offering for us, and a Sacrifice in a strict Sense; in his inward Appearance of his Divine Life in us, being as a *Peace-offering*, and Sacrifice of sweet smelling Incense before *God*; not to Reconcile *God* and us, as is above said; but to apply effectually to us, the Reconciliation made for us by his Death on the Cross.

IV. And that I said (as he again Quotes me) the Seed hath been the same in all Ages, and hath had its Sufferings, under, by, and for the Sins of Men in them all, for the Removing and Abolishing them; This I still hold, that there is a tender Suffering Seed, or Principle in Men, that suffers by Men's Sins, and by its gentle Strivings, prevails and gains the Victory at last in all the Heirs of Salvation. But this suffering Seed, or Principle, I never held it to be *God*, nor was I ever of that Mind, that *God* did *really and properly Suffer by Men's* Sins; although I have known divers to hold such an absurd Opinion, as *G. Whitehead* hath plainly declared to be his Opinion in his *Divinity of Christ*, p. 56. which is as really Repugnant, both to Scripture and sound Reason, as to hold that *God* hath *Bodily Parts and Members*; because the Scripture in many places, in condescension to our human Capacities, speaks of *God's Suffering, Repentance, being grieved*; as it doth of his *Face, Eyes, Ears, Hands* and *Feet*; all which ought not to be properly, but Allegorically understood. And though I hold that this tender Seed suffers in Men by their Sins, that so by its gentle Strivings with them, it may overcome them, and Slay and Crucifie the Body of Sin in them; Yet I hold not that Suffering to be the *Procuring* and *Meritorious Cause of our Justification, and Pardon of Sins before* God; nor do I remember any where that I have so said or writ; if any shall shew me where, I shall readily Correct and Retract it, or any thing in any of my Books that looks that way: And if any Query whether I hold that Seed to be *Christ*, that doth so suffer in Men by their Sins; I Answer, It is not the Fulness of *Christ*, but a Measure proceeding from the Fulness that was, and is lodged in the Man *Christ*; and because the Fulness is not in us, and never was, or shall be in any Man, but in the Man *Christ Jesus* alone, that was Born of the Virgin; therefore he, and he only, because of the Fulness of Grace and Truth that was and is in him, was Ordained and Appointed to be the *Great*, and *only*, and *alone Sacrifice* for the Sins of the World, being *the Head of the Body*, which is his Church, it was only proper that the Sufferings that should be in the Head only, should be that *compleat, only, and alone Satisfactory,*

and

An Appendix.

and Propitiatory Sacrifice for the Sins of Men; As the Arguments above mentioned in my Queries to *G. Whitehead,* and *W. Penn,* do plainly demonstrate: And though in *Christ* when he Suffered for the Sins of the World at his Death, his Godhead did not Suffer, yet all that was in him (the Godhead excepted) did Suffer.

Note again, Reader, That although I find no cause to give an Answer to the Book of *John Pennington,* above-mentioned, called, *The Fig-Leaf Covering,* &c. Because I had said in my second Narrative, p. 33. that very Book, (being a pretended Answer to my Book of *Explications and Retractations*) is such a plain and evident Discovery of his Unjust, and Unfair Proceedings against me (whereof the whole second Days Meeting, who hath approved his Book is Guilty) and of his Ignorance and Perverseness of Spirit, in Perverting my Words; that I see no need to give any other Answer to him, or direct to any other Answer, (either to his *Fig-Leaf,* &c. or his Book *Keith against Keith,* or any other his Books) but his own very Book, and Books compared fairly with my Books, Quoted by him; and particularly that of my *Explications and Retractations;* yet because I find divers Passages in that Book of his, plainly prove him and his Brethren of the second Days Meeting extreamly Erroneous in the great things of the Christian Doctrin, some of them being Fundamental; therefore I shall take notice of the following Passages; partly to give the Reader a tast of his Unfair Dealing towards me, and partly to shew his being still Erroneous in some great Fundamentals of the Christian Faith; together with his Brethren of the second Days Meeting, who have approved his *Fig-Leaf.*

In his 19 and 20 Pages, he will needs fasten a Contradiction on me: That one time, *by the Flesh of Christ,* John 6. I mean an inward invisible Substance, and the Eating an inward invisible Eating. But now in my Retractations, I Assert, that to believe in *Christ,* as he gave his Body of Flesh outwardly to be broken for us, is the Eating of his Flesh, as well as the inward Enjoyment of his Life in us. And to confirm the Contradiction, he Quotes me, saying, *Immed. Revel.* p. 258. *This Body of* Christ, *of which we partake, is not that which he took up when he came in the Flesh outwardly, but that which he had from the beginning.* Ans. First, It is no Contradiction, to say, *the Eating of Christ's Flesh,* John 6. is to believe (not by a bare Historical Belief, but by a living sincere Faith Wrought in us by the Spirit of *Christ*) that *Christ* gave *his outward Body to be broken for us;* and also that it is the inward

Enjoy-

An Appendix.

Enjoyment of his Life in us; as it is no Contradiction, to say, *Chriſt* is our Intire and compleat Saviour; both as he came outwardly in the Fleſh, Dyed and Roſe again, &c. And as he cometh inwardly by his Spirit into our Hearts, and dwelleth in us by Faith: And as concerning that Quotation, *Immed. Rev.* p. 258. by *this Body*, in that place; I did mean that which is only Allegorically called his Body, to wit, that *Middle of Communication*, above-mentioned; that is indeed a Spiritual and inviſible Subſtance, owned by *R. B.* as well as by me, and many others. And I ſay ſtill, this inviſible Spiritual Subſtance in the Saints, is not that viſible Body of *Chriſt* which he aſſumed when he came in the Fleſh outwardly; yet this is not to make two Bodies of *Chriſt*; becauſe the one is called his Body, only in a Metaphorical Senſe. *Anſ.* 2. In my Book of *Retractations*, p. 25. I had plainly Retracted and Corrected that Paſſage, in p. 25. *Recor. Corr. That by Chriſt's Fleſh and Blood*, John 6. 50, 51. He meaneth only Spirit and Life; acknowledging, that it was at moſt an Overſight in me; but how doth this prove me a Changling in an Article of Faith? As he infers very Injurouſly: May not a Man change his Judgment concerning the Senſe of a particular place of Scripture, without changing an Article of Faith? That ſuch a Change may be, without a Change in an Article of Faith, is acknowledged by all Sober Writers and Expoſitors of Scripture. Yea, there are many places of Scripture, that ſome underſtand one way, and others not that way, but another, and others a third way; and yet all have one Faith in point of Doctrin. *Anſ.* 3. What a Man Retracts in one Book, or part of a Book, he ought to be underſtood to Retract the ſame Paſſage, where it can be found in another Part, or Book of his; nor ought he to be Charged with Contradiction, in what he hath Retracted. For as I have formerly ſaid in Print, they are only Chargable with Contradictions that without Re ractation, holds Contradictory Aſſertions, *ſimul & ſemel*, i. e. both together.

Page 22. He will not permit me to uſe that Diſtinction, to ſay, I had not my Knowledge from them, (*viz.* The Scriptures) as being the efficient Cauſe, but I did not deny that I had my Knowledge by them Inſtrumentally: to wit, the Doctrinal Knowledge and Faith I had of Goſpel Truths; he Quibbles upon the Word *from*, as if it could not ſignifie ſometimes the efficient Cauſe, and ſometimes the Inſtrumental, whereas a School Boy knoweth that it hath theſe ſeveral Significations, and more alſo. And ſeeing what I then Writ in my Book of *Immed. Rev.* was owned by the Quakers, it plainly followeth, That according to *J. P.* the Words of Scripture are not a Means ſo much as

Inſtru-

An Appendix.

Instrumentally to our Knowledge of the Truths of Christian Doctrin. But how will he Reconcile this to *W. Penn*; who doth acknowledge that the Scriptures are a Means to know *God, Christ* and our selves ? See his *Rejoynder*, p. 115. where he expresly faith; *we never denied the Scriptures to be a means in* God's *Hand, to Convince, Instruct, or Confirm.* By me, its plain. *W. P.* meant all the Quakers; and consequently *G. K.* being then owned to be one of them.

Page 39. He will not allow, that what I have Quoted out of my *Immed. Revel.* p. 243. to p. 247. proves that I did then hold the Man *Christ* without us in Heaven, to be the *Object of our Faith*; though he grants my Words that I said, *The Man Christ who Suffered in the Flesh at Jerusalem, is the Spring out of which all the living Streams flow into our Souls*, and that he is to be Prayed unto, which he faith none of us deny. And yet with the same Breath as it were he denyeth it; for if the Man *Christ* is to be Prayed unto, being the Spring out of which all the living Streams flow unto our Souls; surely as such he is the *Object* of our Faith; for how can we Pray to an *Object* in whom we *believe not*? But seeing he will not allow me, that I then owned the Man *Christ* without us to be the *Object* of Faith (wherein he is most unjust unto me) and that I Writ then as a Quaker, and my Doctrin was the Quakers Doctrin; It is evident, that according to him, it was not the Quakers Doctrin, that the Man *Christ* without us, is in any Part or Respect the Object of our Faith; why then doth he, and many others Accuse me, that I Bely them, for saying they hold it not necessary to our Salvation, that we believe in the Man *Christ* without us? And it is either great Ignorance, or Insincerity in him, to say, that none of them deny that the Man *Christ* without us in Heaven, is to be Prayed unto; Seeing a Quaker of great Note among them, *William Shewen*, hath Printed it in his Book of *Thoughts*, p. 37. *Not to Jesus the Son of Abraham, David and Mary, Saint or Angel; but to God the Father, all Worship, Honour and Glory is to be given, through Jesus Christ,* &c. This &c. cannot be *Jesus* the Son of *Abraham*, but some other *Jesus*; as suppose the Light within; otherwise there would be a Contradiction in his Words; so here he Asserts two *Jesus's* with a witness; what faith *J. Pennington* to this?

Page 41. In Opposition to my *Christian Assertion*, that the believing *Jews*, before *Christ* came in the Flesh, did believe in *Christ*, as he was to be Born, Suffer Death, Rise and Ascend; and so the Man *Christ*, even before he was Conceived, Born, &c. was the Object of their Faith;

An Appendix.

Faith; He thus most Ignorantly and Erroneously Argueth.——*Could that be the Object of theirs,* (viz. *The believing Gentiles*) *or of the Jews Faith, which our Lord had not yet received of the Virgin, which was not Conceived, nor Born, much less Ascended?* Ans. Yes, That can be an Object of Faith and Hope, which has not a present Existence, but is *quid futurum*, something to come; though nothing can be an Object of our Bodily Sight, or other Bodily Senses, but what is in Being, and hath a real Existence in the present Time. But so Stupid and Gross is he, that he cannot understand this, that the Faith of the Saints could have a future *Object*, in any Part or Respect; this is to make Faith as low and weak a thing as Bodily Sense. Is it not generally acknowledged through all *Christendom*, that the Saints of old, as *Abraham, Moses, David* believed in *Christ*, the Promised Seed as he was to come, and be Born, and Suffer Death for the Sins of the World, according to our Saviours Words, *Abraham saw my Day and was glad*; which is generally understood by Expositors, that as he saw *Christ* inwardly in Spirit, so he saw that he was to come outwardly, and be his Son according to the Flesh; and by what Eye did he see this, but by the Eye of Faith? And that Eye of Faith had *Christ* to come in the Flesh, to be Born, *&c.* for its Object as a thing to come.

And in the same Page 41. He Quoteth me falsly, saying, *Immed. Rev.* p. 132. agreeing with both Papists and Protestants, *That God speaking in Men is the Formal Object of Faith.* This Quotation is False in Matter of Fact, as well as his Inference from it is False and Ignorant. I said in that p. 132. That both Papists and Protestants agree in this; *That the Formal Object of Faith is God speaking*; but quoth the Papist, it is the Speaking in the Church of *Rome*; no, quoth the Protestant; *God* Speaking in the Scriptures, is the Formal Object of Faith. Here I plainly shew the difference of Papists and Protestants, about the *Formal Object of Faith*; though they agree in one Part, that it is *God* Speaking; yet in the other Part they differ; the Papists making it, *God* Speaking in the Church; that is, not in every Believer, but in the Pope and his Counsel. And there in that, and some following Pages, I Plead for Internal Revelation of the Spirit, not only Subjectively, but Objectively Working in the Souls of Believers; to which Testimony I still Adhere. But what then? Doth this prove that *Christ* without us is no Object of our Faith? Will he meddle with *School Terms*, and yet understand them no more than a Fool? Doth neither he, nor his *quondam* Tutor, *T. Ellwood*, understand that the *res credendæ*,

i. e.

An Appendix.

i. e. The things to be believed, are Ingredients in the *Material Object of Faith*; as not only that *Christ* came in the Flesh, was Born of a Virgin; but all the Doctrins, and Doctrinal Propositions set forth in Scripture, concerning *God* and *Christ*, and all the Articles of Faith, are *the Material O'ject of our Faith*; but the *Formal Object of Faith*, is the inward Testimony of the Spirit, moving our Understandings and Hearts to believe and close with the Truth of them: All which are well consistent, and owned by me.

Page 43. He Rejects my Exposition of the Parable, concerning the lost piece of Money, in my late Retractation of my former Mistake, p. 15. Sect. 1. p. 10. *That by the lost piece of Money, is to be understood the Souls of Men; as by the lost Sheep, and the lost Prodigal.* To this he most Ignorantly and Falsly opposeth, by saying: *First, The Lord can find the Soul without lighting a Candle in it.* I Answer, By finding, here is meant Converting the Soul; thus the Father of the Prodigal found him, when he Converted him to himself; this my Son was lost, and is found, *i. e. was departed from God, but now is Converted*, Luke 15. 32. And ver. 6. *I have found the Sheep that was lost.* Now, can this be wrought; or doth *God* Work this Work of Conversion in a lost Soul, without his Lighting a Candle in it? *Secondly*, He saith, the very design of the Parable, was to set forth, not what *God* had lost, but what Man had lost; the Candle being used by Man who needed it, not by *God* and *Christ* who needed it not. How Ignorantly and Stupidly doth he here Argue? How can Man use the Candle, unless *God* light it in his Heart; and doth not *God* use it in order to bring, or Convert Man to himself? It's true, though there were no Candle lighted in Man's Heart, *God* seeth where the Soul is, even when it is involved in the greatest Darkness; but in order to the Souls Conversion, which is principally *God's* Act, it is *God* that lights the Candle in it, and causes his Light to Shine in it. And whereas I have said; they who Expound the *lost Piece of Money*, to be the *Light within*; will find difficulty to shew what the nine Pieces are, which are not lost.——His Answer to this is, as Similes seldom go on all four; so neither must Parables be pursued too far. I Answer, Though every Circumstance of a Parable is not to be pursued, yet every necessary part of it is; whoever Expounds the Parable, is bound to Expound what the nine Pieces are, as well as what the tenth was. But he thinks to pinch me with great Difficulties in my Exposition. As first, He demands whether there be no difficulty to find who the Woman is that had ten Souls,

kept

An Appendix.

kept nine, and loſt one. *Anſ.* There is no difficulty in this, more than in finding who the ninety nine Sheep were that were not loſt; and who the Elder Brother was in the other two Parables: And who they were, I had formerly ſhewn, but that his Prejudice blinds him, that he will not ſee: Many Angelical, Created, Rational Spirits did not Sin, ſo were not loſt; but the Souls of Men did Sin, ſo were loſt.

And the number nine in the one Parable, and ninety nine in the other, anſwer one to another; the Definite Numbers being put for Indefinite, as is ordinary in Scripture. But he thinks it a mighty difficulty according to my Expoſition, to tell what the Houſe was, which in effect has no difficulty at all; the Houſe where the Soul is, as Buried under a great heap of Filth and Sin, is the Body wherein the Soul is Lodged; and the Animal and Natural Faculties, with which alſo the Soul is Defiled; ſo the Houſe, to wit the Body, and Animal and Natural Faculties, being Swept and Cleanſed by him who hath his Fan in his Hand, purely to Purge his Floor, to wit, *Chriſt*, (ſignified here by the Woman) he finds the loſt Soul; for as he ſaid himſelf, *he came to ſeek and to ſave*, (i. e.) *that which was loſt*. For *Chriſt* had not loſt *Chriſt*, nor *God* had not loſt *God*; but they had (in a Senſe) loſt the Souls that had Sinned, as the Souls had loſt *God* and *Chriſt*.

Page 45. 46.) In Oppoſition to me; he will needs have all theſe Places, 1 *Cor.* 2. 2. *Rom.* 66. *Gal.* 2. 20. *Heb.* 6. 6. To be underſtood of *Chriſt*'s being Crucified in Men; elſe why doth he oppoſe me with his Queries? and at this rate we ſhall not find any place in the New Teſtament, where *Paul* Preached *Chriſt* Crucified without Men, but only within; for by the ſame Liberty he may Expound all other Places, only of *Chriſt* Crucified within. But there is no reaſon, why any of theſe places ſhould be underſtood of *Chriſt's* Crucifixion in Men; the Crucifying the Old Man is ſo far from being joyned with the inward Crucifying of *Chriſt*, that it is rather a Sign and Effect of *Chriſt*'s Power, Triumphing Victoriouſly in Man, than of his being Crucified in Man. The Crucifying *Chriſt* afreſh, is not ſo much the Crucifying him within Men, as its Men Acting ſo Unworthily; as if they did Act over again the *Jews* Part, in Crucifying him outwardly.

Page 47. His baſe Reviling me, for my Retracting ſome things in my Book of *Univerſal Grace*, uſed by way of Argument unduly by me, ing, *Thus in him is verified the ſaying of the Apoſtle*, James 1. 8. *A double minded Man is unſtable in all his ways*. By this means he will allow

An Appendix.

low no Man to Amend or Correct his Faults, or Retract his Errors, however truly convinced of them; if he does, he is Condemned by *J. Pennington*, (and not by the Apostle *James*) *to be a double minded Man.* But what if perhaps G. *Whitehead,* or *W. Penn,* should find cause to Retract, or Correct some Passages in their Books, which formerly they thought Divine Openings; must they also be judged double Minded Men, *&c.* Is it not more an Evidence of Sincerity to Retract an Error, than to persist in it? Have not many good Men done it? Yea, have not the Quakers commended some for Retracting and Condemning some things, which formerly they reckoned to be Divine Openings? Must all that Retract from their Errors, be Reputed double Minded Men? Oh unfair Adversary, full of deep Prejudice and Spite! I pray *God* give him Repentance and Forgiveness.

Page. 50. He is so Ignorant and Blind, as not to understand my distinction betwixt Essentials of true Religion Indefinitely, and Essentials of the true Christian Religion *in Specie. Cornelius*'s Religion (being *Gentile* Religion) was true in its kind, before he had the Faith of *Christ* Crucified; but I say, the Faith of *Christ* Crucified, in some degree is Essential to the *Christian Religion,* and otherwise to Assert its plain *Deisme*; yet that Faith may be, where the knowledge of the Circumstances of Times, Places and Persons may be wanting.

Page 52. He blames my saying, upon Supposition that any such thing can be found in my Books, I Retract and Renounce it, (*viz. That any are saved without all Knowledge and Faith of Christ, Explicit or Implicit*) this he saith is Childish all over. And for a Proof he Querieth; Can a Man Retract and Renounce a Passage upon Supposition, and not know what the Passage is?

But his Query is Impertinent, and hits not the Case; a Man may Retract a Saying upon Supposition, that he had said it; yet not knowing that ever he said it; as if he were accused, that he had said, *B.* is a Dishonest Man, and replyeth, I know not that ever I so said; but on Supposition that I so said, I Retract it. This is not Childish, but Manly and Christian; if he had no cause to say, *B.* is a Dishonest Man. It seems, *J. Pennington* never Repented of his Sins of Ignorance; he thinks that's Childish all over: I pity his Childishness.

Page 54. His blaming me for saying in my *Retractations*; *The breaking of the Union betwixt Soul and Body; is more properly a Death, than the breaking the Union betwixt the Life and Spirit of Christ, and the Soul of Man, is the Death of Christ in the Soul.* For of that I was Treating,

P

An Appendix.

ing, and at this rate of his blaming me; when *Christ* Dyed upon the Cross; that was not so proper a Death, as when he is Crucified in Men by their Sins; and consequently his Death in Men is the only proper Sacrifice, for that Mans Sins. His Death without, being not so proper a Death, is not a proper Sacrifice, by his most Ignorant way of Reasoning. But my Reason for my Assertion holds good, and which he has not touched; for when a Man Dyeth, his Soul leaveth the Body, and ceaseth to Act in it, nor is the Body any more sensible; but *Christ* Acteth in a Dead Soul, and the Soul, though Dead, is oft made in some degree sensible of the Spirit of *Christ* Acting in it, in order to its being further quickned; as frequently comes to pass in Thousands and Millions of Souls. Besides, as I Argued; the Union of Soul and Body, is a Personal Union, whereby what the Body doth, is chargable upon the Soul; but the Union betwixt the Spirit of *Christ* and Men, is not a Personal Union; otherwise when those Men Sin, their Sin would be chargeable upon *Christ*.

Page 61. He Ignorantly thinks he hath caught me in a Contradiction, about owning a Condition in one Sense, in Reference to *God's* Willing all Men to be saved; *ex parte Objecti*, and denying a Conditional Election. But this is no Contradiction at all; because the Will of *God* is Conditional Objectively, or *ex parte Objecti, i. e.* Men that are the Object of *God's* Will; and yet not Conditional Subjectively, *i. e.* on *God's* Part; if he understand not this Distinction, I ought not to suffer for his Ignorance, he should not meddle with *School-Terms*, except he understand them; the distinction of Volition, *Conditional Objectively*, and not *Conditional Subjectively*; *and yet the same* Will is common and ordinary in all Authors that Treat on such Subjects.

Page 69. He is Guilty of great Injury against me, in Matter of Fact, by an Unfaithful Reciting of my Words, and thence taking occasion against me.——*In all places in the New Testament, where the word Gospel is used, it signifieth the Doctrin of Salvation by the promised Messiah, that was outwardly to come, and did come in the true Nature of Man,* &c. He quite leaves out my Words, *and did come in the true Nature of Man,* that were necessary to perfect the Sentence, and if he had brought them, would have taken away his occasion of his Quarelling with me so Unjustly; he saith, *here he is out again*; for the *New Testament being written, not when Christ was outwardly come, but after he was outwardly come; the word Gospel there, when it signifieth the Doctrin of Salvation by the promised Messiah*, must needs respect him, as already come, not as

to

An Appendix.

to come. Anf. Where the New Testament faith, the Gospel was Preached to *Abraham,* and to the Children of *Israel* in the Wildernels; Gospel there signified the Doctrin of Salvation by the promised *Messiah* that was then to come, and not already come; but at other times it signifieth the Doctrin of Salvation, by *Christ* already come, as my Words Cautioned it; therefore he is Guilty of Abuse and Forgery, like his *quondam* Master, *Tho. Elwood,* as elsewhere.

Page 70. He most Impertinently opposeth my found Assertion, by Quoting *Paul,* mentioning another Gospel, as 2 *Cor.* 11. 4. and *Gal.* 1. 6, 8, 9. *For by Gospel I understand the true Gospel of Christ, and not a false Gospel; as when I say, every Man is a Rational Creature;* and *J. Pennington,* should Object, a Man Pictured on a Board or Wall, is not a Rational Creature. Is not this a rare Disputant?

But his following Opposition is the most observable, and is a new effectual Proof of my Charge against him and his Brethren of the 2d. Days Meeting, who have approved his Book, he saith by way of Opposition. *Also when the Everlasting Gospel was again to be Preached after the Apostacie (for it seems by the word* again, *it had been discontinued to be Preached; although the History of Christ's Birth, Death had not) doth that place,* Rev. 14. 6, 7. *mention any thing of the Doctrin of Salvation, by the promised* Messiah? *There is not a word of that said there; but saying with a loud voice, fear God, and give Glory to him,* &c. *(Being Preached with Commission from on high,) is called Preaching the everlasting Gospel.* Did G. K. (saith he) *in his diligent search overlook this? if not, how could he say in all places in the New Testament, where the word Gospel is used, it signifieth the Doctrin of Salvation by the promised* Messiah; *he adds to this two other places, as* Rom. 1. 16. *and* Colof. 1. 23. *in both which, he will not have the Gospel to signifie the Doctrin of Salvation by Christ Crucified, with respect to that clear and bright Dispensation the Apostles were under (which was the Sense I gave of the Gospel, in* Col. 1. 23.) *And he saith in* Rom. 1. 16. *That the Gospel cannot be said to be the Power of God unto Salvation, to the Believer, in any other Sense, than as it is a Powerful, Energetical inward Principle; for as it is barely Historical, the Ungodly have that Belief, though they want the Power.* This I say effectually proves again my Charge against them, That they hold it not necessary, for us to believe that *Christ* Dyed and Rose again for our Salvation; why, the Gospel that *Paul* Preached, *Rom.* 1. 16. and *Col.* 1. 23. *Is not the Doctrin of Salvation by Christ Crucified, the promised Messiah, and when the everlasting Gospel was to be Preached,* Rev. 14. 6, 7. (Which the Quakers think they have given them to Preach

An Appendix.

(with Commission from on High) the Doctrin of Salvation by *Christ* Crucified, was not that Gospel; the Consequence is plain, that therefore the Faith of *Chr st* Crucified, is not necessary to their Hearers for Salvation. It is not the Everlasting Gospel that is given them to Preach; If they Preach it, they go beyond their Commission, they do a needless Work. But saith *J. P.* Fear *God* and give Glory, to him is called Preaching the Everlasting Gospel. But is not that also a Doctrin? yes, surely; so then the Doctrin, Fear *God*, &c. being Preached, is a Preaching the Everlasting Gospel; but the Doctrin believe that *Christ* Died for our Sins, and Rose again, being Preached is not Preaching the Everlasting Gospel; according to *John Pennington,* and his Brethren of the Second Days Meeting.

This Sufficiently sheweth, that those Quakers are *semper idem,* always the same; they are the same still, as formerly; though many that hear them of late, say, their Way of Preaching is changed; they had wont formerly, before the Difference arose betwixt them and *G. K.* to Preach only the Light within, and Obedience to it; but now they Preach the Man *Christ*, and his Death and Sufferings without, and how beneficial they were to Mankind; and that the Faith of it is Beneficial. Yet by *J. P.* his Affirmation approved by the Second Days Meeting of the Friends of the Ministry, in and about *London,* whereof *G. W.* and *W. Penn* are Members, and where frequently they are present, The Doctrin of Salvation by *Christ* Crucified, is none of the Everlasting Gospel that is given them to Preach; but fear *God*, and give Glory to him, *&c.* But how comes it, that believe in the Light within, obey the Light within, and that shall suffice to your Salvation, is not mentioned in the Angels Commission to Preach the Everlasting Gospel, no more than believe in *Christ* Crucified without you? Perhaps *J. P.* will reply, though not mentioned or expressed; yet it is implyed, and understood. But how prove they it is implyed; that believing in the Light within alone, and obeying it, is sufficient to Salvation, without Faith in *Christ* Crucified? Is not the Blindness of these Men (for all they talk of Light within) exceeding Great, and the Darkness that's over them, like the Darkness of *Egypt* that might have been felt? *John* (*Rev.* 14. 6, 7.) did not say the Angel had nothing else to Preach, but fear *God*, and give Glory to him; that Doctrin being a general Doctrin, common both to Law and Gospel, and both to *true* Gentile *Religion,* as well as *true Christian Religion.* The Apostacie having been so great, that many called Christians were Degenerated below the Heathens, and their Religion scarce so good, as that of some *Heathens* that did fear God, and Worship him only; the Angel might Preach

that

An Appendix.

that general Doctrin, as being very proper and necessary to call Apostate and Degenerate Professors of Christianity, from their Idolatry and Profanity, as a necessary Introduction to the Everlasting Gospel; as well as in one Sense it is a necessary part of it, but not the whole Doctrin of the Gospel; for Faith and Love are as necessary Doctrins of the Gospel, as Fear, though neither of them are expresly mentioned, yet implyed, together with all the other Christian Virtues. But *J. P.* in his Words above Cited, will have it, *That the Gospel cannot be said to be the Power of God unto Salvation, to the Believer in any other Sense, than as it is a Powerful energetical inward Principle; for as it is barely Historical, the Ungodly have that Belief.* I Answer, How Foolishly doth he here Argue, and Impertinently? whoever said, that the bare Historical Relation, or Report of *Christ* Crucified, is the Power of *God* unto Salvation? Or if any have said it is the Gospel, I am sure I never said nor thought it. But what hath *J. P.* against this Sense of the Gospel, *Rom.* 1. 16. *That it is the Doctrin of Salvation, by the promised Messiah, accompanied with the Spirit of God and Christ inwardly Revealed, making it effectually to be Believed and Obeyed, in all that shall be Saved by it; and thus the Gospel that* Paul *and the other Apostles Preached, is not a bare Form of Doctrin without the Spirit and Power, nor the Spirit and Power without the Doctrin.* And how Non-sensical is he to Argue; *that as it is barely Historical, the Ungodly have that Belief?* But they have not the Saving Belief of the Doctrin of *Christ* Crucified; for that only is wrought in the Godly, by the Power and Spirit of *Christ.* And though the Ungodly may have the Gospel Preached unto them; yet while they remain Ungodly, they receive it not, neither do they truly believe it, nor obey it. A bare Historical Faith, is no more a True Faith, than the bare Picture of a Man, is a Man. Therefore he is Idle to Argue against the Saving Faith of *Christ* Crucified; because the Ungodly may have the bare Historical Belief of it; which differs as widely, as a Dead Body from a a Living Man.

But it is not enough for *J. P.* to Pervert my Words; but he will be bold to Pervert the Words of the Scripture, and not only put a false Gloss on them; but alledge that to be said in Scripture, which is not said, but is his own Addition. For as I have above Cited him, he saith, also when the Everlasting Gospel was again to be Preached; and he adds in Parenthesis; for it seems by the Word *again*, it had been discontinued to be Preached; although the History of *Christ's* Birth, Death had not. Now, Reader, open the Bible, and Read that place,

Rev.

An Appendix.

Rev. 14. 6, 7. and thou wilt find the Word *again* is not there to be found; (but in *G. Fox's Some Principles*, p. 22. it is found) and yet he Grounds his Argument upon this Pillar, *again*; by which he inferreth, that to his seeming, the Everlasting Gospel had been discontinued to be Preached, although the History of *Christ's* Birth, Death had not. And this discontinuing of the Preaching the Everlasting Gospel, he and his Brethren think did remain, until *G. Fox* and the Quakers began to Preach it. For *saith G. Fox and his Brethren, in the Book,* called, Some Principles of the Elect People of God, *Printed at* London, 1671. In p. 48. *But many People speak after this manner; Have we not had the Gospel all this time till now?* Ans. *We say no, you have had the Sheeps Cloathing, while you are Alienated from the Spirit; and so not living in the Power, which is the Gospel,* &c. But as in *Rev.* 14. 6, 7. The Word *again* is not to be found, nor will the *Greek* bear it; so nor is it implyed, that there was a discontinuing of the Preaching of it altogether; for had the Gospel ceased, the Church had ceased also, and Faith and Salvation had ceased. The most that can be inferred, is, that the Preaching of it was not so common and frequent, as formerly; it had met with a great Stoppage and Opposition in many parts of the World, even under a Christian Profession, because of the Apostacie; which had it not come, the Gospel would have spread much more than it yet hath done; but as the Apostacie goes out, the Everlasting Gospel, the same that the Apostles Preached, will be Preached to every Nation and Kindred, and Tongue, and People, *John* 14. 6. That is, universally; this doth not prove the discontinuing of it, as *J. P.* falsly Argueth; but that the more General, and indeed the Universal Spreading of it, hath not hitherto been as yet. His Argument, *That the Gospel that* Paul *Preached to the* Colossians, *was not the Doctrin of Salvation, by the promised* Messiah, *Christ Crucified; because the Gospel he was speaking of, was Preached to, or in every Creature under Heaven.* Therefore (saith he) it could not be meant of the Doctrin of Salvation, by *Christ* Crucified,——but of that Gospel which had been Preached to, or in every Creature under Heaven. I say this his Argument is Vain and False; but it is a good and effectual Proof to confirm my Charge against them. These Quakers Preach not any Gospel for Salvation, but that which is Preached *to, or in every Creature* under Heaven; but (saith *J. P.*) that is not the Doctrin of Salvation, by *Christ* Crucified; therefore that is none of the Gospel these Quakers Preach; what can be required more, *habemus Confitentem reum*; we have the

Guilty

An Appendix.

Guilty Confessing Matter of Fact. But surely the Gospel that *Paul* Preached to the *Colossians*, was the Doctrin of Salvation, by *Christ* Crucified, as appears plainly from 1 *Col. v.* 14. to the end of the Chapter. And his Arguing from the Words *to, or in every Creature* (which sort of Argument hath deceived many) is no more valid to prove that the Gospel, either then, or formerly had been Preached to every Man and Woman, in the full and adequate Sense of the Word *every*, as it signifieth every individual; than that because *Paul* said, *v.* 28. of that same Chapter *whom we Preach, Warning every Man, and Teaching every Man* in all Wisdom, that we may present every Man Perfect in *Christ Jesus*, that *Paul* and his Brethren, then living, did Teach every Man, that ever lived, or is now living on Earth. If yea, then surely *John Pennington*, and all other Men now on Earth, were then living; and this will be the Doctrin of the *Revolution*, or *Transmigration* of Souls with a witness, (which he so frequently would cast upon me, though he has no just ground so to do, nor any other Man; if nay, then he must quit his Post, and cease any more to Argue from his place of Scripture; that the Gospel that *Paul* Preached, was not the Doctrin of Salvation, by *Christ* Crucified; but the true Sense of that place, *Col.* 1. 23. I had formerly given, as he Quotes me, p. 71. Saying, *though it was not at the same time actually Preached to all Men, yet it was begun to be Preached, and after the Prophetical Stile, that which was to be done, is said to be done*: He Quibbles against this, saying, *where that Prophetical Phrase is, or how it is used, he Assigns not*. Indeed it was not necessary to shew to any but a little Skilled in the Letter and true Sense of Scripture, where that Prophetical Phrase is; for it is so general in Scripture Prophecies, that no Man that is not Brutish, but must be sensible of it, when he Reads them. When *Isaiah* Prophecied of *Christ's* Death and Sufferings, and Birth, yea, and Burial, it is all said *in præterito*; as if it had been, which yet was not some hundred Years after. And so it is almost in the whole Prophecie of the Book of the *Revelation*, and particularly that 14. *Rev.* 6. 7. brought by him, which yet he applyeth, not to *John's* Time, but to his and his Brethrens Preaching (not the Doctrin of Salvation, by *Christ* Crucified; if we must believe *J. P.*) (behold your Patron, all Sober Persons among the Quakers) *but the Light in every Creature* under Heaven. And p. 22. *Some Principles of the Elect People*. And now saith *G. F.* the Gospel must be Preached again to all Nations; and this saith *J. P.* is not the Doctrin of Salvation, by *Christ* Crucified, but the Light or inward Principle

in

An Appendix.

in every Creature, and his, and his Brethrens Argument is Weak; that becaufe *Paul* called the Gofpel the Power of God to Salvation; therefore it is nothing elfe but the inward Principle; for he called the Preaching of the Crofs the Power of God, 1 *Cor.* 1. 18. And yet that Preaching was an outward Preaching, and he called it the Power of God becaufe it was made Effectual to many that heard it, by the Power of God that accompanied it.

Thus Reader, I have given thee a Taft of this Man's Ignorance and Anti-Chriftian Doctrin, which is the fame with that of his Brethren of the Second Days Meeting, who have approved his Books againft me. I fhall not naufeate thee with his other many Impertinencies, and Extravagancies, as well as his Grofs Errors in other Particulars of Doctrin; nor take notice of his Bafe and Scurrilous Revilings, that are equally Unjuft and Malicious; As his calling me not Sincere, but a Belly-Convert, and his infinuating; If I be difappointed among Proteftants, I may feek a Living from the Papifts, which is like his and his Brethrens other falfe Prophecies.

Note, Reader, That having fome Years ago feen a Book of *Thomas Lawfon*, a Quaker, againft *Water-Baptifm*; I have made fearch for it, but cannot find it any where, to have it; however, I fuppofe it hath nothing of Argument in it, but what in effect is contained in thofe above Examined and Anfwered; and I do not think that any of their Books on that Subject, will be found to have any other Arguments in them againft *Baptifm* and the *Supper*, but what is in effect contained in thofe above-mentioned.

F I N I S.

The E R R A T A.

P. 2. l. 18. for *thereof*, r. *therefore*, p. 2 l. 24. for *becomes*, r. *becaufe*, p. 3. l. 30. after *Whitehead*, r. *only*, p. 5. l. 17. r. *judged*, p. 13. l. 18. before *have*, r. *they have*, and l. 19. for *art*, r. *act*, p. 30. l. 38. for *there*, r. *thrice*, p. 68. l. 13. for *vifible*, r. *invifible*.

Primitive Heresie
REVIVED,
IN *Ant. Johnson*

The Faith and Practice
Of the PEOPLE Called
QUAKERS:
Wherein is shewn, in *Seven* Particulars, That the *Principal* and most *Characteristick* Errors of the *Quakers*, were *Broached* and *Condemned*, in the Days of the *Apostles*, and the first 350 Years after *Christ*.

To which is Added,

A *Friendly Expostulation* with *William Penn*, upon Account of his *Primitive Christianity*, lately Published.

By the Author of *The Snake in the Grass*.

LONDON:
Printed for *C. Brome*, at the *Gun*, at the *West*-End of St. *Paul's*. *W. Keblewhite*, at the *Swan* in St. *Paul's* Church-Yard. And *H. Hindmarsh*, at the *Golden-Ball* over-against the *Royal Exchange*. 1698.

The Contents.

not Difference *enough betwixt us, to Justifie their* Separation: *Whence an Invitation to them to* Return.

The Friendly Expostulation, Concerning,
1. *Mr.* Penn's *Notion of the* Light within.   p. 20.
2. *This not sufficient to Justifie his* Separation.   p. 28.
3. *For he owns that we are of one* Religion.   p. 29.
4. *His Exposition of* Justification *in his* Primitive Christianity *most* Orthodox, *and agreeing exactly with us. And his whole* ix. Chapt. *of the* Inward *or* Spiritual *Appearance of* Christ *in the* Soul.

Some Objections *of his solv'd, so far as not to be any Justifiable Causes of a* Separation, *as Concerning,*
1. Forms *of* Prayer.   p. 30.
2. *The* Spirituality *of the* Ministry.
3. *Their being* Witnesses *of* Christ.   p. 31.
4. *Their* Receiving Hire (*as he calls it*) *for their* Preaching.
5. Tythes.
6. Swearing.
7. War.
8. Holy-Days.   p. 32.

Errata.

Page 11. l. 29. f. one r. only.   P. 17. l. 21. r. Discriminating.   P. 21. l. 11. dele ?

Primi-

Primitive Hereſie *Reviv'd*, &c.

IN my Diſcourſe of *Baptiſm*, I promis'd ſomething upon this Subject, in hopes that the *Quakers*, ſeeing the *Original* of their *Errors*, may bethink themſelves, and Return from whence they have Fallen.

And particularly, as to *Baptiſm*, that I might confirm my Expoſitions of the H. *Scriptures*, with the Concurrent Teſtimony of the H. *Fathers*, who were *Co-temporarys* with the *Apoſtles*, and learn'd the *Faith* from their mouths; and thoſe who immediately followed them, to 150 Years after *Chriſt*. Though we have very little Remaining of the Writings of the *Fathers* in that early Age. Yet I would deſcend no lower (where I might have had *Clouds* of *Witneſſes*) to avoid a Groundleſs *Cavil*, which the *Quakers* have learn'd from our Elder *Diſſenters*, to Run down the *Primitive Church*, by whole-ſale, becauſe it was ſo Full of *Biſhops*, and, in all the Pretences of their *Schiſm*, went ſo Directly contrary to them. But the *Fathers* of the *Firſt* Age, that next to the *Apoſtles*, and of which the *Apoſtles* were a Part, tho' as much *Biſhops*, and as much againſt them as thoſe following, yet for *Decency* ſake, they Pretend to *Reverence*, left in throwing them off, they ſhould ſeem to throw off the *Apoſtles* with them, from whom they could not be parted.

And becauſe, even in this *firſt* Un-controverted Age, we have Proofs ſufficient, I would avoid Needleſs Diſputes, and Argue from *Topicks* that are allowed on all hands.

The Greateſt Part of the following Diſcourſe was wrote at the time with the *Diſcourſe of Baptiſm*, and Intended to have been Annex'd to it, but being Prevented at that time, it has ſince been neglected. Till I was ſtirr'd up afreſh by a Book lately Publiſhed (though ſaid to be Printed in 1696.) Intituled, [*Primitive Chriſtianity Reviv'd in the Faith and Practice of the People called Quakers*.] This came Directly to my Subject, therefore I have

have Examin'd it thorowly, and leave the Reader to Judge, whether the *Primitive Christianity* or *Heresie* does belong most to them: At least, whether it did, before the late *Representations* of *Quakerism*, which have given it quite another *Turn* and *Face* than it ever had before. Such a *Turn*, as has left nothing on their side, whereby to justifie their *Schism*. And therefore we hope that their *Conversion* is nigh; or if already *Converted*, their Full *Reconciliation* to the *Church*. That the Present *Quakers*, chiefly the Valuable Mr. *Penn*, may have the Honour, and the Happiness to Heal up that *Breach*, which now for 48 Years has so Miserably *Torn* and *Divided* this once most *Christian* and Renowned *Church* of *England*.

In this following Discourse, I will not take up the Reader's time to Prove the several Positions which I name upon the *Quakers*; only Briefly Recite them, and Refer to the Places in *The Snake in the Grass*, and *Satan Dis-Rob'd*, where they are prov'd at large. And to Repeat them Here, would swell this to an unreasonable Bulk. And this being intended in the Nature of a *Supplement* to these, it would be Needless. The proper Business of this, is, to Compare the *Quaker-Heresies* with those of the first 150 Years of *Christianity*.

Where I Quote *The Snake*, the Reader is desired to take notice, that it is the *Second Edition*.

And now to our Task. The *Seven* Particulars wherein the *Quakers* have, if not copy'd after, at least Jump'd with the Condemn'd *Hereticks* before mention'd.

I. The *First* is, as to their Denyal of the *Incarnation* of *Christ*. They confess that *Christ* or *The Word* took *Flesh*; that is, That He *Assum'd* or *Dwelt* in an *Human Body*, *i. e.* the *Body* of that Man *Jesus*; who was therefore called *Christ*, because that *Christ* or the *Word* Dwelt in Him. And for the same Reason, they take the Name of *Christ* to themselves; and say that it belongs to every one of the *Members* as well as unto the Head, *i. e.* as well as to that Man *Jesus*, who was Principally and Chiefly called *The Christ*, because that *Christ* Dwelt in Him, or did *Inspire* Him in a Greater *Measure* than other Men. But they *Utterly Deny* that the Man *Jesus* was Properly the *Son* of God. In a large Sense, every *Christian* may be call'd a *Son* of God; and so, and no otherwise, they allow *Jesus* to be the *Son* of God. But that He

was

was Properly *the Son of God, we utterly Deny,*—says their *serious Apology*, p. 146. which was Printed 1671. See this Proved at large in *The Snake in the Grass, Sect.* x.

Now I Proceed to shew, That this *Heresie* was *Broach'd* and *Condemn'd* in the Days of the *Apostles*. This is it which St. *John* Reprehends, 1 *Joh.* iv. 3. *Every Spirit that confesseth not that Jesus Christ is come in the Flesh,* &c. or as *Socrates* (Hist. Eccl. l. 7. c. 32.) tells us it was wrote in the Ancient Copys, *Every Spirit which separateth Jesus from God, is not of God.* And he observes that this Text, and other Parts of this *Epistle* were alter'd by those who would separate the *Divinity* of *Christ* from His *Humanity*. Tho' as it now stands in our Copys, it means the same thing; for he that denys *Christ* to have been *made* Flesh, only says that he took it upon Him for a *Cloak* or a *Veil*, as *Angels* assume *Bodys* when they appear in them: He denys *Christ's* coming in the *Flesh*, so as to become *Truly* and *Really* a *Man*; he takes away the *Humanity* of *Christ*, and so separates *Jesus* from *God*: Which, in the sense of this *Text*, is to Deny His *coming in the flesh*. St. *Polycarp*, in his *Epist.* to the *Philippians*, n. 7. Disputes against these *Anti-Christs*, in the words of his *Master* St. *John*, whose *Disciple* he was, πᾶς γὸ (*says he*) ὃς ἂν μὴ ὁμολογῇ Ἰησοῦν Χριστὸν ἐν Σαρκὶ ἐληλυθέναι, Ἀντίχριστός ἐστι. *i. e. Whosoever does not confess that Jesus Christ is come in the Flesh, is an Anti-Christ.*

II. The *Second* point is the *Quakers* Denyal of the *Truth* and *Reality* of the *Death* and *Sufferings* of *Christ*. This is Consequential to the former *Heresie*; for if *Christ* took not the *Body* of *Jesus* into his own *Person*, but only dwelt in the *Body* of another Man, as he dwells in his *Saints*; if *Christ* and *Jesus* are two *Persons*; if the *Body* of *Jesus* was only a *Veil* or *Garment* for *Christ* to shrowd himself in, as the *Quakers* speak; then, tho' *Jesus* suffer'd, yet *Christ* could not; and the *Sufferings* of *Christ* were but in *Appearance* and *shew*, as if a Man's *Cloak* or *Garment* only were *Crucify'd*.

What are then those *Sufferings* of *Christ* which the *Quakers* do own as *Meritorious* in the sight of *God*, for the *Atonement* of our *sins*? Why, an ALLEGORICAL *Suffering, Death,* and *shedding* of the *Blood* of their *Light within*; which they call *Christ*; of which *Jesus*, or the outward *Christ*, they say was but a *Type*; and that his *Sufferings* were only an *Historical* Transaction of the greater

[4]

Greater *Mysterie* of the *Sufferings* and *Atonement* perform'd by their *Light within*, as I have fully shewn in *The Snake in the Grass*, Sect. x. p. 127. and *Satan Dif-Rob'd*, Sect. xii. p. 11.

But now I am to shew, That the *Devil* had *Broached* these *Heresies*, against the *Truth* of the *Incarnation* of *Christ*, and consequently against the *Reality* of his *Death* and *Sufferings*, within the first 150 Years after *Christ*: and that they were then Condemned by the Holy *Fathers* of the *Church*.

Ignatius that Glorious *Martyr* of *Christ*, Bishop of *Antioch*, who flourish'd about the Year 70 after the Birth of *Christ*, and was Disciple to St. *John* the *Evangelist*, writes thus in his Epistle to the *Magnesians*, instructing their Faith, in what sort of Sufferings of *Christ* we were to *Believe* and *Trust*, not these *Inward* in our *hearts*, but to-distinguish most effectually from these, those that He suffered under *Pontius Pilate*. *I would have you Preserved, that you fall not into the snare of vain Doctrin; but that ye may abound, and be filled with the knowledge of the Birth, Passion, and Resurrection, which truly, and firmly were of Jesus Christ our hope, in the time of the Government of* Pontius Pilate, *from which let none of you be turned away.*

Θέλω προφυλάσσειν ὑμᾶς, μὴ ἐμπεσεῖν εἰς τὰ ἄγκιστρα τῆς κενοδοξίας, ἀλλὰ πεπληροφορεῖσθε ἐν τῇ γεννήσει, ᾗ καὶ πάθει, καὶ τῇ ἀναστάσει τῇ γενομένῃ ἐν καιρῷ τῆς ἡγεμονίας Ποντίου Πιλάτου, πραχθέντα ἀληθῶς καὶ βεβαίως ὑπὸ Ἰησοῦ Χριστοῦ τῆς ἐλπίδος ἡμῶν. ἧς ἐκτραπῆναι μηδενὶ ὑμῶν γένοιτο.

Stop your ears therefore (says he in his Epistle to the *Trallians*) *when any shall speak to you without Jesus Christ.*

Κωφώθητε οὖν, ὅταν ὑμῖν χωρὶς Ἰησοῦ Χριστοῦ λαλῇ τις.

What *Christ* was this? the *Outward* Man *Jesus*, or the *Light within*? That Jesus, *who was of the stock of* David, *who was of* Mary, *who was truly Born, did both Eat and Drink; was truly Persecuted under* Pontius Pilate, *was truly Crucify'd and Dyed — And who truly Rose from the Dead, his Father Rai-*

τοῦ ἐκ γένους Δαβίδ, τοῦ ἐκ Μαρίας, ὃς ἀληθῶς ἐγεννήθη, ἔφαγέ τε καὶ ἔπιεν, ἀληθῶς ἐδιώχθη ἐπὶ Ποντίου Πιλάτου, ἀληθῶς ἐσταυρώθη, καὶ ἀπέθανεν —— ὃς καὶ ἀληθῶς ἠγέρθη ἀπὸ νεκρῶν, ἐγείραντος αὐτὸν τοῦ Πατρὸς αὐτοῦ, κατὰ τὸ ὁμοίωμα, ὡς καὶ ἡμᾶς

sing

sing of him; *and his Father will, after the like fashion, Raise us up in Jesus Christ, who believe in him, without whom we cannot truly live.*

τὰς πιστεύοντας αὐτῷ ὅπως ἐγείρῃ ὁ Πατὴρ αὐτοῦ ἐν Χριστῷ Ἰησοῦ, οὗ χωρὶς τὸ ἀληθινὸν ζῆν οὐκ ἔχομεν.

But some *Athiests*, that is, *Infidels, do say, That He only appear'd to be a Man, but took not a Body in Reality, and in appearance only seemed to Suffer, and dye*, &c.

Εἰ δὲ ὥσπερ τινὲς Ἄθεοι ὄντες, τουτέστιν Ἄπιστοι, λέγουσι, τῷ δοκεῖν γεγενῆσθαι αὐτὸν Ἄνθρωπον, οὐκ ἀληθῶς ἀνειληφέναι σῶμα, κὰι τὸ δοκεῖν τεθνηκέναι, πεπονθέναι οὐκ ὄντι, &c.

And in the beginning of his Epistle to the *Smyrnæans*, after having Describ'd that *Christ* who is the Object of our Faith, in the fullest manner, to obviate the Deceit of applying it to an *Inward* Christ, by calling Him the *Son of David, Born* of the *Virgin*, and *Baptized* of *John*, truly *Crucified* under *Pontius Pilate*, and *Herod* the Tetrarch; none of which can be apply'd to *The Light within*. He adds that we can only be saved by the Faith in this OUTWARD Jesus. *By the Fruits of whose Divinely Blessed Passion, we are Saved —— For he suffer'd all these things for us, that we might be saved.*

ἀφ' οὗ καρποῦ ἡμεῖς ἀπὸ τοῦ θεομακαρίστου αὐτοῦ πάθους ——
ταῦτα γὰρ πάντα ἔπαθεν δι' ἡμᾶς ἵνα σωθῶμεν.

And to Obviate the two *Heretical* Pretences, of making the *Meritorious* Suffering of *Christ*, to be His Suffering within us. And that His *outward* Sufferings, were not *Real*, but, in *appearance* only, as not being Really a Man, but only Residing in that Man *Jesus*, as in a *Veil* or *Garment*. *Ignatius* adds in the next words. *And he truly suffered, and truly Raised himself; not, as some Unbelievers say, that he only appeared to suffer, they but appearing to Exist. And as they Believe, so shall it be unto them, when they come to be out of the Body, and in the state of Spirits*; that is, they shall justly Forfeit the *True* and *Real* Benefits

Καὶ ἀληθῶς ἔπαθεν, ὡς καὶ ἀληθῶς ἀνέστησεν ἑαυτόν, οὐχ ὥσπερ ἄπιστοί τινες λέγουσιν τὸ δοκεῖν αὐτὸν πεπονθέναι, αὐτοὶ τὸ δοκεῖν ὄντες, καὶ καθὼς φρονοῦσιν καὶ συμβήσεται αὐτοῖς, οὖσιν ἀσωμάτοις, καὶ δαιμονικοῖς.

Benefits Purchased for *True Believers*, by the *death* of *Christ*; since they will have it to be only in *Appearance* or *False shew*; and take the *Merit* from the *Outward death* of *Christ*, which he suffer'd upon the *Cross*, and place it in a Fancy'd Suffering of the *Light within* them.

And as He asserts the Faith in *Christ*'s outward *Death*, so does he, in His *Resurrection*; not the *Inward Rising* of *Christ* in our *hearts*, but in His *Outward Resurrection*, that which was proved by their *Handling* of Him, and *Feeling* of His *Flesh*, and His *Eating* and *Drinking* with them, after His *Resurrection*.

But, in the next Paragraph, he has a Prophetick Exhortation, which looks terribly upon the *Quakers*, among others. He tells the *Smyrnæans*, that he gives them these Admonitions, not that he thinks them Guilty of these Heresies. But *I Guard you before hand* (says he) *against Beasts in Human shape, whom you ought not only not to Receive; but if it be possible, not so much as to meet with them, only to pray for them, if they may at last Repent, which will be difficult.*

προσφυλάσσω ἢ ὑμᾶς ἀπὸ τῶν θηρίων τῶν ἀνθρωπομόρφων, οὓς οὐ μόνον δεῖ ὑμᾶς μὴ παραδέχεσθαι, ἀλλ᾽ εἰ δυνατόν ἐςι μηδὲ συναντᾶν, μόνον δὲ προσεύχεσθαι ὑπὲρ αὐτῶν, ἐάν πως μετανοήσωσιν, ὅπερ δύσκολον.

And again, says he, speaking of our Lord *Jesus Christ, Whom some not knowing, do deny, or rather, are denyed by him, being the Preachers of Death, rather than of Truth.*

Ὅν τινες ἀγνοῦντες ἀρνοῦνται, μᾶλλον δὲ ἠρνήθησαν ὑπ᾽ αὐτοῦ, ὄντες συνήγοροι τοῦ Θανάτου μᾶλλον ἢ τῆς Ἀληθείας.

They abstain from the Eucharist, (that is, The *Sacrament* of the *Lord's Supper) and from the Prayers* (of the Church) *because they do not confess that the Eucharist is the flesh of our Saviour Jesus Christ, which suffered for our sins; and which the Father in his Goodness Raised up. But these speaking against this Gift of God, die in their Inquiries.*

Εὐχαριστίας κ̀ προσευχῆς ἀπέχονται, διὰ τὸ μὴ ὁμολογεῖν τὴν Εὐχαριστίαν σάρκα εἶναι τοῦ σωτῆρος ἡμῶν Ἰησοῦ Χριστοῦ, τὴν ὑπὲρ ἁμαρτιῶν ἡμῶν παθοῦσαν, ἣν τῇ χρηςότητι, ὁ πατὴρ ἤγειρεν. Οἱ οὖν ἀντιλέγοντες τῇ δωρεᾷ τοῦ Θεοῦ συζητοῦντες ἀποθνήσκουσι.

And *vain* and *Death* must those *Inquiries* be, which, leaving the *Gifts of God*, the *Sacraments* of his own *Institution*, and to which
His

[7]

His *Promises* are Annex'd, Seek for *Salvation* in ways and means of their own Devising.

But it was unavoidable, that they who had left the Body of Christ, as a forsaken *veil* or *garment*, to Rot for ever in the Grave; or are careless what is come of it, as a thing now of no Vertue or Consequence to us, should Reject the *Sacrament* of it, which is a continual Exhibition of its *vertues* and *efficacy* to us: Or that they who hope for no *Resurrection* of their *Bodies* out of the *Dust*, should continue the use of those *Sacraments* which were ordained as *signs* and *pledges* of it.

But, if it please God that they ever Return to the *Faith*, it is to be hoped that they will then Re-assume these *Guards*, and *Confirmations*; which are the outward *vehicles*, and *assurance* of it.

III. The *Third* point is their Denyal of the *Resurrection* and *Future Judgment*. For the Proof of this upon the *Quakers*, I Refer to *The Snake in the Grass*, Sect. xii. p. 152. and to *Satan Dis-Rob'd*, Sect. iii. and iv. beginning at p. 26. and p. 21. of the *Gleanings*.

Now we find full Proof, that this *Heresie* was Broached in in the Days of the *Apostles*; and by them Condemn'd, as is plain from 1 *Cor.* xv. 12. *&c.* and 2 *Tim.* 2. 18. in which last Text, the very *Quaker-salvo* is expresly set down, by which they have Betray'd themselves into this Fatal *Heresie*, *viz.* Saying that the *Resurrection* is *Past already*, that is, Perform'd Inwardly, to those who follow the *Light*, (see *Satan Dis-Rob'd*, p. 21. of the *Gleanings*) and Mr. *Penn* understands that Full and Elegant Description of the *Resurrection*, 1 *Cor.* xv. all of this *Inward* and *Allegorical Resurrection*; for in his Book, Intituled, *The Invalidity of* John Faldo's *Vindication*, &c. Printed 1673. repeating *ver.* 44. of this *Chapt. viz. It is sown a Natural Body, it is Raised a Spiritual Body*, he says p. 369. *I do utterly deny, that this Text is concern'd in the Resurrection of Man's carnal Body, at all.* And p. 370. *I say this doth not concern the Resurrection of carnal Bodys, but the two states of Men under the first and second* Adam. And though as he objects, the 47 and 49 verses *seem to imply a Bodily* Resurrection, But (says he) *let the whole verse be considered, and we shall find no such thing.*

To the Arguments of the *Apostles* against this *Heresie*, let me add some Testimonys of others their *Co-temporary Fathers*,

or

or rather explain the Texts of the *Apostles* by their *Comments*, who learned this *Article* of the *Faith* from their mouths. The Texts above Quoted were wrote by St. *Paul*, who (*Phil*. iv. 3.) mentions *Clement* as his *Fellow Labourer*, *and whose Name is in the book of Life*: And he was as likely to know St. *Paul*'s meaning, as Mr. *Penn*, whom I desire to read his 2d. Epist. to the *Corinthians*, where, N. ix. he will find these words.

Let none of you say, that this same flesh is not judged, nor shall rise again. Understand, in what have ye been saved; was it not while ye were in this flesh? therefore it behoveth us to keep our flesh, as the temple of God. For as ye have been called in the flesh, so shall ye come in the flesh. Jesus Christ the Lord, who saveth us, was first a Spirit, and then made flesh, and so he called us. So shall we Receive our Reward, in this very flesh.

Καὶ μὴ λεγέτω τις ὑμῶν, ὅτι αὕτη ἡ Σὰρξ ὁ κρίνεται ὐδὲ Ἀνίςαται· Γνῶτε ἐν τίνι ἐσώθητε, ἐν τίνι Ἀνεβλέψατε, εἰ μὴ ἐν τῇ Σαρκὶ ταύτῃ ὄντες. Δεῖ ἂν ἡμᾶς ὡς ναὸν Θεῦ φυλάσσειν τ Σάρκα. ὅν ζρόπον γδ ἐν τῇ Σαρκὶ ἐκλήθητε, ἢ ἐν τῇ Σαρκὶ ἐλεύσεσθε. Ὁ Ἰησῦς Χριςὸς ὁ Κύριος, ὁ σώσας ἡμᾶς, ὢν μὲν τὸ πρῶτον πνεῦμα, ἐγγνέτο Σάρξ, ἐ ὕτως ἡμᾶς ἐκάλεσεν. ὕτως ἐ ἡμεῖς ἐν ταύτῃ τῇ Σαρκὶ ἀποληψόμεθα τ μιθὸν.

St. *Polycarp*, *Bishop* and *Martyr*, who *flourished* about the Year of *Christ*, 70. and was Disciple to St. *John* the *Evangelist*, in his Epistle to the *Philippians*, n. 7. says that *Whoever does not confess the Martyrdom or suffering of* Christ *upon the Cross, is of the Devil: And he that will wrest the Oracles of* Christ *to his own Lusts, and say that there is no Resurrection nor Judgment to come, he is the* First-Born *of Satan*.

Καὶ ὃς ἂν μὴ ὁμολογῇ τὸ Μαρτύριον τῦ Σταυρῦ, ἐκ τῦ Διαβόλυ ὅςι, ἐ ὃς ἂν μεθοδεύῃ τὰ λόγια ϐ Χριςῦ πρὸς τὰς ἰδίας ἐπιθυμίας, ἢ λέγῃ μήτε Ἀνάςασιν, μήτε Κρίσιν ἔι, ὅϜς πρωτότοκος ὅςι ϐ Σατανᾶ.

And *Hegesippus*, who lived near to the Days of the *Apostles*, in his Fifth Book; as Quoted by *Eusebius* (Hist. Eccl. l. 2. c. 23.) speaking of these Ancient *Hereticks*, says, that they did not believe either the Resurrection, or the coming of Christ to render to every one according to his Works.

αἱ ϟ Αἱρέσεις πρφρειρημέναι, ὐκ ἐπίςευον ὅτε Ἀνάςασιν, ὅτε ἐρχόμενον ἀποδοῦναι ἑκάςῳ κατὰ τὰ ἔργα αὐτῦ.

IV. The

IV. The Fourth Point, is their abstaining from the *Sacraments* and *Prayers* of the *Church*. And for this, I have before quoted *Ignatius* to the *Smyrnæans*, where he tells of those who Abstained *from the* Prayers *of the Church, and the* Lord's Supper, *because they did not believe it to be the* Flesh *of* Christ, *which* Suffered *for our sins, and was* Raised *up,* &c. For how could they who (as the *Quakers*) made no more of the *flesh* of *Christ*, than a *Garment* or a *Vail*, but no part of his *Person*, and consequently could *never call the Bodily Garment*, *Christ*: And thought their own *Flesh* and *Blood* to be the *Flesh* and *Blood* of *Christ*, as well as the *Flesh* and *Blood* of that Man *Jesus*, in whom they say that *Christ* or the *Light* dwelt, as in themselves (see *Satan Dis-Rob'd*, Sect. ii. n. 2. and 3. p. 2. and 3. of the *Gleanings*) and plac'd the *Meritorious* Cause of our *Redemption*, and *Justification*, not in the *Blood* of *Christ* outwardly shed; but in the *Allegorical* or Inward *Blood* of their *Light within*, *Inwardly* and *Invisibly* shed, *&c*. I say, How could these endure a *Sacrament* so contrary to their Belief? For the *Bread* cannot be called the *Flesh* of their *Light within*; but it was of His *Outward Flesh* that *Christ* spake, when he said, *This is my Body,* and His *Outward Blood* was said to be shed for *The Remission of Sins*.

And the *Eucharist* was such a visible *Representation* of this, as could not but shock these *Enthusiast Hereticks*.

And where the *Sacraments* are Practised, such mad *Enthusiasm* cannot take place. And we see, by woful Experience, that where these Guards of the *Truth* and *Importance* of *Christ*'s Outward *Sufferings* are taken away, Men fall, from the True *Faith*, in them.

But the *Quakers* have not only thrown off the Use and Practise of the *Sacraments*, and left them as things Indifferent, or Lawful to be Practised by such as may be conscientiously concern'd for them, but Damn them as *Carnal*, and *Doctrines of Devils*. G. *Fox*, in his *News out of the North*, Printed 1655. p. 14. makes them the like *Witch-craft* as turn'd the *Galatians* to *Circumcision*. *And their Sacrament* (says he) *as they call it, is carnal* —— *And their Communion is carnal, a little Bread and Wine* —— *Which is the Table of Devils, and Cup of Devils, which is in the Generation of Serpents in this Great City* Sodom *and* Gomorrah, *so dust is the Serpents meat,* &c. And p. 39. *You say that* Matthew, Mark, Luke, *and* John, *is the Gospel, which is carnal* —— *You say, that sprinkling Infants is the Baptism, which Baptizeth them into the faith, and so into the Church,* which is carnal: *And you tell People of a Sacrament, bringing them to Eat a little Bread and Wine, and say, that this is a Communion of Saints, which is carnal, and all this feeds the Carnal Mind,* &c. And he *Blasphemously* says in his *Title Page,* that all this was *Written from the mouth of the Lord.*

Edward Burrough, p. 190. of his *Works,* Printed 1672. says, *Their Doctrines are of the devil, who* —— *say sprinkling Infants with water* —— *is Baptism into the faith of Christ, this is the doctrine of the devil.* And p. 191. *These have filled the world with damnable Heresies, as holding forth, That sprinkling Infants with water is Baptism into the faith of Christ,* &c. *These are damnable Heresies, even to the denying the Lord that bought them.* And p. 644. *That it is not lawful for the Saints of God, to join themselves to your Ordinances.*

This Hideous *Blasphemy* and *Outrage* against the *Divine Institutions* of our *Lord,* I hope will appear to be such to the well-disposed among the *Quakers,* who will be at the pains to Read my Discourse of *Water-Baptism.* It seems to have had some Effects already, even with *George Whitehead* himself. For in his Answer to *The Snake* (whereto he adds a *chapter* upon that Discourse of *Baptism*) he seems to come off that former *Rigor* of the *Quakers,* and says, p. 114. That *as for those who are More conscientiously tender in the observation thereof, we are* (says he) *the more tender to these so as not to censure or condemn them meerly for Practising that which they believe is their duty, either in breaking of Bread, or Water-baptism.*

So that, by this, he yields the *Practice* of the *Sacraments* to be at least *Lawful,* contrary to *Burrough, Fox,* and the Primitive *Quakers;* for, if it were not *Lawful,* I suppose he would not have that *Tenderness* for the *Observation thereof,* but would *censure* and *condemn* it, as those others have done. I pray God perfect his Conversion, and let him see the *Necessity* as well as *Lawfulness* of it. And I would desire him to consider that if it be *Lawful,* it must be *Necessary*: For if *Christ* has not commanded *Water-Baptism,* it cannot be less than *Superstition* to Practice that as a *Sacrament,* and consequently as a *Means* of *Grace,* which he has not Commanded: Even the *Church* of *Rome* does not pretend to a Power to *Institute* a *Sacrament,* that can be done by none but *God* alone: Therefore if *Water-Baptism* was not *Instituted* by *Christ,* it cannot be *Lawful* to Practice it: And if he did *Institute* it, it is not only *Lawful,* but *Necessary,* and a *Duty.* Now, in Aid of *George Whitehead,* and

by

by way of *An Antidote against the venome of* G. Fox, Burrough, *and other foure Quakers*; and to purſue the Deſign of this preſent Paper, I will, to the Authoritys of H. Scripture, which I have Produc'd in The *Diſcourſe of Baptiſm*, add in this place, as a ſure Comment and Explanation of them, the Teſtimonys of ſome of thoſe Fathers, whoſe Works we have Extant within the Compaſs of Years propoſed, that is, 150 Years after *Chriſt*, in witneſs to this *Divine Inſtitution* of *Water-Baptiſm*, and to ſhew what ſtreſs they laid upon it.

St. *Ignatius*, who was (as before-mentioned) bred under Saint *John* the Beloved Diſciple, makes our *Baptiſm* not only the *Badge*, but the *Arms* and *Defence* of our *Faith*; and the quitting of it to be a Deſerting of Chriſt.

Let no one of you (ſays he, in his *Epiſt.* to St. *Polycarp*) *be found a Deſerter, but let your Baptiſm remain as your Armor.*

μή τις ὑμῶν δεσέρτωρ εὑρεθῇ, τὸ Βάπτισμα ὑμῶν μδυίτω ὡς ὅπλα.

And St. *Barnabas*, who was St. *Paul*'s Fellow-Traveller, mentioned ſo often in the *Acts*, ſpeaking, in his *Catholick Epiſtle*, chapt. xi. concerning Water and the Croſs, ſays, that, *It is written concerning Water to the People of Iſrael, that they ſhould not receive that Baptiſm which was ſufficient to the Pardon of ſins.* Which they did not under the *Moſaical* Diſpenſation. But they Inſtituted a *Baptiſm* to themſelves, whereby to admit Men as *Proſelites* to the Law: But that was not the *Baptiſm* which could take away Sin. No, nor the *Baptiſm* of *John*: That was the *Peculiar* one of the *Chriſtian Baptiſm*.

περὶ μὲν ὅ ὕδατ@ γέγραπται ἐπὶ τ̄ Ἰσραήλ, πῶς τὸ Βάπτισμα, τὸ φέρον εἰς ἄφεσιν ἁμαρτιῶν, ὁ μὴ προσδέ- ξωντ' ἀλλ' ἑαυτοῖς οἰκοδομήσοσι.

A little after St. *Barnabas* ſays, that God had joyned the *Croſs* (that is, the Faith in CHRIST Crucified) and the *Water* (that is, *Baptiſm*) together, *viz.* the *Inward* Faith, and the *Outward* Profeſſion and Seal of it.

Conſider (ſays he) *how He* (God) *has appointed the Croſs and the* Water *to the ſame end. For thus he ſaith, bleſſed are they who hoping in the* Croſs, *have gone down into the* Water.

ἀιᾶωιεθε πῶς τὸ ὕδωρ, ἢ τ̄ σαυρὸν ἐπὶ τὸ αὐτὸ ἄρισι. τοῦτο γὰρ λέγει· μακάριοι οἱ ἐπὶ τ̄ σαυρὸν ἐλπίσαν- τες, κατέβησαν εἰς τὸ ὕδωρ.

And

[12]

And again, pursuing the same Argument, he Magnifys the great *Efficacy* and *Power* of Baptism, when duly Received, a few lines after what is above quoted, saying,

For we go down into the Water *full of sins and filthiness ; and come up again bearing fruit in our hearts by the fear and hope which is in* Jesus, *which we have in the* Spirit.	ἡμεῖς μὲν καταβαίνομεν εἰς τὸ ὕδωρ γέμοντες ἁμαρτιῶν ὲ ῥύπε ; ὲ ἀνα- βαίνομεν καρποφοροῦντες ἐν τῇ καρδί- ᾳ, διὰ τ̅ φόβον κ̀ τὴν ἐλπίδα εἰς τ̅ Ἰησῶν ἔχοντες ἐν ᾧ πνεύματι.

After the same manner, and in the like words speaks St. *Hermas* (whom St. *Paul* salutes *Rom.* 16. 14.) in that only Remaining Work of his, called *The Shepherd of* St. *Hermas*, there in the 3*d.* Book, and 9*th.* Similitude, he speaks thus :

Before a Man receives the Name of the Son *of God, he is designed unto death : but when he receives that seal, he is delivered from death, and given up to life. Now that seal is* Water, *into which Men go down, lyable to death, but come up again, assigned over unto life.*	Antequam enim accipiat homo nomen Filii Dei, morti destinatus est : at ubi accipit illud sigillum, liberatur a morte, & traditur vitæ. Illud autem sigillum Aqua est, in quam descendunt homines morti obligati, ascendunt vero vitæ assignati.

I have taken this out of the Ancient *Latin* Translation, according to the *Oxford* Edit. 1685. For the *Greek* was, in great part, lost, and came not down to us intire, as this old *Latin* Version did.

St. *Clement*, in his 2*d. Epist.* to the *Corinthians, Paragr.* 8. calls *Baptism* by the same name of our Seal, and applys to it that Text, *Isa.* lxvi. 24. which he renders thus. *They that have not kept their seal, their worm shall not die,* &c. Or, as he expresses it in the *Paragr.* before this, *Unless we keep our* Baptism *pure and undefiled, with what assurance can we enter the Kingdom of God ?*

τῆς γὰρ μὴ τηρησάντων τὴν σφρα- γῖδα, ὁ σκώληξ αὐτῆς ᾀ τελευτήσει, &c.

ἡμεῖς ἐὰν μὴ τηρήσωμεν τὸ βάπ- τισμα ἁγνὸν κ̀ ἀμίαντον, ποίᾳ πεποι- θήσει εἰσελευσόμεθα εἰς τὸ βασίλειον τῦ Θεῦ

V. The Fifth Point is their *forbidding to Marry, and Preaching up of fornication*. I charge not *All* the *Quakers* with this ; no, nor the *Greatest Number* of them. Only those called *New-Quakers* in *America*, of whom, and this their *Principle* and *Practice*, an Account
is

is given in The *Snake in the Grafs* Sect. vi. n. x. Par. 11. p. 74. and Sect. xii. p. 160. But the *Quakers* are thus far anfwerable, That all this *Wild Extravagance* is a Natural Confequence of their *Common Principle* and *Notion* of The *Light within,* as fuch an *Abfolute Rule* and *Judge,* that is not to be Controled by Scripture, or any Law or Rule whatfoever: Which leaves every Man in fuch an Un-limited Latitude, that there is no *Reftraint* to whatever the *Wildeft Imagination* (fo it be Strong enough) can fuggeft: Nor any Cure (upon their Foundation) but to bid him follow it ftill on. Liften to that *within* you. That is all their *Advice,* and all their *Rule.*

But befides, I would fain know what Anfwer the *Old Quakers* can give to the *New* ones, upon their Principle; for the *New* threw off their *Wives,* becaufe they found it Written, That *the children of the Refurrection neither marry, nor are given in marriage.* Now, as fhewn in *The Snake,* Sect. xii and before fpoke to, the *Quakers* General Notion is that the *Refurrection* is Spiritual, and that every *Regenerate* Man has obtained it already. And fome of the Chief and Oldeft of them have declared, that they expect no other than what they have obtained already, or at leaft, fhall attain before they leave this body. See *Satan Dis-Robed* p. 21. of the *Gleanings.*

Now let me ask the *Old Quakers*: Are they the *Children of the Refurrection*? They muft anfwer *Yea,* or go againft their own avowed *Principles.* And if *Yea,* then the Text is plain againft their Marrying.

Let me ask again. Are they *the Children of this World?* They will all fay, *Nay,* for that is the common Epithet by which they defcribe the *Wicked*; and is a Term that they put in oppofition to *the Children of the light,* which they beftow upon *themfelves.* Now it is written, That *the children of this world marry.* Therefore, fay the *New Quakers,* Marriage is a Wicked Thing, and confequently of the Devil: And the *Old Quakers* have not yet anfwered their Arguments, that I can hear of. And the *New Quakers* do vouch themfelves to be the only True and Genuine *Quakers,* who follow their Principles up to the height. Nor do they want *Antiquity* in all this: The *Gnoftick Quakers,* who boafted in their Light beyond all other Men, and called themfelves (as the *Quakers* do) the *Pureft* and moft *Perfect* of Chriftians; held thefe fame Principles, and Practifed them, in the very days of the *Apoftles,*. And
- they

[14]

they are Reprehended, and our Later *Hereticks*, who should follow their steps, Prophesied of 1 *Tim.* iv. 1, 2, 3.

VI. The Sixth Point is, *Their Contempt of Magistracy and Government*. This is shewn, as to the *Quakers*, in *The Snake.* p. 94. and in Sect. xviii. and xix. more largely. *George Fox* in his *Great Mistery*, Printed 1659. p. 76. says, *The Power of God* ——— *strikes down Government of Men and Governours*. And p. 90. *And so* (says he) *for the* Lord's *sake the Saints cannot be subject to that Power*. And he Argues (though very falsly) that, *The* Jews *of old time could not obey the* Heathen *Magistrates* — *Nor the* Apostles *could not bow to the Authority of the* Jews — *Nor that among the* Gentiles, *held up by the* Magistrates. I say all this is most False; for the *Jews* did obey the *Heathen* Magistrates; and the *Apostles* both the *Jews* and and *Gentiles*, and that, not only for *Wrath*, but also for *Conscience* sake. But it shew'd what *Fox* meant, *viz.* That the Saints are not under the Dominion of the Worlds Rulers, whom they think to have no other Authority than that of the Devil. Accordingly *Fox* says *(ibid.) For it was the* Beasts *Power hath set up your Tythes, Temples, and Colledges*. This will include all the *Governments* upon the Earth: For there is none but have some of these; hardly any but have them *All.* And then down go All, if the *Quakers* prevail.

But to come to our Point. This *Wicked Heresie* was born into the World in the days of the *Apostles*, and set up by the then *Quakers*, That the Receiving of Christianity did Exempt Men from the Service of *Un-believers*, whether Masters or Magistrates. Which occasioned the many Repeated Exhortations in the Epistles, especially of the *Apostle* of the *Gentiles*, to be subject both to Masters and Magistrates, though *Un-believers*. And there were those *Jews* in our Saviours time, who, upon the same account, thought it not Lawful to give Tribute to *Cæsar*, being then an *Heathen*. They thought that the *Jews* were not to submit to the Dominion of the *Heathen*. And *Judas* of *Galilee*, mentioned in *Act.* 5. 37. drew away much People after him, upon the same Pretence, of not paying Taxes to the *Romans*, *Joseph*. (de *Bell. Jud.* l. 2. *c.* 7.) says, he Taught that no Tribute should be paid to the *Romans*. But he went further (a thorow *Quaker*) for he would have had all Magistrates taken away, and *God* only to be *King*. I suppose (as the *Quakers*) he would have been Content that the

Govern-

Government should have come into his own hand, and to some *Saints* under him, as *Deputys* from *God*! Such he made his *Gaulonites* or *Galileans* who followed him. For the meaning of those who find fault with the *Government* of others, is commonly to seize upon it for themselves, (and they seldom mend the matter) tho' their pretence is always to set up the Kingdom of *God* and His *Saints*.

Such *Gaulonites* or *Galileans* are the *Quakers*, who, in a *Declaration* to the *Present distracted Nation of* England, (Printed 1659. Penn'd by *Edw. Burrough*, and subscrib'd by *Fifteen* of the Cheif of the *Quakers*, in the name of all the rest) p. 8. do Proclaim that they have chosen a *King*, (*viz.* their own *Light within*, which they call the *Son* of *God*) and that it is *His only Right to Rule in Nations*, and their *Heirship* (as being only his Faithful Subjects) *to possess the uttermost parts of the Earth* : And that *He may command thousands and ten thousands of* (these) *his Saints, at this day, to* Fight — mark that, to *Fight*, even with the *Carnal* Sword, to Regain their *Right*. But in the Reprinting of *Burrough*'s Works, 1672, it was thought convenient to leave out this Passage (p 603. of his works) tho' it was said to be given forth by the *Spirit* of God, and in *His Name*. It is set down more at large in *The Snake*, p. 209.

The same *Universal Monarchy* and *Heirship* of the *Quakers* is asserted by *Samuel Fisher*, in a Collection that he Printed of several *Messages* which he said he had, *By Commission from God*, to deliver to the then *Protector* and *Government*, 1656. The last of which bears this Title. *The Burden of the Message of the Lord it self*, there p. 32. speaking of the *Quakers* and their *King*, says, *He in them, and they in him shall Rule the Nations with a Rod of Iron, and break them to pieces as a Potters Vessel* —— *And every tongue that riseth up in Judgment against them shall they condemn.* And p. 33. he brings in *God*, saying, *yea, I will never rest till I have made all their Foes their Foot-stool* : *And howbeit the Powers of the Earth are of me* —— *I will utterly subvert and overturn them*; *and bring the Kingdoms and Dominions, and the Greatness of the Kingdom under the whole Heaven into the hands of the Holy Ones of the most High, and give unto my Son, and his Saints to Reign over all the Earth, and to take all the Rule and Authority, and Power that shall stand up against my Son in his Saints.* There is the Mystery couch'd in the last words. *In his Saints*, that is the *Light within* (which they call *Christ*) *in* the *Quakers* : And to which they ascribe all that is said of *Christ* in the Scriptures. *Edw.*

Edw. Burrough writing from *Dublin* in *Ireland* to the *Quakers* in *England*, in the Year 1655. Directs thus, *To the Camp of the Lord in* England. This is p. 64. of his Works. And he was then for their beginning of their *War* to Conquer the whole Earth. He Exhorts them, p. 67. in their *Conquests* to be very *severe* and *bloody*, to spare none. *Give the great Whore* (says he, that is *Rome*) *double into her bosom; as she hath loved blood, so give her blood, and dash her Children against the stones.* This was for all the *Popish* Countrys, and those who partook of their Abominations, which in their Account were all the Protestants too, whom they, in contempt called *Professors*; and *All sects in these Nations,* whom *Burrough* includes in his Epist. to the *Reader,* p. 1. and declares *War* against them. But were the *Heathens* then to escape? No, their Conquest and Empire was to be *Universal,* their *Heirship* did extend to the uttermost parts of the Earth. For thus he goes on, (*Ut supra*) *Let none of the Heathen Nations, nor their Gods escape out of your hands — but lay waste the fenced Cities, and tread down the high walls, for we have proclaimed open War betwixt* Michael *our Prince and the* Dragon — *And cursed be every one that riseth not up, to the help of the Lord against the mighty. Put on your Armour, and gird on your sword, and lay hold on the spear, and march into the Field, and prepare your selves to the Battle, for the Nations doth defie our God, and saith in their hearts, who is the God of the* Quakers, *that we should fear him, and obey his voice? — Our Enemies are whole Nations, and multitudes in number, of a Rebellious People that will not come under our Law* (a great Fault indeed!) *stand upon your feet, and Appear in your terror as an Army with Banners; and let the Nations know your power, and the stroke of your hand: Cut down on the right hand, and slay on the left; and let not your eye pitty, nor your hand spare,* &c. And in his *Trumpet of the Lord sounded,* which he calls *An Alarum and Preparation for War against all Nations where* Gog and Magog *resideth,* Printed 1656. p. 32. he says to the *Quakers, your despised Government shall rule over Kingdoms, and your laws shall all the Nations of the earth become subject unto.* And p. 41. He expostulates with God, *When wilt thou appear to lay their honour in the dust of Confusion? Thy Host and Chosen waiteth for a Commission from thee to do thy will. And thy Camp waiteth to see the honour of Kings and Princes overthrown by thee,* &c. But it seems the *Quakers* would make use of the swords of the *wicked,* till their own were ready. Therefore in the

Year

[17]

Year 1659. they had great Hopes in the *Rebel* Englifh *Army* ; who having Deftroy'd the *King*, and the *Church* in thefe Kingdoms, *Burrough* Hoalloos them (in his Epift. to them, p. 537.) upòn *Italy* and *Spain*, and all the *Popifh* Countrys : *For what are thefe few poor Iflands* (fays he) *that you have run through ? in comparifon of the great Part of* Chriftendom, *in which* Idolatry — *do abound* — *wherefore*, *Hew down the Tops, ftrike at the Branches, make way, that the Ax may be laid to the root of the Tree, that your fword, and the fword of the Lord may neither leave Root nor Branch of* Idolatry ---- *to avenge the blood of the Guiltlefs thro' all the Dominions of the* Pope, *the blood of the Juft it crys thro'* Italy, and Spain ---- *and it would be your honour to be made ufe of by the Lord, in any degree, in order to this matter*. They were to be made ufe of, *in fome degree*, to clear the way for the *Quakers*, who were, at laft, to have *All*. Now whether thefe have not out-ftript their Forerunner *Judas*, and his *Galileans*, I leave the Reader to judge. And Proceed to the next.

VII. The *Seventh* and laft Point which I intend to fpeak of, is now come, and is fo near of kin to the laft, that I fhall difpatch it quickly. It is, *Their ftiffnefs in not taking off their Hats, or giving Men their Civil Titles.* Ther needs no Proof of this, as to the *Quakers*, for they All own it, it is their *Difcriminating Charaƈter*.

And now to find a Precedent for them in *Antiquity*, the fame *Judas Galilæus* is ready at hand. *Jofephus* tells (*Antiq. Jud.* l. 18. c. 2.) that he was the Head of a Fourth *Seƈt* among the *Jews*, which he himfelf (like *George Fox*) Founded. And that as he acknowledg'd but one *Lord* and *Mafter*, that is, *God*; fo as a confequence of this, he would pay honour to none other; and fo *Obftinate* were his *Seƈt* in this, That, as *Jofeph*. tells in the *chapt*. laft quoted, *they would rather expofe themfelves, their Children and Relations to the moft cruel Torments, than call any mortal Man Lord or Mafter*. So that *George Fox* has not the *Honour* of this noble *Invention*, as he would make us believe in his *Journal*, p. 24. where he fays, *When the Lord fent me forth into the world, He forbad me to put off my Hat to any* ---- *And I was required to* Thee *and* Thou *all men and women*. He would call none *Lord* or *Mafter* more than *Judas*. And their *Infpirations* came from the *fame Author* ; the *Spirit* of *Pride*, under the *Guife* of *Humility* ; fo that in this, and all the other Inftances before mentioned, *George Fox* is depriv'd of the *Glory* of being an *Original*, and to be *No man's Copy*, as is Boafted of him, in the *Preface* to his *Journal*, p. 31. I do not fup-

D   pofe

pose that he knew a tittle of these *Ancient Precedents*, only *Good wits Jump'd*; and so exactly, as shews, That they were all *Taught* by the same Master.

The CONCLUSION.

1. What Application now needs to be made, from all that has been said, to the *Quakers*? The thing shews it self. Let them not call it *Malice* and *Envy* and what not, to oppose them. We oppose the Primitive *Heresies* in them. We cannot but *oppose* them: Unless we would *Condemn* the *Apostles* and Primitive *Fathers*, who have *Condemned* them. I charitably believe that the *Quakers*, at least, the *Generality* of them, do not know, nor, may be, have heard of these Ancient *Heresies*, or that they have so literally lick'd them up. But now they do know, let them consider, and see how they have put *Darkness* for *Light*, and *Light* for *Darkness*!

2. But if the *Quakers* say, as of late they have begun to do, That they are *Mis-represented*, that they do not hold these *Vile Heresies*, and *Errors* Charg'd against them, nor ever did hold them. Let the Reader judge of that by the *Quotations* which are produc'd out of their most Approved *Authors*, in *The Snake*, and *Satan Dis-Rob'd*; of all which G. *Whitehead*, in what is called his *Answer*, does not deny one: But pleads *Not Guilty*, without offering to Disprove the *Evidence* brought against them. However, That is not my Business now. I am willing they should *come off* as easily as they can: Provided they do *come off*, and mean not this to *Deceive* us.

3. Let it then be suppos'd, that the Modern Representations they have given of their *Notion* of *The light within*, and of other their *Doctrines* (since the *oppositions* they have lately met with) are the *True* and *Genuin* sense of what they held from the beginning: And, when truly explained and understood, the same, and no more than what the *Ch.* of *England*, and all sober *Christians* have always held.

If so, then they must begin again to give a new Account of their *Separation*, and so violent a *Separation* as they have made, not only from the *Ch.* of *England* but all the *Churches* in the World, as *Edw. Burrough*, p. 416. of his *Works*, *And so all you Churches and Sects, by what name soever you are known in the world, you are the seed of the great Whore.* And p. 17. of his *Epist.* to the Reader he tells him, *Thou mayst fully perceive we differ in Doctrines and Principles; and the one thou must justifie, and the other thou must condemn, as being one clean contrary to the other in our Principles.* And p. 1. he says, *We have sufficient cause*

to

to cry *againſt* them, and to deny their *Miniſtry*, their *Church*, their *Worſhip*, and their whole *Religion*. What ſhall we do now! Now we Agree in nothing! our *Whole Religion* is *Condemned*: And ther is no *Compounding*: we muſt *Condemn* the *One*, and *Juſtifie* the other. Here is Foul-Play on ſome ſide! By ſome *Modern Accounts*, it is hard to diſtinguiſh wherein the *Doctrines* of the *Ch.* of *England*, and thoſe of the *Quakers*, do differ. Particularly in their *Fundamental Principle* of *The Light within*, on which all the Reſt do Depend, as it is Explained by Mr. *Penn* in his late *Primitive Chriſtianity*, and in *The Snake*, Sect. i. and Sect. xxii. except the Particular hereafter excepted, they are the ſame; and Mr. *Penn* asks no more (upon the Main) than what is not only *Allowed*, but *Practiſed*, and always has been, and that *Dayly*, in our *Common Prayers*, by the *Ch.* of *England*; yes, and by our *Diſſenters* too; ſo that now we are very *Good Friends* again! And the *Difference* betwixt us, upon this Point, is no ways ſufficient to Juſtifie any *Separation*. And ſo of the other Points of *Doctrine*, as, of late Explained. And for the *Sacraments*, G. *Whitehead* allows them to be *Lawful*, and let ſuch *Practice* them, as ſo think fit. Then ther is no ground for their *Separation* from us, for our Practice of what themſelves Allow to be *Lawful*. And for *Epiſcopacy*, that is a matter of *Government*, not of *Worſhip*, ſo that we might join in Worſhip for all that. And the *Biſhops* Exerciſe no other *Power* than what is uſed amongſt the *Quakers*, to *Diſown* thoſe who will not walk according to the Rules of the *Society*. And their *Power* herein is much Curbed by the Laws, and *Appeals* lye from their *Sentence* to the *Secular Courts*, which are not Allowed in the *Quaker-Diſcipline*.

Now, to bring this matter to an Iſſue, in a *Friendly* manner, without *Ripping* up or *Confronting* Former *Teſtimonies*, it is deſired, That Mr. *Penn*, or any other for him, would ſhew ſuch Differences betwixt his Explanation of the *Light within*, and that in *The Snake*, as are ſo *Material*, to juſtifie a *Separation*; and ſo of the other Points Treated of in his *Primitive Chriſtianity*.

And herein let him and them Conſider the Grievouſneſs of the Sin of *Schiſm*; even as Enforced by them againſt their own *Separatiſts*; it is a Tearing the *Body* of *Chriſt* in pieces; and

turning the *Heaven* of *Christianity*, into a *Hell* of *Confusion*. Let us
Act herein *Manfully*; for we Fight for our own *Souls*, the *Union* and
Joy of *Christendom*, the *Honour* of *Religion*, and the *Glory* of *God*;
who *knows* our *Hearts*, and will *Reward* our *Sincerity*. He, through
whose Holy *Inspiration* only, we think those things that be Right-
ful, *Prevent* us, in all our *Doings*, with His most *Gracious Favour*;
Further us with His Continual *Help*, and *Pardon* all our *Infirmities*;
in the Prosecution of these Glorious Ends, through *Jesus Christ*, our
Lord; who for these same Ends, *Dyed*, *Rose*, *Ascended*, and will come
again, in that same *Body*, to *Reward*, and to *Judge* every Man according to what he has been *Useful*, or *Prejudicial* to these Ends. To
whom with the *Father*, and the *Eternal Spirit*, be All *Power*, *Honour*, and *Glory*, from All *Creatures*, *Converted Sinners* especially,
now, and for ever. *Amen.*

A Friendly Expostulation *with Mr.* Penn; *upon Account of his*
Primitive Christianity, *lately Published.*

1. I Have said before, how near Mr. *Penn* has brought the *Quaker*
Principles (as he has, of late, Represented them) to the *Doctrin*
of the *Ch.* of *England*, and the *Common Principles* of *Christianity*. But
I would desire to Expostulate a little with him upon one Part of his
Exposition of *The Light within*, p. 29. where he is not satisfied with
what we allow, *viz.* that it does *Influence* and *Assist* our *Natural
Light*; but he will not grant that we have any *Natural Light* at all,
or any other than that *Divine Light* of the *Word*, which is *God*; which
he says, *some, mistakenly, call* Natural *Light*. As G. *Fox* says, in his
Great *Mistery*, p. 42. where he opposes this *Tenet, That no man by
that Native* Light *inherent in him, had Power to Believe,* &c. G. F.
Answers, *The* Light *that doth enlighten every man* (which is their description of the *Light within*) he calls it Native *and* Inherent: *The
names he gives of* Native *and* Inherent, *are his own, out of the Truth.*
Here he denys any *Natural* Light, and will have none other but the
Divine Light *within*. But to go on with Mr. *Penn*, he says, p. 30.
and 31. That the *Scripture* makes no distinction between *Natural*
and *Spiritual* Light, and Provokes any to give so much as one *Text*
to that Purpose; he makes it as Absurd, as to talk of a *Natural* and
Spiritual Darkness *within*. He says, *There are not two Lights from
God in man, that Regard Religion*. Not that *Reproves* or *Condemns*
a Man for *Sin*. But

But how then does he Anfwer the *Objection*, which he puts againſt himſelf, of the many *Falſe Religions* in the world ? It was not the *True Light* which guided men into them. And if they have no other *Light*, how came they by them ? He ſays, it was becauſe they did not follow the *True Light*. But why did they not follow it ? How could they help following of it, if they had nothing elſe to follow ? What was it that Reſiſted It ? Or, What could Reſiſt It, if we have no *Natural Light* or *Underſtanding* to Refuſe its Dictates ? But ſuppoſe our *No Light* or *Underſtanding* could ſhut its eyes, and not follow this *light*; then it might loſe the *True Religion*. But could *no-underſtanding* invent another *Religion* ? For that is ſomething *Poſitive*; and ſomething muſt Guide and Direct Men to it. The *Abſence* of *Light* is *Darkneſs*, not a *Falſe-light*. But an *Ignis Fatuus*, or *Will i'th' Wiſp*, is a *Light* that leads Men *wrong*. Men that are in *Error* follow a *Light*, but it is *Falſe-light*, and they think themſelves to be in the *Right*. Our *Underſtandings* have a *Natural*, which is a *Fallible-light*; and therefore often leads us wrong. What elſe is the meaning of *Prov.* 3. 5. *Truſt in the Lord with all thine heart, and lean not unto thine own Underſtanding.* It is true, that *Underſtanding* and the *Natural light* of it, was given us by *God* : And He made it *Right* and *True*; but *Fallible*, elſe it could never be miſtaken. God has plac'd a *Natural light*, as a *Candle* in our *Hearts*; and His *Super-natural light* does *Influence* and *Direct* it, when we ſeek to Him for it, and ſerve Him according as He has commanded: *Solomon* ſays, Prov. xx. 27. *The Spirit of man is the Candle of the Lord, ſearching all the Inward Parts.* You will not call the *Spirit* of *Man* the Eternal *Light*, which is G O D. This was the Miſtake which drove George *Fox* to make our *Soul* a *Part* of *God,* without *Beginning*, and *Infinite in it ſelf*, &c., as ſhewn in *The Snake*, Sect. ii. and to make us even *Equal* with God, as ſhewn, *Sect.* iii. And Mr. *Penn*, p. 15. of this Book, (*Primit. Chriſtian.*) allows no *Natural light* to the *Underſtanding*, For (ſays he) *Man can no more be a Light to his Mind than he is to his Body* : And thence inferrs, that as the *Eye* has no *Light* in it ſelf, ſo neither the *Underſtanding*: He makes our *Nature* and *Minds* wholly *Dark* of themſelves, only ſucceptible of *Super-natural light*, when ſent into our Underſtanding: And
that

that all the *Light* we have is thus *Super-natural*; and only called *Natural*, because, as he says, *It is Natural to Man to have a Super-natural light.* I will not take advantage of the *Philosophy* of this; for, I suppose his meaning to be, that it is *Natural* to the *Understanding* to Receive a *Light* that is infus'd into it, as for the *Eye* to see by an *Extraneous light*; that is, it is an *Organ* fitted to Receive *Light*, tho' it has none in it self; as the *Understanding* to *Apprehend*, tho' it has no *Reason* or *Light* in it self. Thus he expresses it, p. 50. *All Men have Reason*, (says he) *but all Men are not Reasonable*; which must be taken with the same grains of Allowance. For every Man is a *Reasonable Creature*, that is, the *Definition* of a *Man*. But according to his *Hypothesis*, tho' all men have *Reason*, yet not *Natural*, but *super-naturally* put into their *Understanding*: And so, tho' they have *Reason*, yet are they not *Reasonable*, because that *Reason* is none of their own, only as *Gifted*, that is, *Accidental*, but not *Natural* to them; and so they can no more be called *Rational*, than a *Bagg* can be called *Rich*, that has *Money* in it. For he says, p. 15. *That* God, *is the Light of our Nature, of our minds, and understandings.* If it were meant as an *Assistant*, *Guide* or *Director*, to the *Light* of our *Understanding*, ther were no difference betwixt us: But quite to put out the *Natural light* of our *understandings*, and make it but only *Passive*, that is, *succesptible* of another *light*, that is the point on which I would *Reason* now with Mr. *Penn*. It is said 1 *Cor.* 1. 21. *That the World by Wisdom knew not God.* What *Wisdom* was this? it could not be a *Divine light*; and if Man have no *Natural light*; it must be the *Quaker* third sort of *light*, that is, *No light at all*: But if by *Wisdom* here, you mean Mens *Natural light* or *Reason*, the *Text* is *Plain* and *Easie*.

It is Written, 1 *Joh.* 3. 20. *If our Heart Condemn us,* God *is greater than our heart, and knoweth all things*. Now, by *Heart*, here must be meant the *Natural light*; because, if it means the *Light* which is *God*, God is not Greater than *Himself*. And it is supposed here that the *Heart* does not Know all Things: Therefore this must be meant of our *Natural Conscience*, and not of *God*. And now here is a *Natural light*, which does *Reprove of Evil*, which Mr. *Penn* supposes cannot be shewn, p. 30. Our *Saviour* says, *Luk.* xii. 57. *Yea, and why even of your selves*

judge

judge not what is Right? But why *of your selves*, if we have no *Light* at all *of our selves* whereby to *Judge*?

I find a great *Light* of the *Quakers*, *Edw. Burrough*, owning these *Two* Lights *within*, in his *Warning to Underbarrow*, 1654. p. 16. and 17. of his *Works* Re-printed 1672. where speaking of some of the *Worlds People, whose Light* (says he) *is only Natural and Carnal, and doth only make manifest Carnal Transgressions, and who Judge by the* Natural *light, &c.* This being Objected by *John Stalham*, in his *Reviler Rebuked*, p. 282. as a Contradiction to what other *Quakers* had said of the *Light*. *Richard Hubberthorn* (a *Quaker* of the First Rank) undertakes the Defence of *Burrough*, which you find in his *Works*, Re-printed 1663. p. 144. where he says that *Burrough* was Mis-represented, in that *Stalham* would have had him say, that the *Light* of *Christ* was *Natural* and *Carnal*, which he says *Burrough* did not mean ; but the *Light of Man* (says he) *by which Carnal Men do judge of Carnal Transgressions, is Natural — And Mans light, by which Carnal men do Judge of any thing, is one thing, and the light of* Jesus Christ, *which is Spiritual mens Guide, is another thing*. Here are *Two* Lights *within* most plainly, which Mr. *Penn* does so positively Oppose.

But which of these Lights guided Mr. *Penn*, and which *Hubberthorn* and *Burrough*? For it could not be the same Light that guided to Two Lights, and not to Two!

And now it will be time, to ask from Mr. *Penn* a Solution of the Difficulty which he Proposes p. 29. that is, *To assign us some certain* Medium, *or* Way, *whereby we may truly discern, and distinguish between the Manifestations and Reproofs of the* Natural Light *within, from those of the* Divine Light *within*. He proposed this as a Difficulty upon the Opinion of Two Lights within, a *Natural*, and a *Divine*. And presses it against those who held that the *Natural* Light could *Reprove of Evil* ; if which were granted, he would yield that ther must be Two Lights. But he supposes that nothing but the *Divine* Light could *Reprove of Evil*. The Contrary of which has been shewn from 1 *Joh*. 3. 20. and allowed both by *Burrough* and *Hubberthorn*, who both (in the places above Quoted) do assert that the *Natural* Light does *Reprove* of *Carnal Transgressions* : And therefore, if *Carnal Transgressions* be *Evil*, the *Natural* Light does *Reprove of Evil*.

But that which I would Improve from this, and for which I have been so long upon it, is, to Represent to Mr. *Penn* the Consequence of this Opinion of his. For if I think that my *Understanding* is a Perfect *Blank*, uncapable to *Judge* any thing *of it self*, that is, by the *Natural* Light which *God* has given it : But that every *Thought* of my *Heart*, concerning *Religion*, is *Super-natural*, Darted in there Immediately by *God* Himself, by the very *Life* of *the Word Eternal*, Then must I follow every such *Thought*, even without *Examination*, and Refuse to let it be *Over-Ruled*, either by the *Written Word* of the *Scriptures*, or by All the *Reason* or *Authority* of *Men* or *Angels*. And if such *Thought* be *Erroneous*, I am *Un-moveable* and *Irrecoverable*! This is the most *Desperate Condition* of which Man is Capable in this world. Therefore this *stumbling Block* must be Removed before we can proceed any further. And this is that, which keeps the *Quakers* so Deaf to all Arguments, *Charm* we never so *wisely*!

It was this which Confirm'd *Gilpin*, *Toldervy*, *Milner*, and other *Quakers*, that their *Diabolical Possessions* (owned now as such by all the *Quakers*) and the *Quaker-witches* who Attempted the lives of *Henry Winder* and his Wife (see the Story in *The Snake*, p. 300.) and tho' *Disproved*, *Confuted*, and *Confounded* many ways in all their *Accusations* against them, yet still to stick to it, and could never be brought to *Repentance*, or to own themselves *Mistaken*. Why? Because they had this *Notion*, That *what came into their minds, was the* Light *of* Christ.

And so it must be, if ther be no other *Light* in the *mind* but that of *Christ*, except we allow of a *Diabolical*. And then ther are *three* sorts, *Natural*, *Divine*, and *Diabolical*.

Unless you will say, That a *False-light* (as the *Diabolical* is) ought not to be Reckon'd a *Light*. But that will not do. Because what Guides, or Directs, or Perswades, *that* is called a *Light* : And you may as well say, That a *False-Guide* is no *Guide*, as that a *False-light* is no *Light* : Thus it is, that *Satan* Transforms himself into an *Angel* of *Light*. And, as our *Saviour* has fore-warned us, That the *Light* in some Men is *Darkness*. Not that *Light* is *Darkness*, but what Men take for *Light*; and that is a *Light* or *Guide* to them, though a *False* One. And then how we shall know the one from the other? That is a Material Question which you have ask'd, and which now Returns upon you.

What is that *Spirit* of the *Prophets*, that is Subject to the *Prophets*?

phets? Is it the *Divine* Light *within*? is *God Subject* to the *Prophets*? Muſt you not then allow a *Natural* Light? *Ceaſe from thine own Wiſdom,* Prov. xxiii. 4. Can ther be *Wiſdom* without *Light*? *Wiſdom* is *Light*. Muſt I then *Ceaſe* from the *Divine* Light? or is ther not *Another*? And how ſhall I know *mine own* Light, from the *Divine* Light?

We are Commanded not to *Believe* every *Spirit*, but to *Try* the *Spirits*, 1 *Joh*. iv. 1. How ſhall we *Try* them? By Themſelves! Muſt I Try the *Spirit* or *Light* in my *Heart*, by it ſelf? Ask it, whether it be a *True Light*, or not? It ſays it is. So do all *Deceivers* ſay, ſo does every *Falſe-Spirit* ſay; then I muſt not take its word: But I muſt *Try* it. And I ask again, *How Try it*? Therefore it muſt be by ſomething elſe than it ſelf. And what is that? Now we are near the Truth. For, Mr. *Penn*, the Caſe ſtands thus.

God has given a *Natural Light* to our *Underſtanding*, but a *Fallible* one; therefore it needs *Help*, and our own *Endeavours*. The Principal Help is the *Influence* and *Light* of the *Holy-Spirit* of God, which works together with our *Light*, and Enables it to work. Beſides this, *God* has given us a *Rule* to walk by. Plain Directions in *writing*, which we may *Study*, and have always Before us. That is, The *Holy Scriptures*; and His *Light*, will open, that is, *Help* our *Underſtanding* in the *Reading* and *Studying* of the *Scriptures*; but that Implys we muſt *Read* and *Study*; we muſt uſe our *Endeavours*, elſe He can not *Help* our *Endeavours*: We muſt not Ly in the *Ditch*, and cry *God Help us*; uſe no *Outward Helps*, which God has *Appointed*; but fold our *Arms*, and *ſit ſtill*, and *gape* for *Extraordinary Inſpirations*, which is a *Tempting* of God, inſtead of *waiting* upon *Him*.

Then God has Appointed other *Helps* beſides the *Scriptures*, He has Conſtituted a *Church*, and an *Order* of Men to *Teach* us, to Help us to *Underſtand* the *Scriptures*; and to Adminiſter the *Sacraments* to us, which *Chriſt* has Commanded; and Promiſed the Aſſiſtance of His H. *Spirit* to thoſe who ſhall Reverently, as He has Appointed, approach unto them.

We have likewiſe the *Helps* of *Hiſtorys*, and *Humian-Learning*, to know former Times, to obſerve the *Riſe* and *Growth* of *Hereſies*, and to beware, left we Fall into the like *Snares* of the *Devil*.

But if we will *Neglect* all theſe *Helps*; nay, *Vilifie* and *Deſpiſe* them, cry out upon them as *Low, Carnal*, and what not; and Direct *God* to work *Miracles* for us, while we Refuſe to work, to ſend ſuch an

Irre-

Irresistable and *Infallible Light* into our *Hearts*, as may, without any Pains on our side, secure us *Absolutely*; and ther is an End on't! If we will thus Alter our own *Frame*, and the whole *Method* of *God*'s Dispensations, it is but just with *God* to give us up to follow our own *Imaginations*, and let us feel the Effect of our *Folly*.

But now, on the other hand, if we will be Content to follow *God* in His way: To acknowledge what we *Feel* and *Know*, that we have a *Free-will* within us, and an *Understanding*, which has *Natural* Powers, to *Judge*, and *Discern*, and *Consider*; and will use the *Helps* God has given us; then, and not till then, are we in a Capacity to be *Reason'd* with; to Judge and Try our own *Spirits*, and other Mens, by the Plain *Rule* of *God*'s H. Word; and if we find they speak not according to that, then to Reject them. Then may we Expect the Assistance of God's B. *Spirit* to Inform our *Understandings*, and lead us into All Truth necessary for us.

For, whatever the *Quakers* think, the *Ch.* of *England* has always Acknowledg'd the *Influences* and *Inward Operation* of the B. *Spirit* of God upon our *Hearts*, as the Cause of All the Good that is wrought in us; which is sufficiently shewn in *The Snake*, Sect. xxii.

And this has been all along the Doctrin of the *Catholick Church*, which I might Prove at length; but that is not the Point in which we are, at Present, engag'd: Yet for the satisfaction of the *Quakers* who may not know this, I will set down two *Canons* of the *Council* of *Carthage*, which was held in the year of our Lord, 419.

Can. 113. *Whoever says, That the grace of God, by which a man is Justify'd through Jesus Christ our Lord, avails only for the Remission of sins that are already past, but does not also give strength to resist sin for the future, Let him be Anathema. For the grace of God does not only give us the knowledge of what we ought to do, but also inspires us with love, whereby we may be enabled to Perform those things which we know to be our duty. Likewise*

Ὅστις δήποτε εἴποι τ̄ χάριν τῦ Θεῦ ἥ τινι δικαιῶ διὰ Ἰησῦ Χριςῦ τῦ Κυρίυ ἡμῶν, πρὸς μόνlω ἄφεσιν ἁμαρτιῶν ἰχύειν τῶ ἤδη πεπλημμελημένων, ἐ μὴ παρέχειν ἔτι μlω βοήθειαν πρὸς δ̄ μὴ ἔτερα πλημμελεῖϑαι, Ἀνάϑεμα ἔιη. ὅτι ἡ χάρις τῦ Θεῦ ἐ μόνον γνῶσιν παρέχι, ὧν δεῖ πράττειν, ἀλλὰ ἐ Ἀγάπlω ἔτι μlω ἐμπνεῖ ἡμῖν, ἵνα ἐ ἐὰν ἐπιγνώσκωμ{ν, κ̄ πληρῶσαι ἰχύωμ{ν. ὁμοίως, ὅστις δή-

who-

whosoever shall say, that this grace of God, which is thro' Jesus Christ our Lord, does help us to avoid sin, only as the knowledge of sin is made manifest to us by it, whereby we know what we ought to seek after, & what to avoid; but that strength is not given us by it, that what we know we ought to do, we may also love it, and be enabled to perform it, Let him be Anathema.

Can. 114. *Whosoever shall say that the grace of Justification was therefore given unto us, that what we could perform by our own free-will, we may do the more easily by grace; insomuch, that tho' grace had not been given, we might, tho' with difficulty, perform the divine Commandments without it, Let him be Anathema. For, concerning the fruits of the Commandments, The Lord did not say that without me, ye shall do them with difficulty; but He said, without me, ye can do nothing.*

 This Constant Doctrin of the Church, the *Quaker Infallibility* did not know that she had ever held; and therefore set it up as a New *discovery* of their own, and broke with the Church for it. And to Advance *Divine Grace*, they would extinguish *Human Reason*, which is a *Divine Grace* it self, and the Subject given unto us by God, whereupon His B. Spirit should work.

 And to Divest us of it, is to make us cease to be *Men*, instead of being *Saints*.

 It makes God the sole *Author* of all our *Sin*; for if we have no *Natural-Light*, we can have no *Free-will*; are only *Passive* in God's Hands, acted by Him, but do nothing of our selves; and therefore are not answerable for any thing that we do; more than a *Sword* or a *Pen* are Blame-worthy for whatever use is made of them.

This Arraigns the Wisdom of God, in all the *Institutions* and *Ordinances* that ever He gave to Men. For, what need of such Helps to the *Divine* Light! and Mr. *Penn* says we have no other. Why then does he Preach? To whom doth he Preach? To the *Divine* Light in Men? (as G. *Fox*, and the *Primitive Quakers* us'd to speak) Can he *Teach* that? Cannot that *guide* Men without his Preaching? If he says that he only Preaches to perswade Men to follow that *Light*. But cannot the *Light* Teach even that too? Or has it Forgot it? Does it need *Help* in that? Then why not in other things? then is it not *self-sufficient* without *something else*.

Nay, by this Principle, ther was no need of *Christ's* coming into the World, at least of His *dying* for us: For Men had the *Divine* Light before. And what could the Man *Jesus* add to that? Was it not *sufficient* without *Him*? If not, then you want something else besides your *Light within*: But if it was *sufficient* without *Him*, then could not His Coming be *Necessary*. I desire to know what you differ herein from the *Deists*? They hold a *Divine Light* Planted by *God* in the Heart of Man, which they call *Reason*: And that this is *sufficient*, without any thing else, to Teach a Man all that he ought to *Know* or *Do*. This *Divine Light* you call the *Light within*: So that you Differ from them but in *Words*: Both of you Reject the Necessity of any *Outward Revelation*, that is, of a *Christ without*. And so are the same with all the *Pagan* or *Gentile* World. For they too (and the latter *Mahometans*) allow *Jesus* to have been a Good Man; and to have had this *Divine Light* (which you call *Christ*) within Him, as all other Men have: But this does not make Him *Properly the Son of God*; which you also *utterly deny* Him to be, as said before, p. 3. This is Literally that *Anti-Christianism* which is Reprehended, 1 *Joh*. 2. 22. of Denying *Jesus* to be the *Christ*. For having of the *Light* in me, does not make me to be the *Light*: But *Jesus* not only had the *Light* in Him, but He was the *Light*, or *Christ*; which it is *Blasphemy* to say of any other. And yet, if Man have no other *Light* in him but the *Divine*, and that be made Part of his *Nature*, it must follow that he is *God*: For whoever does *Properly* partake of the *Divine Nature*, is so.

2. But now whatever Mr. *Penn* thinks of my *Reasoning*, (which by his own Principle, must be the Immediate Dictate of the *Holy Ghost*, if I have no *Natural* Light which taught it me) yet he can have no Reason to break *Communion* with us, upon

this

this Account, more than with *Hubberthorn, Burrough*, or other *Quakers* who held the same, as *James Naylor*, and others I cou'd shew, if that were worth the while. And though *James Naylor* was Censur'd by the *Quakers* for other things, yet never for this; and he was Receiv'd again into Favour, and Liv'd and Dy'd in their *Communion*.

3. This hinders not, by Mr. *Penn*'s own Acknowledgment, they and we being all of one *Religion*. For he says, p. 62. *I know not how properly they may be call'd of divers* Religions, *that assert the* True God *for the Object of* Worship; *The Lord* Jesus Christ, *for the only Saviour; and the* Light *or* Spirit *of* Christ, *for the* Great Agent *and* Means *of* Mans Conversion *and* Eternal Felicity.

Now all this, Mr. *Penn*, the *Church* of *England* does most sincerely and heartily *Believe*, and ever have *Profess'd* it: And therefore, if we be not of divers *Religions*, why of divers *Communions*!

4. Again, your Exposition of *Justification*, p. 79. That you acknowledge Justification *only for the sake of the Death and Sufferings of Christ; and nothing we can do,* (say you) *though by the* Operation *of the* Holy Spirit, *being able to Cancel old Debts, or wipe out old Scores: It is the Power and Efficacy of that Propitiatory offering, upon* Faith *and Repentance, that Justifies us from the sins that are past; and it is the Power of* Christ's *Spirit in our hearts, that* Purifies, *and makes us Acceptable before God.* All this is most *Sound* and *Orthodox*. And your whole *Ninth* Chapter concerning the *Inward* and *Spiritual* Appearance of *Christ* in the *Soul*, I not only *Approve*, but do very much Congratulate with you, that you have so *Christianly* and *Pathetically* Press'd it. I know you will not suspect me of *Flattery*: For, where ther is occasion, I speak Plain enough. This *Cause* Requires not *Dodging*. Let us Contend for the *Truth*, on whatever side it lys. It is for our own *Souls*. And we must give an Account.

How do you keep up a *Schism*, if you agree with us in these *Fundamentals* of *Religion*! *Small Matters*, you know, are not sufficient to excuse a *Schism*. *Great* things are to be *done*, and *much* to be *Born* to Compass such *good* of *souls*.

Therefore let me consider All your Objections.

1. Chap.

1. Chap. x. Sect. 1. You Insist much upon the *Spirituality* and *Life* of *Prayer*. In the name of God, carry that as High as you can, you shall find no opposition from us: For without this, *All Prayer*, in whatever *words*, whether *Ex-tempore*, or *Pre-meditated*, are but *Dead Forms*. And an *Ex-tempore* Prayer, is only *Ex-tempore* as to the *Speaker*, if he has not thought of it before: But it is as much a *Form* to the *Hearers*, as if he had thought of it; if they join with him, they are ty'd to his *words* and *method*, and every thing else of his *Prayer*. So that the Question is ill stated, to call *Pre-meditated* Prayer a *Form*, and the other not. Both are *Forms*, and equally *Forms* to the *Hearers*: But the True State of the Question is this, whether an *Ex-tempore*, or a *Pre-meditated* FORM, is most Beneficial to the *Hearers*? Which can be freed from most *Defects*? And which best fitted to the Common Exigencies of the People?

If the Heart cannot be suppos'd to be *Spiritually* lifted up in the use of any *Form*, then must All *Publick* Prayer cease. Then was *The Lords Prayer* Un-fitting ever to be us'd; or the *Psalms* of *David*, which were daily Read in the *Temple*, and composed for that End.

But if the *soul* may be *spiritually* lifted up in the Use of a *Form*, then is it Great Un-Charitableness to *Censure* those who use it: And this can be no sufficient Cause for a *separation*.

Besides that it is Impossible for any of your *Hearers* to know whether they make use of (that is, join in) an *Ex-tempore*, or a *Pre-meditated Form*: For how do they know whether the *Speaker* has thought of it before? These are too slender Causes for a *Separation*.

But in our *Churches*, the *Ministers* are not ty'd to the *Common-prayer*, but take the same Liberty as yours, to Pray according to their own Conceptions before and after *Sermon*. So that herein you may join quite free from this Exception.

2. Your next *Exception*, Sect. 2, and 3. is concerning the *Ministry*, That they who undertake it, ought to be *Guided* and *Influenced* by the *Holy-Spirit*. Herein you differ not from us. We assert the same. And it is Demanded in the Examination of Persons to be *Ordain'd*, Whether they are perswaded that they are moved thereto by the *Holy Ghost*? If Men will be-ly their own Consciences, and thrust themselves Unworthily into the *Ministry*, that is not to be objected against the *Constitution*: And, Mr. *Penn*, you know that your *Communion* has Laboured under this Inconvenience as well as ours. I need not go to Instances. I know you will not put me to it. Therefore this is no Cause for *Separation*. 3. Your

3. Your 4. *Sect.* That *Ministers* are *Christ's* Witnesses, and applying to this 1 *Joh.* 1. 1, 3. *That which we have heard, seen with our Eyes, and our hands have handled,* &c. seems Strange; for this was spoken by St. *John* in relation to the *Person* of *Christ*, whom they had *seen, felt,* &c. And such sort of Witnesses I suppose you do not Pretend to be: You Pretend not to have *seen* our *Lord* in the *Flesh.* But if you take this *spiritually,* (as I perceive you do) then we Witness it as much as you. And here can be no Cause of *Separation.*

4. Your 5. *Sect.* against Mens *offering money to be made Ministers.* I would fain know what Caution you can advise against *Symony* that is not taken. But if you think it utterly unlawful for *Ministers* to Receive ought from the *People,* to whom they *Preach,* How got *G. Fox* so much Money? And I would desire to know how you answer 1 *Cor.* ix. 7, 11, 14. *Gal.* vi. 6. *Phil* iv. 14. 16. However, here can be no Cause of *Separation.*

5. Chap. xii. *Sect.* 1. You say nothing against *Tythes,* but that you will not Support our *Ministry:* And that depending upon what is said before as to them, I dismiss it. Though you might Grudge them their Tythes, and yet not break *Communion:* For you are no less Lyable to them now, than if you were in our *Communion.* And, not now to enter upon the *Jus Divinum* of *Tythes,* (which I think is very Plain) yet till you can shew it to be a Sin for the *King* and *Parliament* to give *Allowances* or *Estates* to the *Clergy,* as well as to other Men, you can never countenance a *Separation* upon the account of *Tythes.* Ther are many in our *Communion* who are not yet perswaded of the *Divine Right* of *Tythes.*

6. As to your 2. *Sect.* against *Swearing.* You have obtained an *Act of Parliament* to Swear in your own *Form.* Therefore that *Objection* is taken out of the way. At least it can be made no Pretence for a *Separation.*

7. As to your 3. *Sect.* concerning *War,* you say no more of it, than that it ought to Cease among *Christians.* And who does not wish it? But that it may sometimes be *Necessary* and *Lawful* you have allow'd, in Engaging to the Government to maintain Souldiers in *Pensilvania.* But however you may keep that opinion, and yet not make a *Separation.* As you may, what you mention Sect. 4, 5, 6, and 7. That is, The *Salutations* of the Times. *Plainness* of *Speech.* Not to Marry from among your selves. *Plainness* in *Apparel.* And to Refrain *Sports* and *Pastimes.*

8. As

8. As to *Sect.* 8. against our Publick *Fasts* and *Feasts*, they are little enough observ'd amongst our selves. You'll not be much Quarrell'd for that. But your Reason against them, because they are of *Human* Institution, needs another Reason why that is one, which you do not Give us. All *Churches*, both before and since *Christ*, have done the same. And ther is no *Prohibition* against it. However, if you cannot comply with it, you may stay at home on those days. That is no Reason for a *General* Separation.

And these are all the *Causes* you have *Instanc'd* or *Hinted* at in your Book. And I hope, upon serious Consideration, you will not think that any or all of them are sufficient for a *Separation*.

Remember what you said to your own *Separatists* of *Harp-Lane*, when they desired to put up past *Quarrels*; you bid them then to *Return from their* Separation. Take the *Good Advice* you have given. Sure the *Cause* is more Important. And our *Church* can Plead more *Authority* over you, than you could over them.

And if you think that she has *Errors* and *Defects*, (wherein I will join with you) yet Consider, that no *Errors* can justify a Breach of *Communion*, but those which are Impos'd as Conditions of *Communion*.

We shall have many things to *Bear* with, to *Bemoan*, to *Amend*, to *Struggle* with, while we are upon this Earth.

And he that will make a *Separation* for every *Error*, will fall into much greater *Error* and *Sin* than that which he would seek to Cure. It is like tearing *Christ*'s seamless *Coat*, because we like not the *colour*, or to mend the Fashion of a Sleeve.

God Direct you, and us all. To His Grace I commend you, and the *Influences* of His *Blessed* Spirit, to shew you what Great things it is in your Power to do for Him and His Church; and give you a Heart to do them, that it be not laid to your Charge.

ADVERTISEMENT.

I Would not have the *Reader* or the *Quakers* think, because I have instanced but in *Seven* Particulars, wherein the *Quakers* have Copy'd after the *Ancient Hereticks* within the first 150 Years of *Christianity*, that therefore ther are no more. But I would not swell this matter to too great a bulk. I have shewn in *The Snake*, Sect. ix. how *George Fox* falls in with the *Patripassians*, who Deny'd any Distinction of *Persons* in the *God-head*; and consequently held that it was *God* the *Father* who was Born of the B. *Virgin*, and *Dyed* for us. And whoever will compare the Tenets of the *Quakers* with the Account which *Epiphanius* and others later, have given of the *Gnosticks*, and other *Hereticks* of those times, will find many other Particulars wherein they agree. But because the *Quakers*, and others of our *Dissenters*, have (for no cause but their own *Guilt*) excepted against the Account of former *Heresies*, given by those of After Ages, I have, to take away all Umbrage, fetched my Authoritys from those who were *Co-temporaries* with those *Hereticks* which they mention.

FINIS.

A *Tho. Johnson*

DISCOURSE;

SHEWING,

Who they are that are now Qualify'd to Administer *Baptism* and the *Lord's-Supper*.

Wherein the Cause of

EPISCOPACY

Is briefly Treated.

By the Author

OF

A DISCOURSE

Proving the Divine Institution of *Water-Baptism*.

No Man taketh this Honour unto himself, but he that is called of God, as was Aaron, Heb. 5. 4.

LONDON,
Printed for *C. Brome* at the *Gun*, at West-end of St. *Paul's*; *W. Keble* white at the *Swan* in St. *Paul's* Church-Yard; and *H. Hindmarsh* at the *Golden-Ball* over-against the Royal Exchange, *Cornhill*. 1698.

THE
PREFACE.

THIS *Discourse* was Promis'd in that which I formerly Publish'd, proving the *Divine Institution* of *Water-Baptism*; And was intended to have been Annex'd to that, but some Delays prevented it.

I can give no good Reason why it has stay'd thus long, having made but little Addition to what was then done: But other things Interven'd, and, as it is usual in Delays the first in Design proves the last in Fact.

The Subject of this has led me directly upon the larger Theme of *Episcopacy*; which having been so *Elaboratly* and so *Often* treated of, I intend not in this to Branch out into so wide a Field; but in a short compendious Method, to lay before the *Quakers*, and others of our *Dissenters*,

The Preface.

ters from *Episcopacy*, the Heart of the Cause, so far particularly as it concerns our present Subject, the *Right* of *Admimistring* the *Sacraments* of *Christ*.

And to avoid the length of Quotations, when brought into the Discourse, and Dilated upon, I have, at the end, Annex'd a small *Index* of Quotations out of the Primitive *Fathers* and *Councils* of the first 450 Years after *Christ*, to which the Reader may Recur, as ther is occasion. And having them all in one view, may consider them more Intirely, and Remember them the better.

I have Translated them for the sake of the *English* Reader, but have put the *Originals* in another *Column*, to justifie the Translation; and for their sakes who may not have the Books at hand.

The

The CONTENTS.

SECT. I.

The Necessity of an Outward *Commission to the* Ministers *of the* Gospel.

The Case is Stated, as to those Quakers, *for whose satisfaction this is Intended.* Page 1

I. *Of* Personal *Qualifications requisite in the* Administrators *of the* Sacraments. 2
II. *Of the* Sacerdotal *Qualification of an* Outward *Commission, as was given to* Christ *by* God.
III. *By* Christ *to the* Apostles, *&c.*
IV. *By the* Apostles *to others.*
V. *Those others Impower'd to give it to others after them.*

SECT. II.

The Deduction of this Commission *is continu'd in the Succession of* Bishops, *and not of* Presbyters.

I. *Either way it operates against the* Quakers. 3
II. *The Continuance of every* Society *is Deduc'd in the Succession of the* Chief Governours *of the Society, not of the* Inferior Officers. 4
III. *This shewn, in Matter of Fact, as to the* Church *and the Succession of* Bishops *from the* Apostles *times to our Days; particularly here in* England.
IV. *The* Presbyterian *Plea consider'd; that* Bishopricks *were but single* Parishes; *and consequently, that every* Presbyter *was a* Bishop; *and their vain* Logo-machy *upon the words* Ἐπίσκοπος *and* Πρεσβύτερος. 5
V. *Argu'd from the* Type *of the* Levitical Priesthood; *which shewn to be the Method of* Christ, *the* Apostles, *and Primitive* Fathers. 7

VI. *Whence*

The Contents.

VI. *Whence the Cafe of* Korah *and the* Presbyterians *fhewn to be the fame. And the* Epifcopal Supremacy *as Plainly and Fully Eftablifhed, as was that of* Aaron *and his Succeffors.* 8
VII. *No Succeffion of* Presbyters *can be fhewn from the* Apoftles. 9
VIII. *The Pretence of Extraordinary* Gifts, *no Ground or Excufe for making of a Schifm.* 11

SECT. III.

Objection from the Times of Popery *in this Kingdom; as if that did* Un-church, *and confequently break the* Succeffion *of our* Bifhops.

I. *This fhewn to be a* Popifh *Argument.* 17
II. *That* Idolatry *does not* Un-church. *Prov'd*
  1. *Becaufe a* Chriftian *may be an* Idolater. 18
  2. *From the Type of the* Church *under the* Law. 19
III. Epifcopacy *the moft oppofite to* Popery. *ibid.*
IV. Male-Adminiftration *does* Forfeit, *but not* Vacate *a* Commiffion, *till it be Re-call'd.* 21
V. *Defects in* Succeffion, *no Bar to the* Poffeffors, *where ther are none who* Claim *a Better Right.* 23

SECT. IV.

The Affurance *and* Confent *in the* Epifcopal Communion, *beyond that of any other.*

I. *The* Epifcopal Communion *of much greater* Extent, *and more* Univerfal *than all thofe who oppofe it.* 24
II. *And than the* Church of Rome, *if join'd with them.* ib.
III. *The* Diffenters *from* Epifcopacy, *do all* Deny *the* Ordination *or* Call *of each other.* 25

IV. *If*

The Contents.

IV. *If the* Quakers *receive* Baptism *from any of these Dissenters, they have no Reason to expect the same Allowances as may be given to those of their own Communions.*

V. *The Episcopal Ordinations, and consequently their Right to* Baptize, *is own'd by both* Papists *and* Presbyterians.

SECT. V.

The Personal Sanctity *of the* Administrator *of the* Sacraments, *tho' highly Requisit on his Part, yet not of* Necessity, *as to the* Receivers, *to convey to them the Benefits of the* Sacraments: *Because*

I. *The* Vertue *comes not from the* Minister, *but from* God *alone.* 26

II. *For this Cause (among others)* Christ *chose* Judas *to be an* Apostle. 27

III. God's *Power is Magnify'd in the* Meaness *of His* Instruments.

IV. *St.* Paul *Rejoyc'd at the* Preaching *of* Evil *Men* 28

V. *This confirm'd by dayly Experience.*

VI. *The* Argument *stronger as to the* Sacraments. 29

VII. *The Fatal Consequences of making the* Personal Holiness *of the* Administrator *Necessary towards the* Efficacy *of the* Sacraments.

1. *It takes away all* Assurance *in our Receiving of the* Sacraments.

2. *It renders the* Commands *of* Christ, *of none* Effect. 30.

3. *It is contrary to the tenure of* God's *former Institutions; and puts us in a more uncertain Condition than they were under the* Law.

4. *It was the Ancient Error of the* Donatists; *and Borders upon* Popery.

VIII. *As*

The Contents.

VIII. *As great* Sanctity *to be found in the* Clergy *of the* Church *of* England, *as among any of our* Dissenters. 32

IX. *Ther is, at least, a* Doubt, *in Receiving* Baptism *from any of our* Dissenters. *Which, in this case, is a* Sin: *Therefore security is only to be had in the* Episcopal *Communion.*

X. *The Advantage of the* Church *of* England, *by Her being the* Established Constitution, *ever since the* Reformation.

XI. *That therefore nothing can excuse* Schism *from Her, but Her Enjoyning something, as a* Condition *of* Communion, *that is contrary to the Holy* Scriptures; *which cannot be shewn.* 33

XII. *Therefore to Receive* Baptism *from the* Church *of* England, *is the greatest security which the* Quakers *can have of Receiving it from Proper Hands.*

XIII. *An* Answer *to the* Objection, *That* Baptism *has not such* Visible Effects *amongst us, as the* Quakers *wou'd desire,* 34

The Supplement.

I. *Some* Authorities *for* Episcopacy, *as* Distinct *from, and* Superior *to* Presbytery , *taken out of the* Fathers *and* Councils *in the first* 450 *Years after* Christ. 35

II. *That the whole* Reformation ; *even* Calvin, Beza, *and those of their* Communion, *were zealous* Asserters *of* Episcopacy. 58

A

A DISCOURSE

Shewing, who they are that are now qualify'd to Administer BAPTISM, and the LORD's SUPPER.

SECT. I.

The Necessity of an Outward Commission *to the* Ministers *of the* Gospel.

Some *Quakers* having perus'd my *Discourse of Baptism*, think the *Quaker* Arguments against it sufficiently Answered: And they have but one Difficulty remaining, that is, who they are (among the various Pretenders) that are duly Qualify'd to *Administer* it.

And if satisfaction can be given to them herein, they promise a perfect Compliance to that *Holy Institution*.

The Chief thing they seem to stand upon is the *Personal Holyness* of the *Administrator*; thinking that the *Spiritual* Effects of *Baptism* cannot be convey'd by the means of an *Unsanctify'd Instrument*.

But yet they Confess, that there is something else Necessary, besides the *Personal Holiness* of the *Administrator*: Otherwise, they wou'd think themselves as much Qualify'd to *Administer* it as any others; because, I presume, they suppose themselves to have as great a Measure of the *Spirit* as other Men.

This *Requisit* which they want, is that of *Lawful Ordination*.

But the *Presbyterians, Independents*, and *Baptists* do pretend to this. Therefore their *Title* to it is to be Examin'd.

B And,

And, that we may proceed the more clearly in this Matter, with Respect still to that Difficulty upon which the *Quakers* lay the stress; we will Inquire concerning those *Qualifications* which are Requisite in any Person that shall take upon him to *Administer* the *Sacraments* of *Christ*'s Institution. And,

These Qualifications are of two sorts, *Personal* or *Sacerdotal*.

I. *Personal.* The *Holiness* of the *Administrator.* And, though this is a great Qualification to *Fit* and *Prepare* a Man for such an Holy Administration, yet this *Alone* does not sufficiently Qualifie any Man to take upon him such an Administration.

II. But there is moreover requir'd, 2ly, A *Sacerdotal* Qualification, that is, an *Outward Commission*, to Authorize a Man to execute any *Sacerdotal* or *Ministerial* Act of Religion. For, *This Honour no Man taketh unto himself, but he that is called of God, as was* Aaron; *so also Christ glorify'd not himself to be made an High-Priest; But he that said unto him, thou art my Son ——— Thou art a Priest,* &c.

Heb. v. 4.

Accordingly we find that *Christ* did not take upon Him the Office of a *Preacher*, till after that *Outward Commission* given to Him by a *Voice* from *Heaven*, at His *Baptism*; for it is written, *Matth.* iv. 17. *From that time* Jesus *began to Preach*: Then He *Began*; and He was then *about Thirty Years of Age,* Luke iii. 23. Now no Man can doubt of *Christ*'s Qualifications, before *that time*, as to *Holiness, Sufficiency*, and all *Personal* Endowments. And if all these were not sufficient to *Christ* Himself, without an *Outward Commission*, what other Man can pretend to it upon the Account of any *Personal* Excellencies in Himself, without an *outward Commission?*

III. And as *Christ* was outwardly Commissionated by *His Father,* so did not He leave it to His Disciples, every ones Opinion of his own sufficiency, to thrust himself into the *Vineyard*, but Chose Twelve *Apostles* by Name; and after them, Seventy others of an Inferior Order, whom He sent to *Preach.*

IV. And as *Christ* gave *outward Commissions*, while He was upon the Earth, so we find that His *Apostles* did Proceed in the same Method, after His Ascension. *They ordained them Elders in every Church.*

Act. xiv. 23.

V. But had they, who were thus Ordained by the *Apostles*,

Power

Power to Ordain others? Yes, *For this cause left I thee in* Crete, *that thou shouldest* —— *Ordain Elders in every City. Lay hands suddenly on no Man,* &c. St. *Clement,* in his first *Epistle* to the *Corinthians,* writing concerning the *Schism* which was then risen up amongst them, says, Parag. 44. *That the Apostles fore-knowing there wou'd be Contests concerning the Episcopal Name (or Office) did themselves appoint the Persons: And not only so, lest that might be said to be of force, only during their time. But that they afterwards established an Order how, when those whom they had Ordained shou'd Die; others, fit and approved Men, shou'd succeed them in their Ministry.* Par. 43. *that they who were intrusted with this work, by God, in Christ, did Constitute these Officers.*

Tit. 1. 5.
1 Tim. V. 22.

Καὶ οἱ Ἀπόστολοι ἡμῶν ἔγνωσαν διὰ τοῦ Κυρίου ἡμῶν Ἰησοῦ Χριστοῦ, ὅτι ἔρις ἔσται ἐπὶ τοῦ ὀνόματος τῆς Ἐπισκοπῆς. διὰ ταύτην οὖν τὴν αἰτίαν πρόγνωσιν εἰληφότες τελείαν, κατέστησαν τὸς προειρημένους, & μεταξὺ ἐπινομὴν δεδώκασιν, ὅπως ἐὰν κοιμηθῶσιν, διαδέξωνται ἕτεροι δεδοκιμασμένοι ἄνδρες, τὴν λειτουργίαν αὐτῶν. — οἱ ἐν Χριστῷ πιστευθέντες παρὰ Θεοῦ ἔργον τοῦτο, κατέστησε τὸς προειρημένους.

But this Matter depends not upon the Testimony of him, or many more that might be produced. It is such a Publick Matter of Fact; That I might as well go about to quote particular Authors, to prove that there were *Emperors* in *Rome,* as that the *Ministers* of the *Church* of *Christ* were *Ordained* to succeed one another; and that they did so succeed.

SECT. II.

The Deduction of this Commission *is continu'd in the Succession of* Bishops *and not of* Presbyters.

BUT here is a Dispute, whether this *Succession* was preserv'd in the Order of *Bishops* or *Presbyters?* or whether both are not the same?

I. *Answ.* 1. This is the Contest betwixt the *Presbyterians* and us: But either way it operates against the *Quakers,* who allow of no *Succession* deriv'd by *outward Ordination.*

II. *Answ.* 2. But becaufe the Defign of this *Difcourfe* is to fhew the *Succeffion* from the *Apoftles*, I anfwer that this *Succeffion* is preferv'd and deriv'd only in the *Bifhops*: As the continuance of any *Society*, is deduc'd in the *Succeffion* of the *Chief Governors* of the *Society*, not of the *Inferior Officers*. Thus in Kingdoms, we reckon by the *Succeffion* of the *Kings*, not of *Sheriffs* or *Conftables*; and in *Corporations* by the *Succeffion* of the *Mayors* or other *Chief Officers*; not of the Inferiour *Bailiffs* or *Serjeants*: So the *Succeffion* of the *Churches* is Computed in the *Succeffion* of the *Bifhops*, who are the *Chief Governours* of the *Churches*; and not of *Presbyters*, who are but *Inferiour Officers* under the *Bifhops*.

III. And, in this, the Matter of Fact is as Clear and Evident as the Succeffion of any *Kings* or *Corporations* in the World.

To begin with the *Apoftles*, we find not only that they Conftituted *Timothy* Bifhop of *Ephefus*, and *Titus* of *Crete*, as in the Subfcriptions of St. *Paul's* Epiftles to them: But, in *Eufebius* and other *Ecclefiaftical Hiftorians*, you have the *Bifhops* Nam'd who were Conftituted by the Apoftles themfelves, over the then famous Churches of *Jerufalem, Antioch, Rome*, and *Alexandria*, and many other Churches; and the *Succeffion* of them down all along.

St. *Polycarp*, Bifhop of *Smyrna*, was Difciple to St. *John* the Apoftle; and St. *Irenæus*, who was Difciple to St. *Polycarp*, was Conftituted *Bifhop* of *Lyons* in *France*.

I mention this, becaufe it is fo near us; for, in all other Churches, throughout the whole World, where-ever *Chriftianity* was Planted, *Epifcopacy* was every where Eftablifh'd, without one Exception, as is Evident from all their Records.

And fo it was with us in *England*, whither it is generally fuppos'd, and with very good Grounds, that St. *Paul* firft brought the Chriftian Faith. *Clemens Romanus*, in his *Firft Epift.* to the *Corinthians*, Paragr. 5. Says, that St. *Paul* went Preaching the Gofpel to the fartheft bounds of the *Weft*; ἐπὶ τὸ τέρμα τῆς Δύσεως. by which Term *Britain* was then Underftood. And *Theodoret* exprefly Names the *Britains* among the Nations Converted by the *Apoftles*. (To. 4, ferm. 9. p. 610.) And *Eufebius* in his *Evangelical Demonftration*, (l. 3. c. 7. p. 113.) Names likewife the *Britains*, as then Converted.

But

But whether St. *Paul*, or, as some Conjecture, *Joseph* of *Arimathea*, or any other *Apostolical* Person was the first who Preached *Christ* in *England*, it matters not, as to our Present Purpose; who Enquire only concerning *Episcopacy*; And it is Certain by all our Histories, that as far up as they give us any Account of *Christianity* in this *Island*, they tell us likewise of *Bishops*; and the Succession of this *Church* of *England* has been Deduc'd in the Succession of *Bishops*, and not of *Presbyters*. And particularly in the *Diocess* of *London*, which was the first *Archi-Episcopal See*, before *Augustin* the *Monk* came hither, after which it was Establish'd in *Canterbury*. And the *Saxon* Writers have Transmitted the Succession of their *Bishops* in *Canterbury, Rochester, London*, &c.

And in Countries so Remote and Barbarous as *Island* it self we find the same care taken; *Ara* or *Aras* an *Islandish* Priest Surnam'd *Hinfrode* the *Learned*, who flourish'd in the *Eleventh Century*, and was 25 Years Old when *Christianity* was brought thither, in his Book of that Country written in *Islandish*, has Transmitted to Posterity, not only the *Succession* but the *Genealogies* of the *Bishops* of *Skalholt* and *Hola* (the two Episcopal Sees of *Island*) as they Succeeded one another in his Time. I mention this of *Island*, to shew that *Episcopacy* has Extended it self Equally with *Christianity*, which was carry'd by it, into the Remotest Corners of the Earth; upon which account the *Bishops* of *Skalholt* and *Hola*, and their *Succession*, are as Remarkable Proofs of *Episcopacy*, tho' not so Famous as the *Bishops* of *Canterbury* and *London*.

IV. If the *Presbyterians* will say (because they have nothing left to say) that all *London* (for Example) was but one *Parish*; and that the *Presbyter* of every other *Parish* was as much a *Bishop* as the *Bishop* of *London*; because the words Ἐπίσκοπος and Πρεσβύτερος, *Bishop* and *Presbyter*, are sometimes us'd in the same sense; They may as well prove that *Christ* was but a *Deacon*, because He is so call'd, *Rom*. xv. 8. Διάκονος, which we rightly Translate a *Minister*. And *Bishop* signifies an *Overseer*, and *Presbyter* an *Ancient Man*, or *Elder Man*; whence our Term of *Aldermen*. And this is as good a Foundation to Prove that the *Apostles* were *Aldermen*, in the *City* acceptation of the Word; or that our *Aldermen* are all *Bishops* and *Apostles*, as to Prove that *Presbyters*

byters, and *Bishops* are all one, from the Childish *Gingle* of the Words.

It wou'd be the same thing, if one shou'd undertake to Confront all Antiquity, and Prove against all the Histories, that the *Emperors* of *Rome* were no more than *Generals* of *Armies*, and that every Roman *General* was *Emperor* of *Rome*; because he cou'd find the word *Imperator* sometimes apply'd to the *General* of an *Army*.

Or as if a *Common-wealth-man* shou'd get up, and say, that our former *Kings* were no more than our *Dukes* are now; because the Stile of *Grace*, which is now given to *Dukes*, was then given to *Kings*.

And suppose that any one were put under the Pennance of Answering to such Ridiculous Arguments; what Method wou'd he take, but to shew that the *Emperors* of *Rome*, and former *Kings* of *England*, had *Generals* of *Armies* and *Dukes* under them, and Exercis'd Authority over them?

Therefore when we find it given in Charge to *Timothy*, the first *Bishop* of *Ephesus*, how he was to Proceed against his *Presbyters*, when they Transgressed; to Sit in *Judgment* upon them, Examine *Witnesses* against them, and pass *Censures* upon them, it is a most Impertinent *Logomachy* to argue from the *Etymology* of the Words, that notwithstanding of all this, a *Bishop* and a *Presbyter* are the same thing. Therefore that one Text, i *Tim.* v. 19. is sufficient to silence this Pitiful Clamour of the *Presbyterians*; our *English* reads it, *against an Elder*, which is the *Literal* Translation of the word *Presbyter*, κατὰ πρεσβυτέρου, *against a Presbyter receive not an Accusation, but before two or three witnesses;* and, *them that sin Rebuke before all, that others also may fear*. Now, upon the *Presbyterian* Hypothesis, we must say that *Timothy* had no *Authority* or *Jurisdiction* over that *Presbyter*, against whom he had Power to Receive *Accusations*, Examine *Witnesses*, and pass *Censures* upon him: And that such a *Presbyter* had the same *Authority* over *Timothy*— which is so Extravagant and against Common Sense, that I will not stay longer to Confute it; and think this enough to have said concerning the *Presbyterian* Argument from the *Etymology* of the words *Bishop* and *Presbyter*.

And

(7)

And this likewise Confutes their other *Pretence*, which I have mention'd, that the Ancient *Bishopricks* were only *Single* and *Independent Congregations*, or *Parishes*. This is a *Topick* they have taken up but of late (being Beaten from all their other Holds) and Launched by Mr. *David Clarkson*, in a Book which he Entitules *Primitive Episcopacy*; which has given occasion to an Excellent Answer, by Dr. *Hen. Maurice*, call'd *A Defence of Diocesan Episcopacy*, Printed 1691. which, I suppose, has ended that Controversie, and hindred the World from being more troubl'd upon that Head. And their other little Shift, and as Groundless, that the Primitive *Bishops* were no other than their *Moderators*, advanced more lately by *Gilb. Rule* late *Moderator* of the *General Assembly* in *Scotland*, has been as *Learnedly*, and with great Clearness of *Reason*, Confuted by the Worthy *J. S.* in his *Principles of the Cyprianick Age*, Printed 1695.

But, as I said, that Text, 1 *Tim.* v. 19. has made all these *Pretences* wholly useless to the *Presbyterians*: For supposing their most Notorious false supposition, as if the *Bishopricks* of *Jerusalem*, *Rome*, *Alexandria*, or *London*, consisted but of one single Congregation, and that such *Bishops* had no *Presbyters* under them; but that all *Presbyters* were Equally *Bishops*; I say, supposing this, then it must follow from what we Read of *Timothy*, that one *Bishop* or *Presbyter* had *Jurisdiction* over other *Bishops* or *Presbyters*, which will Destroy the *Presbyterian* Claim of *Parity*, as much as their Confession to the *Truth*, and plain *Matter of Fact*, that *Bishops* had *Presbyters* under their *Jurisdiction*; and that they were Distinct *Orders*: Notwithstanding that a *Bishop* may be call'd Διάκονος a *Deacon*, or *Minister* of *Christ*; and likewise πρεσβύτερος, an *Elder* or *Grave* Man, which is a Term of *Magistracy* and *Dignity*, and not ty'd to *Age*. And a *Presbyter* may likewise, in a sound Sense, be call'd a *Bishop*, that is, an *Overseer* or *Shepherd*, which he truly is over his Particular Flock; without denying at all his Dependance upon his *Bishop* and *Overseer*:

V. As under the Term of *Priest*, the *High-Priest* was Included, without Destroying his *Supremacy*, over the other *Priests*. Against which *Korah* and his *Presbyters*, or Inferiour *Priests* arose. And if the *Presbyterians* will take his word, whom, of all the Fathers, they most Admire, and Quote often on their side, that is, St. *Jerom*, he will tell them, in that very E-
pistle

Pistle (ad *Evagr.*) which they Boast favours them so much, That what *Aaron*, and his *Sons*, and the *Levites* were in the *Temple*, that same are *Bishop*, *Presbyter*, and *Deacon* in the *Church*.

And long before him, *Clemens Romanus* in his 1 *Epist.* to the *Corinthians*, makes frequent Allusion to the *Episcopacy* of the *Levitical Priesthood*, and argues from thence to that of the *Christian* Church. Thus Paragraph 40. Τῷ γὰ Ἀρχιερεῖ ἰδίαι λειτουργίαι δεδομέναι εἰσί· καὶ τοῖς Ἱερεῦσιν ἴδιΘ. ὁ τόπΘ· προσῆπται, καὶ Λευΐταις ἰδίαι διακονίαι ἐπίκεινται· λαϊκὸς ἄνθρωπος τοῖς λαϊκοῖς προστάγμασιν δέδεται. *To the High-Priest* (says he) *were allotted his proper Offices; to the Priests, their proper place was assigned; and to the Levites their services were appointed; and the Lay-men were Restrain'd within the precepts to Lay-men.* And Paragraph 42. he applies that Scripture, *Isa. LX.* 17. to the Officers of the *Christian* Church, and renders it thus; *I will Constitute their* Bishops *in Righteousness, and their* Deacons *in Faith.* The *Greek* Translation of the LXX has it thus. *I will give thee Rulers* (or Princes) δώσω τοὺς ἄρχοντάς σε ἐν εἰρήνῃ, καὶ τοὺς Ἐπισκόπους σε ἐν δικαιοσύνῃ. *in Peace; and thy* Bishops *in Righteousness*.

It was the frequent Method of these Primitive Fathers to Reason thus from the Parallel 'twixt the *Law* and the *Gospel*, the one being an Exact *Type* of the other, and therefore being fulfill'd in the other. And in this they follow'd the Example of *Christ*, and the *Apostles*, who argu'd in the same manner, as you may see *Matth.* v. I *Cor.* x. the whole *Epistle* to the *Hebrews*, and many other Places of the *New Testament*.

VI. Now the *Presbyterians* are desir'd to shew any one Disparity betwixt their Case and that of *Korah*; who was a *Priest* of the *second Order*, that is, a *Presbyter*; and withdrew his Obedience from the *High-Priest* with other Mutinous *Levites*: For, ther was no matter of *Doctrine* or *Worship* betwixt them and *Aaron*; nor any other Dispute but that of *Church-Government*. And, by the Parallel betwixt the *Old Testament* and the *New*, *Korah* was a *Presbyterian*, who Rose up against the *Episcopacy* of *Aaron*. But this Case is brought yet nearer home; for, we are told (*Jude* xi.) of those under the *Gospel,who perish in the gain-saying of Korah*: And in the *Epist.* of *Clem. Rom.* to the *Corinthians*, before Quoted, Paragraph 43. He plainly applys this Case of *Korah*, to the state of the *Christian Church*; shewing at large, that as *Moses*, by the

Com-

Command of God, Determin'd the Pretensions of the Twelve *Tribes* to the *Glory* of the *Priesthood*, by the Miraculous Budding of *Aaron*'s Rod, which was after the *Schism* and *Punishment* of *Korah* and his Company. *So likewise*, he lays, the *Apostles* fore-knowing, by *Christ*, that Dissentions wou'd arise also in the *Christian Church*, by various Pretenders to the *Evangelical Priesthood*, did Settle and Establish, not only the Persons themselves; But gave *Rules* and *Orders* for continuing the *Succession* after their Deaths, as I have before Quoted his Words. So that it is plain from hence, That the *Evangelical Priesthood*, is as *Positively*, and *Certainly* Establish'd, and Determin'd, in the *Succession* of *Ecclesiastical Ordination*, as the *Levitical* was, in the *Succession* of *Aaron*. And consequently, that the *Rebellion* of *Presbyters* from under the Government of their *Bishops*, is the same Case as the *Rebellion* (for so it is call'd, *Numb.* xvii. 10.) of *Korah* and his *Levites*, against *Aaron*; who had as good a Pretence against him from the word *Levite*, which was Common to the whole *Tribe*; as the *Presbyterians* have against *Bishops*, from the Name *Bishop* and *Presbyter*, being us'd sometimes promiscuously, and apply'd to the *Clergy* in General; which is a Term that Includes all the *Orders* of the *Church*, as *Levite* did among the *Jews*.

VII. But, to leave the fruitless Contest about *words*, let this Matter be Determin'd, as other Matters of Fact are.

If I pretend to succeed any Man in an *Honour* or *Estate*, I must name him who had such an *Estate* or *Honour* before me; and the Man who had it before him; and who had it before him; and so up all the way to him who first had it; and from whom all the rest do derive; and how it was lawfully deduc'd from one to another.

This the *Bishops* have done, as I have shewn; and can name all the way backward, as far as History goes, from the Present *Bishop* of *London*, (for example) to the first Plantation of *Christianity* in this Kingdom: So, from the present *Bishop* of *Lyons* up to *Irenæus* the Disciple of St. *Polycarp*, as before is told. The Records are yet more certain in the Great *Bishopricks* of *Rome*, *Antioch*, *Alexandria*, and others, while they lasted in the World. And tho' the Records may not be Extant of every small *Bishoprick*, which was less taken notice of; as the Names of many *Kings* are lost, in obscure Nations; of many *Mayors* or *Sheriffs*, who, notwithstanding have as certainly

tainly Succeeded one another, as where the Records are Preserv'd. I say, tho' every *Bishop* in the World cannot tell the Names of all his *Predecessors* up to the *Apostles*, yet their *Succession* is certain:. And in most Christian Nations there are *Bishops* who can do it; which is a sufficient Proof for the rest, all standing upon the same Bottom, and being Deriv'd in the same Manner.

Now, to Ballance this, it is Desir'd, that the *Presbyterians* wou'd shew the Succession of any one *Presbyter* in the World, who was not likewise a *Bishop*, in our acceptation of [the Word, in the like manner, from the *Apostles*.

Till when, their small *Criticisms* upon the *Etymology* of the Words, *Bishop* or *Presbyter*, is as poor a Plea, as if I shou'd pretend to be Heir to an Estate, from the likeness of my Name to somebody who once had it.

And here I cannot choose but apply the Complaint of our *Saviour*, *John* v. 43. If any come, in the Name of *Christ*, that is, by a Commission from Him, deriv'd down all the way, by Regular *Ordination*, him ye will not Receive: Nay, tho' he be otherwise a Man without Exception, either as to his *Life* and *Conversation*, or as to his *Gifts* and *Sufficiency* for the *Ministry*; you make this his *Commission* an *Objection* against him: For that *Reason alone*, you will not accept him. But, if another come in *his own Name*, that is, with no *Commission*, but what he has from himself; his *own Opinion* of his *own Worthiness*; *giving out that himself is some Great One*, (Act. viii. 9.) him ye will Receive, and Follow and Admire him; *Heaping to your selves Teachers, having Itching Ears*, as it was Prophesy'd of these most degenerate Times, 2 *Tim.* iv. 3.

But as to those well-dispos'd *Quakers*, for whose Information Chiefly I have wrote this *Discourse*, I must suppose that their Inquiry is wholly concerning the several *Titles* of *Bishops*, *Presbyterians*, *Independents*, &c. to the true *Succession* from the *Apostles*: That it may *thereby* be known, to which of all these they ought to go for *Baptism*.

This I have shewn, in behalf of *Episcopacy*; and put the *Presbyterians* to prove their *Succession*, in the Form of *Presbytery*, which they can never do: Because, as I have said before, the *Chronology* of the *Church* does not Compute from the *Succession* of the

Presbyters,

Presbyters, but only of the *Bishops*, as being the *Chief Governors* of the *Church*. And therefore, tho' in many *Bishopricks*, the *Roll* of their *Bishops* is preserv'd from the *Apostles* to this Day; yet there is not one bare *Presbyter*, that is, the *Minister* of a *Parish*, and no more, no not in all the World, who can give a *Roll* of his *Predecessors*, in that *Parish*, half way to the *Apostles*, or near it: For, from the first Plantation of *Christianity*, the *Church* was Divided into *Bishopricks*; this was necessary for the *Government* of the *Church*: But it was not so early Sub-divided into *Parishes*. The *Presbyters*, at first, attending upon the *Bishop*, were sent out by him, to such *Places*, and for such *Time* as he thought fit; and Returning, gave Account of their *Stewardships*, or were *Visited*, and *Changed* by him, as he saw Cause: And therefore, tho' one might come after another, in the Place where he had *Ministred* before; yet they cou'd not *Properly* be said to *Succeed* one another; as to speak Intelligibly to the *Quakers*) many of them do Preach after *G. Fox*, yet none of them are said to *Succeed* him.

I have been thus long upon the *Presbyterians*, because they only, of all our *Dissenters*, have any *Pretence* to *Succession*. And what I have said, as to them, must Operate more strongly against the later *Independent*, *Baptist*, &c. who have not the Face to Pretend to *Succession*, but set up merely upon their own pretended *Gifts*.

VIII. But what are these *Gifts*, which they so Highly *Boast*?

1. An *Inward*, and more than *Ordinary* Participation of the *Graces* of the Holy *Spirit*.

2. A *Fluency* and *Powerfulness* in *Preaching* and *Praying*.

I know of no other *Gifts* that any of our *Dissenters* pretend to; unless they will set up for *Miracles*, as *G. Fox*, &c. And other *Dissenters* did likewise pretend to the same, at their first setting out, to amuse the People; but (as the *Quakers*) have let it drop afterwards, to stop any further Examination of it; having already serv'd their Turn by it.

But, as to these pretended *Gifts*, if we may trust to our *Saviour's* Rule, of knowing the *Tree* by its *Fruits*, we cannot think it the *Holy Spirit* of which these Men did partake, who fill'd these *three Nations* with *Blood* and *Slaughter*; and whose *Religion* was never otherwise Introduc'd, than by *Rebellion*, in any Country whither-soever it has yet come.

And as to that *Volubility* of *Tongue*, which they Boast, as the main *Proof* of their *Miss.n*, we have found it by Experience, that a little *Confidence* and *Custom*, will Improve very slender *Judgments*, to great *Readiness* in that sort of *Talent*.

And the *Powerfulness* which is found in it by some, who are affected with a Dismal *Tone*, Wray *Faces*, and Antick *Gestures*, is not *more* but *less*, if there be either *Method* or *Sense* in the *Discourse*: Which shews their *Passion* to proceed not from *Reason*, but *Imagination*.

The *Scots Presbyterian-Eloquence* affords us *Monstrous* Proofs of this; but not so many, as you may have from *Eye* and *Ear-Witnesses*.

Such *Course*, *Rude*, and *Nasty* Treatment of *God*, as they call *Devotion*; as in it self, it is the highest *Affront* to The *Divine Majesty*; so has it Contributed, in a very great Measure, to that wild *Atheism*, which has always attended these sort of *Inspirations*: It seeming to many, more Reasonable to Worship no *God* at all, than to let up one, on purpose to *Ridicule* Him.

But this sort of *Enthusiasm* presumes upon a *Familiarity* with *God*, which breeds *Contempt*, and Despises the *Sobriety* of *Religion*, as a low Dispensation. I Recommend to the Reader that Excellent *Sermon*, upon this Subject, of Dr. *Hicks*, call'd *The Spirit of Enthusiasm Exorcis'd*. And I desire those to consider, who are most taken with these seeming Extraordinary Gifts of *Volubility* and *Nimbleness* in *Prayer*, that the most *Wicked* Men are capable of this Perfection; none more than *Oliver Cromwell*, especially when he was about some *Nefarious Wickedness*: He continu'd most Fluently in this *Exercise*, all the time that his *Cut-throats* were *Murthering* of his *Royal Master*. And his *Gift* of *Prayer* was greatly Admir'd. *Major Weir* of *Edinborough*, was another great Instance, who was strangely Ador'd for his *Gifts*, especially of *Prayer*, by the *Presbyterians* in *Scotland*; while, at the same time, he was wallowing in the most *Unnatural* and *Monstrous* Sins. See his Stupendous Story in *Ravillac Redivivus*.

There are many Examples of this Nature, which shew that this *Gift* is attainable by *Art*. Dr. *Wilkins* (the Father of the *Latitudinarians*) has given us the *Receipt*, in his *Gift of Prayer*.

Yet none of the Performances of these *Gifted men* are any ways Comparable (as to the wonderful *Readiness* in which they Boast) to the *Extempore Verses* of *Westminster School*, which *Isaac Vossius* cou'd not believe to be *Extempore*, till he gave the *Boys* a *Theme*, which was *senes bis Pueri*, and he had no sooner spoke the Words, but he was immediately Pelted with Ingenious *Epigrams* from four or five Boys.

So that this *Volubility* in *Prayer*, which is the *Gift* our *Dissenters* do most Glory in, may be deduc'd from an *Original* far short of *Divine Inspiration*.

But suppose that they had really those wonderful *Gifts* which they pretend to, yet were this no ground at all to Countenance or Warrant their makeing a *Schism*, upon that Account.

This Case has been Rul'd in a Famous and most Remarkable Instance of it, which God was pleas'd to permit, (for the future Instruction of His Church) at the first setting out of the *Gospel*, in the very Days of the *Apostles*.

Then it was that *Christ*, having *Ascended up on High*, gave many and *miraculous Gifts* unto Men; which was necessary towards the first Propagation of His *Gospel*, in Opposition to all the Established *Religions* and *Governments* then in the World, and under their Persecution.

But these *Gifts* of *Miracles* did not always secure the *Possessors* from *Vanity*, and an high Opinion of themselves, to the disparagement of others; and even to break the *Order* and *Peace* of the *Church*, by advancing themselves above their *Superiors*; or thinking none *Superior* to themselves.

The Great *Apostle* of the *Gentiles* was not free'd from the *Tentation* of this; whom the *Messenger of Satan was sent to buffet, least he shou'd be Exalted above measure, thro' the Abundance of the Revelations which were given to him*, 2 Cor. xii. 7. Nay more, our Blessed Saviour tells of those who had *miraculous Gifts* bestow'd upon them, and yet shou'd be finally *Rejected*, Matth. vii. 22, 23. Therefore He Instructs His Disciples not to Rejoyce in those *Miraculous Gifts* which he bestow'd upon them, but rather *that their Names were written in Heaven, Luke* x. 20. which supposes, that they might have such *Gifts*, and yet their *Names* not be written in *Heaven*.

And when He taught them how to *Pray*, He added no Petition for such *Gifts*, but only for the Remission of their *Sins*, and the *Sanctifying Graces* of the Holy *Spirit*; which are, as most *Profitable* to *Us*, so most *Precious* in the sight of *God*.

Now

(14)

Now some who had these *Miraculous Gifts* made ill use of them, and occasion'd a great *Schism* (the first in the *Christian* Church) at *Corinth*. They were *Exalted* above *Measure*, in their own *Gifts*; and therefore Refus'd to submit themselves to those who were their *Superiors* in the *Church* (who, perhaps, had not such *Gifts* as they had) but set up for themselves, and drew Parties after them, who were Charm'd with their *Extraordinary Gifts*; thinking that the Participation of the *saving Graces* of the Holy *Spirit* must there Chiefly be Communicated, where God had bestow'd such *wonderful Gifts*. And they laid more stress upon the *Personal Qualifications* of these *Ministers* of *God*, than upon the observance of that *Order* and *Constitution* which He had Commanded; which was, in Effect, preferring *Men* to *God*, and trusting to the *Instruments* rather than to the *Author* of their *Religion*; as if thro' the Power and *Holiness* of the *Administrators* of God's *Institutions*, and not from *Him* alone, the *Graces* which were Promis'd to the due Observance of them, were convey'd. *Act*. iii. 12.

And this, as it turn'd Men from *God*, to Trust in *Man*, so, as a necessary Consequence of it, it begot great *Emulations* among the People for one *Teacher* against another, even (sometimes) when it was not the Fault of the *Teachers*. For People being once let loose from *Government* and *Order*, to follow the *Imaginations* of their own *Brain*, will run farther than their first *Seducers* did Intend; and will Carve for themselves.

Thus, in the *Schism* of the *Church* at *Corinth*, one was for *Paul*, another for *Apollos*, another for *Cephas*, &c. much against the Minds of these good *Apostles*; but having been once unsettl'd by the *Pride* and *Ambition* of *Seducers*, they *Heaped to themselves Teachers, having itching Ears*; and made *Divisions* among themselves, Pretendingly in behalf of *Christ* and His *Apostles*, but in Effect, tending to Divide *Christ* and His *Apostles*, as all *Schisms* do.

Against these St. *Paul* Disputes with wonderful force of *Reason* and *Eloquence*; particularly in the xii *Chap*. of his first *Epistle* to these same *Corinthians*; wherein, from the Parallel of the *Unity* of *Members* in the same *Body*, he admirably Illustrates, That the many Different and *Miraculous Gifts* which were then Dispensed all from the same *Spirit*, cou'd be no more an Argument for any to Advance himself beyond his own Station in the *Church*, than for one *Member* of the *Body*, tho' an *Eye* or a *Hand*, the most *Useful* or *Beautiful*,

to

to Glory it felf againſt the *inferior Members* (who are all Actuated by the ſame *Soul*) or not to be Content with its *Office* and *Station* in the *Body*, and due *Subordination* to the *Head*. Thence the *Apoſtle* goes on, and makes the Application in the xiii*th*. *Chap*. That the moſt Exalted *Spiritual* or even *Miraculous Gifts* cou'd not only not Excuſe any *Schiſm* to be made in the *Body*, that is, the *Church*; But that if any who had ſuch *Gifts*, did not employ them for the Preſervation of the *Unity* of the *Church*, which is very properly Expreſs'd by *Charity*, i. e. *Love* for the whole *Body*, ſuch *Gifts* wou'd Profit him *Nothing*, looſe all their *Vertue* and *Efficacy*, as to the *Poſſeſſor*, and be rather an *Aggravation* againſt him, than any *Excuſe* for him, to withdraw his Obedience from his lawful *Superiors*, and Uſurp the Office of the *Head*; and ſo make a *Schiſm* in the *Body*, upon the account of his *Gifts*; which tho' they were as great as to ſpeak with the *Tongues* of *Men* and *Angels* ; to underſtand all *Myſteries*, and all *Knowledge*; to have all *Faith*, even to Remove *Mountains*; and ſuch a *Zeal* as to give all his *Goods* to the *Poor*, and his very *Body* to be *Burned*, yet, if it be done in *Schiſm*, out of that *Love* and *Charity* which is due to the *Body*, and to its *Unity*, all is *Nothing*, will profit him nothing at all.

And no wonder, when all that *Heavenly Glory* in which *Lucifer* was Created, cou'd avail him nothing, when he *kept not his firſt Principality*, but Aſpir'd *Higher*, and made a *Schiſm* in the *Hierarchy* of *Heaven*. Jude 6.

How then ſhall they who have (as St. *Jude* expreſſes it) *left their own Habitation*, or *Station* in the *Church*, and advanc'd themſelves above their *Biſhops*, their lawful *Superiors*, the *Heads* and *Principles* of *Unity*, next and immediately under *Chriſt*, in their Reſpective *Churches*, upon pretence of their own Perſonal *Gifts* and *Qualifications*, and thereby make a *Schiſm* in the *Terreſtrial Hierarchy* of the *Church*; which is the *Body of Chriſt*, the *Fulneſs of him who Filleth all in all*: How ſhall they be Excus'd for this, whoſe pretended *Gifts* are in nothing *Extraordinary*, except in a *Furious Zeal* without *Knowledge*, and a *Volubility* of *Tongue*, which proceeds from a Habit of *Speaking* without *Thinking* ; and an *Aſſurance* that is never out of *Countenance* for Ten Thouſand *Blunders*, which wou'd *Daſh* and *Confound* any Man of *Senſe* or *Modeſty*, or that conſider'd the *Preſence* of *God*, in which he ſpoke ? Eph. 1. 23.

If

If those truly *Miraculous Gifts*, which were made a Pretence for the *Schism* at *Corinth*, were not sufficient to justifie that *Schism*: How *Ridiculous* and much more *wicked* is the *Pretence* of our Modern *Gifted-men*, who have pleaded their Delicate *Gifts* as a sufficient Ground for all that *Schism* and *Rebellion* which they have Rais'd up amongst us ?

If the real *Gifts* and *Inspirations* of the Holy *Spirit* were *Stinted* and *Limited* by the *Governors* of the *Church*, to avoid *Schism* and *Confusion* in the *Church* : If the *Prophets* were *Confin'd* as to their 1 Cor. xiv. *Number*, to *Two*, or at the most *Three* at a time; some from v. 26. ordered to *hold their Peace*, to give place to others; others to *keep silence* for want of an *Interpreter* ; and the *Women* (tho' 1 Tim. II. 12. *Gifted* or *Inspir'd* as many then were) totally *silenc'd* in the *Church*, or *Publick Assemblies*: What *Spirit* has Possess'd our *Modern Pretenders* to *Gifts*, that will not be subject to the *Prophets*, nor to the *Church*, nor to any *Institutions* whether *Divine* or *Humane* ! But if their *Superiors* pretend to *Direct* them in any thing, they cry out; what ! will you *stint* the *Spirit* ! And think this a sufficient Cause to break quite loose from their *Authority*, and set up an open *Schism* against them, upon Pretence of their wonderful *Gifts* forsooth !

That first *Schism* in the *Church* of these *Corinthians* was vigorously oppos'd by the *Apostles* and *Bishops* of the *Church*, at that time. They, like good *Watch-men*, wou'd not give way to it, knowing the fatal Consequences of it.

This produc'd *Two Epistles* from St. *Paul* to the *Corinthians*, and *Two* to them from St. *Clement*, then *Bishop* of *Rome*, which are preserv'd, and handed down to us. It was this same occasion of *Schism*, which so early began to Corrupt the *Church*, that led the Holy *Ignatius* (who flourish'd in that same Age) to press so Earnestly in all his *Epistles* to the several *Churches* to whom he wrote, the Indispensable obligation of a strict *Obedience* to their Respective *Bishops*. That the *Laity* shou'd submit themselves to the *Presbyters* and *Deacons*, as to the *Apostolical College* under *Christ*; and that the *Presbyters* and *Deacons*, as well as the *Laity*, shou'd *Obey* their *Bishop*, as *Christ* Himself, whose Person he did Represent: That therefore whoever kept not *Outward Communion* with his *Bishop*, did forfeit his *Inward Communion* with *Christ*: That no *Sacraments* were *Valid*, or *Acceptable* to *God*, which were not celebrated

brated in Communion with the *Bishop*. That nothing in the *Church* shou'd be done, nor any *Marriage* Contracted without the *Bishop's* Consent, *&c.* As you will see hereafter.

These clear Testimonies forc'd the *Presbyterians* (because they were not in a Temper to be Convinc'd) to deny these *Epistles* of St. *Ignatius* to be Genuine. But they have been so fully Vindicated, particularly by the most Learned Bishop of *Chester*, Dr. *Pearson*, as to silence that Cavil, and leave no Pretence remaining against *Episcopacy* in that *Primitive* and *Apostolical* Age.

SECT. III.

Objection from the Times of Popery *in this Kingdom; as if that did* Un-Church, *and consequently break the Succession of our* Bishops.

I must now Account for an Objection, which with some, seems a mighty one, even enough to overthrow all that I have said concerning the *Succession* of our *Bishops*: And that is, the long *Mid-night* of *Popery*, which has, in old Time, Darken'd these Nations.

Well. The *Succession*, of which I have been speaking, was no Part of that Darkness; and we have, by God's Blessing, recover'd our selves, in a great Measure, from that Darkness. But that Darkness was such, as, with some, to Destroy the *Episcopal Succession*; because, as they say, such *great Errors*, especially that of *Idolatry*, does quite *Un-church* a People; and consequently must break their *Succession*.

I. This, by the way, is a *Popish* Argument, tho' they that now make it, are not aware of it. For the Church of *Rome* argues thus, That *Idolatry* does *Un-church*; and therefore, if she was *Idolatrous*, for so long a time as we charge upon her, it will follow that, for so many Ages, there was no *Visible Church*, at least, in these *Western* Parts of the World. And *Arianism* (which is *Idolatry*) having broke in several times upon the *Church*; if *Idolatry* did quite *Un-church*, and Break the *Succession*, there would not be a *Christian Church* hardly left in the World. The Consequence of of which wou'd be as fatal to the *Church* of *Rome*, as to us: Therefore let her look to that Position, which she has advanced against us, that *Idolatry* does *Un-church*.

II. But that it does not *Un-church*, I have this to offer against those *Papists*, *Quakers*, and *Others* who make the Objection.

1. If it does quite *Un-church*, then cou'd no *Christian* be an *Idolater*; because, by that, he wou'd, *ipso facto*, cease to be a Member of the *Christian Church*: But the *Scripture* does suppose that a *Christian* may be an *Idolater*: Therefore *Idolatry* does not *Un-church*. The *Minor* is prov'd, 1 *Cor*. v. 11. *If any Man that is called a Brother* (that is, a *Christian*) *be a Fornicator, or Covetous, or an Idolater*——Nay, *Eph*. v. 5. *a covetous man* is call'd an *Idolater*; and *Col*. iii. 5. *Covetousness* is *Idolatry*. So that, by this Argument, *Covetousness* does *Un-church*. If it be said, that *Covetousness* is call'd *Idolatry*, only by Allusion, but that it is not *Formal* Idolatry: I know no Ground for that Distinction. The *Scripture* calls it *Idolatry*, and makes no Distinction. But,

2*dly*, In the first Text quoted, 1 *Cor*. v. 11. both *Covetousness* and *Idolatry* are Nam'd; so that, you have both *Material* and *Formal*, or what other sort of *Idolatry* you please to fansie.

I grant, that, in one sense, *Idolatry* does *Un-church*; that is, while we continue in it, it renders us Obnoxious to the *Wrath* of *God*; and forfeits our Title to the *Promises* which are made to the *Church* in the *Gospel*: But, so does *Fornication*, *Covetousness*, and every other *Sin*, till we *Repent*, and *Return* from it. But none of these Sins do so *Un-church* us, as to Exclude our Returning to the *Fold*, by sincere Repentance; or to need a second *Baptism*, or *Admission* into the *Church*: Neither does *Idolatry*. Do I then put *Idolatry* upon the level with other common Sins? No, far from it. Every *Scab* is not a *Leprosie*; yet a *Leper* is a *Man*, and may Recover his Health. *Idolatry* is a fearful *Leprosie*; but it does not therefore quite *Un-church*, nor throw us out of the *Covenant*. For, if it did, then wou'd not *Repentance* heal it; because *Repentance* is a great Part of the *Covenant*. And therefore, since none deny *Repentance* to an *Idolater*; it follows that he is not yet quite out of the *Covenant*. Some of the Ancients have deny'd Repentance to *Apostacy*, yet granted it to *Idolatry*; which shews that they did not look upon *Idolatry* to be an absolute *Apostacy*; for every *Sin* is an *Apostacy*, in a Limited sense.

2. Let

2. Let us, in this Disquisition, follow the Example before mention'd, of the *Apostles* and *most Primitive Fathers*, to measure the *Christian Church* with its exact *Type*, the Church under the *Law*; which are not *Two Churches*, but Two *States* of the same *Church*, for it is the same *Christian* Church, from the first Promise of *Christ*, *Gen.* iii. 15. to the End of the World. And therefore it is said, *Heb.* iv. 2. That the *Gospel* was Preached unto *Them*, as well as unto *Us*. And these two *States* of the Church, *before* and *after* Christ, do Answer, like a pair of *Indentures* to one another; the one being, to an *Iota* fulfilled in the other. *Matth.* v. 18.

Now we find frequent Lapses to *Idolatry* in the *Church* of the *Jews*: Yet did not this *Un-church* them; no, nor deprive them of a competent measure of God's Holy Spirit; as it is written, *Neh.* ix. 18, 20. *Yea, when they had made them a molten calf, and said, this is thy God——yet thou, in thy manifold Mercies, forsookest them not ——Thou gavest thy good spirit to instruct them*, &c.

And let it be here observ'd, That tho' God sent many Prophets to Reprove the great *Wickedness* and *Idolatry*, as well of their *Priests* as *People*; yet none of these *Holy Prophets* did separate Communion from the *Wicked Priests*: They wou'd not joyn in their *Idolatrous* Worship; but in all other Parts, they joyn'd with them; and set up no opposit *Priesthood* to them. So little did the *Prophets* think that their *Idolatry* had either *Un-church'd* them, or broke the *Succession* of their *Priests*; or that it was Lawful for any, how *Holy* soever, to usurp upon their *Priesthood*, and supply the Deficiencies of it to the *People*. And apply to this, what I have before shewn, in the words of St. *Clement, whose Name is written in the Book of Life*, That the *Evangelical Priesthood*, is as surely fixed, in the *Bishops* of the *Church*, and its *Succession* continu'd in those *Ordain'd* by them, as the *Levitical Priesthood* was confirm'd by the Budding of *Aaron's Rod*, and to be continu'd in that *Tribe*.

III. And here let our *Korahites*, of several sizes, take a view of the Heinousness of their *Schism*; and let them not think their Crime to be nothing, because they have been taught, with their Nurses Milk, to have the utmost abhorrence to the very Name of a *Bishop*; tho' they cou'd not tell why. Let them rather consider seriously the misfortune of their Education, which shou'd make them Strangers, to all the rest of the Christian World but them-

themselves in a Corner; and to all the former Ages of *Christianity*.

They have been told that *Episcopacy* is *Popery*; because the *Papists* have *Bishops*.

So have they *Presbyters* too, that is, *Parish Priests*: They have the *Creed* likewise, and the Holy *Scriptures*; and all these must be *Popish*, if this be a good *Argument*.

But, are they willing to be undeceived? Then they must know that *Episcopacy* has none so great an Enemy as the *Papacy*; which wou'd Engross the whole *Episcopal* Power, into the single See of *Rome*; by making all other *Bishops* absolutly dependent upon that, which only they call the *Apostolical* Chair. And no longer since than the *Council* of *Trent*, the *Pope* endeavor'd, with all his Interest, to have *Episcopacy*, except only that of the *Bishop* of *Rome*, to be declar'd not to be *Jure Divino*. By which non other *Bishops* cou'd claim any other Power, but what they had from Him. But that *Council* was not so quite Degenerated as to suffer this to pass.

And the *Jesuits*, and Others, who Disputed there on the *Pope's* part, us'd those same Arguments against the *Divine Right* of *Episcopacy*; which from them, and the *Popish Canonists* and *Schoolmen* have been lick'd up by the *Presbyterians* and others of our *Dissenters*. They are the same Arguments which are us'd by *Pope* and *Presbyter* against *Episcopacy*.

When the *Pope* cou'd not carry his Cause against *Episcopacy* in the Council of *Trent*, he took another Method, and that was, to set up a vast Number of *Presbyterian* Priests, that is, the *Regulars*, whom he Exempted from the *Jurisdiction* of their respective *Bishops*; and fram'd them into a *Method* and *Discipline* of their own, accountable only to *Superiors* of his, and their own contrivings; which is exactly the *Presbyterian* Model.

These *Usurpations* upon the *Episcopal* Authority, made the Famous Archbishop of *Spalato*, quit his great Preferments in the *Church* of *Rome*, and Travel into *England*, in the Reign of King *James* I. to seek for a more *Primitive* and *Independent Episcopacy*. Himself, in his *Consilium Profectionis*, gives these same Reasons for it: And that this shameful *Depression* and *Prostitution* of *Episcopacy*, in the *Church* of *Rome*, was the cause of his leaving her.

He

He obſerv'd truly, that the further we ſearch upward in *Anti-quity*, there is ſtill more to be found of the *Epiſcopal*, and leſs of the *Papal* Eminency.

St. *Ignatius* is full, in every line almoſt, of the high Authority of the *Biſhop*, next and immediately under *Chriſt*; as all the other Writers in thoſe Primitive Times: But there is a profound ſilence in them all of that *Supremacy* in the *Biſhop* of *Rome*, which is now claim'd over all the other *Biſhops* of the *Catholick Church*: Which cou'd not be, if it had been then known in the World. This had been a ſhort and effectual Method, whereby St. *Paul*, or St. *Clement* might have quieted the great *Schiſm* of the *Corinthians*, againſt which they both wrote, in their *Epiſtles* to them; to bid them refer their Differences to the *Infallible Judge* of *Controverſy*, the *Supreme Paſtor* at *Rome*. But not a word like this. Eſpecially conſidering that St. *Peter* was one, for whom ſome of theſe *Corinthians* ſtrove. (1 Cor. i. 12.) againſt thoſe who preferred others before Him.

The *Uſurp'd Supremacy* of the later *Biſhops* of *Rome* over their *Fellow-Biſhops*, has been as Fatal to *Epiſcopacy*, as the Rebellion of our yet later *Presbyters* againſt their Reſpective *Biſhops*.

And indeed, whoever wou'd write the true Hiſtory of *Presbyterianiſm*, muſt begin at *Rome*, and not at *Geneva*.

So very *Groundleſs*, as well as *Malicious*, is that popular Clamour of *Epiſcopacy* having any Relation to *Popery*. They are ſo utterly Irreconcilable, that it is impoſſible they can ſtand together: For that moment that *Epiſcopacy* were Reſtor'd to its Primitive Independency, the *Papacy*, that is, that *Supremacy*, which does now diſtinguiſh it, muſt *ipſo facto* ceaſe. But enough of this, for I muſt not digreſs into various Subjects.

I have ſhewn, in Anſwer to the Objection of the Ages of *Popery* in this Kingdom, that all thoſe *Errors*, even *Idolatry* it ſelf, does not *Un-church*, nor break *Succeſſion*. And 2*dly*, I have Exemplifi'd this from the Parallel of the *Jewiſh Church*, under the *Law*. Then applying of this to our Caſe, I have vindicated *Epiſcopacy* from the Imputation of *Popery*. I will now go on to further *Reaſons*, why the *Succeſſion* of our preſent *Biſhops* is not hurt by that Deluge of *Popery*, which once cover'd the face of this Land.

IV. The end of all *Government*, as well in the *Church* as *State*, is to preſerve *Peace*, *Unity*, and *Order*; and this cannot be done, if the *Male-administration* of the *Officers* in the Government, did *Vacate* their *Commiſſion*, without its being Re-call'd by thoſe who gave ſuch *Commiſſion* to them. For then, 1*ſt*. Every Man muſt be Judge, when ſuch a *Commiſſion* is *Vacated*; and then no Man is bound to obey longer than he pleaſes. 2*dly*, One may ſay it is *Vacated*, another not; whence perpetual Contention muſt ariſe.

A Man may *Forfeit* his Commiſſion, that is, do thoſe things, which give juſt Cauſe to his *Superiors* to take it from him: But it is not actually *Vacated*, till it be actually *Recall'd* by thoſe who have lawful Power to take it from him: Otherwiſe their cou'd be no *Peace* nor *Certainty* in the World, either in *Publick* or in *Private* affairs. No *Family* cou'd ſubſiſt. No Man enjoy an *Eſtate*. No *Society* whatever cou'd keep together: And the *Church* being an *Outward Society* (as ſhewn in the *Diſcourſe* of *Water Baptiſm*) muſt conſequently ſubſiſt by thoſe *Laws* which are indiſpenſible to every *Society*. And tho' *Idolatry* does juſtly *Forfeit* the *Commiſſion* of any *Church*, in this ſenſe, that God's Promiſes to Her being *Conditional*, He may juſtly take her *Commiſſion* from her, and *Remove* her *Candleſtick*: Now tho' her *Commiſſion* be thus *Forfeitable*, yet it ſtill *Continues*, and is not actually *Vacated*, till God ſhall pleaſe *actually* to Recall it, or take it away: For no *Commiſſion* is *Void*, till it be ſo *Declar'd*. Thus, tho' the *Jews* did often fall into *Idolatry*, yet (as before has been ſaid) God did bear long with them; and did not *Un-church* them, tho' they had juſtly *Forfeited*. And theſe wicked *Husband men*, who ſlew thoſe whom the *Lord* ſent for the Fruits of His *Vineyard*, yet continu'd ſtill to be the *Husband-men* of the *Vineyard*, till their *Lord* did Diſpoſſeſs them, and gave their *Vineyard* unto others.

Sect.iii.r.1.

And *natural Reaſon* does enforce this: If a *Steward* abuſe his Truſt, and oppreſſes the *Tenants*, yet are they ſtill oblig'd to pay their *Rent* to him, and his *Diſcharges* are ſufficient to them againſt their *Landlord*, till he ſhall *Superſede* ſuch a *Steward*.

If a *Captain* wrong and cheat his *Soldiers*, yet are they oblig'd to remain under his Command, till the *King*, who gave him his *Commiſſion*, or thoſe to whom he has Committed ſuch an Authority, ſhall *Caſhier* him.

And thus it is in the *Sacerdotal Commiſſion*, Abuſes in it, do not take it away, till God, or thoſe to whom He has Committed ſuch an Authority, shall *Suspend, Deprive,* or *Degrade* (as the *Fact* Requires) such a *Bishop* or a *Priest.*

And there is this higher Consideration in the *Sacerdotal Commission,* than in those of Civil Societies; That it being immediately from *God,* as *none* (therefore) *can take this Honour to himself, but he that is called of God, as was* Aaron; so can none take it away, but he that is as *Expresly* and *Outwardly* called thereunto, as *Aaron* was to be a *Priest.* For this wou'd be to U*surp* upon *God's* immediate *Prerogative,* which is to Constitute His own *Priests.* Upon this Foundation I argue.

V. As the *necessity* of *Government,* and the general Commands in *Scripture,* of *Obedience* to *Government* do require our Submission to the Government in being, where there is no *Competition* concerning the *Titles,* or any that *Claims* a *better Right* than the *Possessor:* So where a *Church,* once Establish'd by *God,* tho' suffering many Interruptions, does continue, Her *Governers* ought to be acknowledg'd, where ther is no *better Claim* set up against them.

This was the Reason why our *Saviour* and His *Apostles* did, without scruple, acknowledge the *High-Priest* and *Sanhedrin* of the *Jews* in their time; tho' from the days of the *Maccabees,* ther had been great *Irruptions,* and *Breaches* in the due *Succession* of their *Priests:* and before *Christ* came, and all His time, the *Romans,* as *Conquerors,* dispos'd of the *Priesthood* as they pleas'd; and made it *Annual* and *Arbitrary,* which *God* had appointed *Hereditary* and *Unmovable.*

But ther was then no *Competition:* The *Jews* did submit to it, because they were under the subjection of the *Romans,* and cou'd have no other. No *High-Priest* claimed against him in Possession, but all submitted to him.

And our *Saviour* did confirm His Authority, and of the *Sanhedrin,* or Inferior *Priests* with him, *(Mattb.* xxiii. 2.) *saying, the Scribes and Pharisees sit in Moses's seat. All therefore, whatsoever they bid you observe, that observe and do.* And St. *Paul* own'd the Authority of the *High Priest,* *Act.* xxiii. 5.

Many Objections might have been rais'd against the Deduction of their *Succession* from *Moses:* But ther being none who claim'd any better Right than they had; therefore their *Right* was Uncontroverted; and by our *Saviour's* Authority was Confirm'd.

Now

Now suppose some *Interruptions* had been in the *Succession*, or *Corruptions* in the *Doctrine* and *Worship* of our *English Bishops*, in former Ages, yet (as in the Case of the *Scribes* and *Pharisees*) that cou'd have no Effect to Invalidate their *Commission* and *Authority* at the present.

SECT. IV.

The Assurance *and* Consent *in the* Episcopal *Communion, beyond that of any other.*

1. THE whole *Christian* World, as it always has been, so at this Present, it is *Episcopal*, except a few *Dissenters*, who, in less than Two Hundred years last past, have arisen, like a *Wart* upon the Face of the *Western* Church. For little more Proportion do our *Dissenters* here, the *Hugonots* in *France*, the *Presbyterians* in *Holland*, *Geneva*, and thereabouts, bear to the whole Body of the *Latin* Church, which is all *Episcopal*. But, if you compare them with the *Catholick* Church all over the World, which is all *Episcopal*, they will not appear so big as a *Mole*.

II. If our *Dissenters* think it much, that the Church of *Rome* shou'd be reckon'd in the List against them; we will be content to leave them out: Nay more, if we shou'd give them all those *Churches*, which own the *Supremacy* of *Rome* to be joyn'd with them (as they are the nearest to them) it will be so far from casting the Ballance on their side, that the other *Episcopal* Churches will, by far, out-number them both.

Let us then, to these *Dissenters* against *Episcopacy*, add the *Churches* of *Italy*, and *Spain* entire, with the *Popish* Part of *Germany*, *France*, *Poland* and *Hungary* (I think they have no more to reckon upon,) against these we produce the vast *Empire* of *Russia* (which is greater in Extent than all these *Popish* Countries before nam'd) *England*, *Scotland*, *Denmark*, *Sweden*, and all the *Lutheran* Churches in *Germany*, which will out-number both the *Papists* and *Presbyterians* before-mention'd. And this comparison is only made as to the *Latin* Church. But then, we have all the rest of the *Christian* World, wholly on the *Episcopal* side, against both the *Supremacy*

macy of *Rome*, and *Parity* of the *Presbyterians*. The whole *Greek* Church, the *Armenians*, *Georgians*, *Mingrelians*, *Jacobites*, the *Christians* of St. *Thomas*, and St. *John* in the *East-Indies*, and other *Oriental* Churches. Then in *Africa*, the *Cophties* in *Egypt*, and great Empire of the *Abyssins* in *Æthiopia*. These all are *Episcopal*, and never own'd the *Supremacy* of *Rome*: And over reckon, out of fight, all that difown *Episcopacy*, and all that own the *Supremacy* of *Rome* with them.

III. Let me add, that among our *Dissenters*, every Class of them does Condemn all the rest; the *Presbyterian* Damns the *Quaker*, the *Quaker* Damns him, *Independent*, *Baptist*, &c. All Damn one another, and Each denys the others *Ordination* or *Call*.

So that, the *Ordination* of every one of them, is difown'd by all the rest; and all of them together by the whole *Christian* World. And if their *Ordinations* are not Valid, then they have no more Authority to administer the *Sacraments*, than any other *Lay-men*; and consequently, ther can be no security in Receiving *Baptism* from any of them.

IV. What allowances God will make to those who think their *Ordination* to be good enough, and that they are true *Ministers* of the *Gospel*; and, as such, do receive the *Sacraments* from them, I will not determine.

But they have no reason to expect the like allowances who are warned of it before-hand, and will notwithstanding venture upon it; before these *Dissenters* have *fully* and *clearly* acquit themselves of so *Great* and *Universal* a Charge laid against them; such an one, as must make the whole *Christian* World *wrong*, if they be in the *Right*! Not only the present *Christian Churches*, but all the Ages of *Christianity* since *Christ*. Of which the *Dissenters* are desir'd to produce any one, in any Part of the World, that were not *Episcopal*——any one Constituted *Church* upon the Face of the Earth, that was not Govern'd by *Bishops*, distinct from, and Superior to *Presbyters*, before the *Vaudois* in *Piedmont*, the *Hugonots* in *France*, the *Calvinists* in *Geneva*, and the *Presbyterians* thence Transplanted, in this last Age, into *Holland*, *Scotland* and *England*.

V. If it shou'd be retorted, that neither is the *Church of England* without *Opposers*; for, that the *Church* of *Rome* opposes Her, as do likewise our *Dissenters*.

E *Ans*.

Ans. None of them do oppose Her, in the Point we are now upon, that is, the Validity of *Episcopal* Ordination, which the *Church of Rome* does own; and the *Presbyterians* dare not deny it, because they wou'd (thereby) overthrow all their own *Ordinations*; for the *Presbyters* who *Reformed* (as they call it) from *Bishops*, receiv'd their *Ordination* from *Bishops*.

And therefore, tho' the *Episcopal* Principles do *Invalidate* the *Ordination* by *Presbyters*, yet the *Presbyterian* Principles do not *Invalidate* the *Ordination* by *Bishops*: So that the *Validity* of *Episcopal* Ordination stands safe, on all sides, even by the Confession of those who are Enemies to the *Episcopal Order*: and, in this, the *Bishops* have no opposers.

Whereas, on the other hand, the *Validity* of the *Presbyterian Ordinations*, is own'd by none but themselves; and they have all the rest of the World as opposite to them.

Therefore, to state the Case the most Impartially; to receive *Baptism* from these *Dissenters*, is, at least, a *hazard* of many *Thousands* to *One*; as many as all the rest of *Christianity* are more than they: But to receive it from the *Bishops*, or *Episcopal* Clergy, has no *hazard* at all, as to its *Validity*, even as own'd by the *Presbyterians* themselves.

SECT. V.

The Personal Sanctity *of the* Administrator *of the* Sacraments, *tho' highly Requisite on his Part, yet not of* Necessity *as to the* Receivers, *to Convey to them the* Benefits *of the* Sacraments.

I. THE only Objection of those *Quakers*, who are otherwise convinc'd of the *Obligation* of the *Sacraments*, is the *Necessity* they think ther is of great *Personal* Holiness in the *Administrators*; without which, they cannot see how the *Spiritual* Effects of the *Sacraments* can be convey'd. But I wou'd beseech them to consider, how, by this, instead of referring the Glory to God, and *lessening* the *Performance* of *Man*, which I charitably

pre-

presume (and I am confident as to some of whom I speak) that it is their true and sincere Intention; but instead of that, I do, in great Good-will, invite them to reflect whither their well-intended Zeal has turn'd the Point of this Question——even to o- ver-magnifie *Man*, and transfer the Glory of *God* unto His *weak Instrument*; as if any (the least Part) of the *Divine* Vertue which God has annexed to His *Sacraments* did proceed from His *Minister*. If this be not the meaning (as sure it is not) why so much stress laid upon the *Sanctity* of the *Ministers*? as if thro' their *power or holiness* the *Holy Ghost* was given! Act. iii. 11.

II. To obviate this pretence, our Saviour *Christ* chose a *Devil* (*John* vi. 70.) to be one of His *Apostles*; and he was sent to *Baptize* and work *Miracles* as well as the rest: And those whom *Judas* did *Baptize*, were, no doubt, as well *Baptized*, and did partake of the Communication of the *Spirit* (according to their Preparation for it) as much as any who were *Baptized* by the other *Apostles*; unless you will say that *Christ* sent him to *Baptize*, who had no Authority to *Baptize*, and that none shou'd receive Benefit by his *Baptism*, which wou'd be to Cheat and Delude the People; and is a great Blasphemy against *Christ*, and a distrust of His *Power*; as if it were *Limited* by the poor Instrument He pleases to make use off; whereas,

III. His *Greatness* is often most *Magnify'd* in the *meaness* of the *Instruments*, by which He works. Thus He destroy'd *Egypt* by *Frogs* and *Lice*; and the *Philistines* by *Emerods* and *Mice*; and sent His Armies of *Flies* and *Hornets* to dispossess the *Canaanites*. *Out of the mouths of babes and sucklings hast thou ordained strength, because of thine enemies, that thou mightest still the enemy, and the avenger*; i.e. That the Enemies of God might be confounded, when they saw His great Power Exerted by such weak and contemptible *Instruments*. The Walls of *Jericho* (the *Type* of *Spiritual* wickedness) were thrown down by the blast of seven *Rams Horns*, when blown by the *Priests* whom He had commanded: And He rebuked the Iniquity of *Balaam* by the mouth of an *Ass*, to shew that no *Instruments* are *Ineffectual* in His Hands; and made use of the mouth of *Balaam* to Prophesie of *Christ*. For this cause, says St. *Barnabas*, in his *Catholick Epistle*, c. 5. did *Christ* choose Men who were *Exceeding great Sinners* to be His A- ὑπὲρ πᾶς ἁμαρτίαν ἀνομωτέρους.

Psal. viii. 2.

postles;

postles; to shew the Greatness of His *Power* and *Grace*; and put the Ineftimable *Treasure* of His *Gospel* into *Earthen Vessels*, that the Praise might be to *God*, and not to Men.

Phil. i. 16. IV. St. *Paul* rejoyced in *Christ* being Preached, tho' not *sincerely* by those who did it; because God can bring *Good* out of *Evil*; and by wicked *Instruments*, Propagate His *Gospel*; turning their *malice* (even of the *Devil* himself) to the furtherance of the *Faith*: Otherwise the *Apostle* cou'd have no cause to *Rejoyce* in the Preaching of *wicked* Men, if none cou'd receive benefit by it. And he plainly suppoſes, 1 *Cor.* ix. 27. That a Man may save others by his *Preaching*, and yet himself be a *cast-away*.

V. And ſo far as we can know or judge any thing, we ſee daily Experience of this; That God has touched Mens Hearts upon hearing the *Truth* ſpoken, tho' by Men who were great *Hypocrites*, and very *wicked*. And what reaſon can be given to the contrary? *Truth* is *Truth* whoever ſpeaks it: And if my Heart be prepared, the *good Seed* receives no evil *Tincture* of the Hand that ſowed it: And who can Limit *God*, that His *Grace* may not go along with me in this?

I have heard ſome of the *now separate Quakers* confeſs, that they have formerly felt very ſenſible Operations of the *Spirit*, upon the *Preaching* of ſome of thoſe whom they have ſince Detected of *gross Errors* and *Hypocrisies*; and they now think it ſtrange. But this were enough to convince them, that *the wind bloweth where it liſteth*: otherwiſe they muſt condemn themſelves, and confeſs that, in all that time, they had no true Participation of the *Spirit* of God, but that what they miſtook for it, was a meer *Delusion*: Or elſe confeſs that by the *Truths* which were ſpoken by theſe *Ministers* of *Satan* (for they ſpeak *some* Truths) God might work a good Effect upon the Hearts of ſome *well-dispos'd*, tho' then *Ignorant*, and much *Deluded* People. If not ſo, we muſt judge very ſeverely of all thoſe who live in *Idolatrous* or *Schismatical* Countries; ther were *great Prophets* and *good Men* among the *Ten Tribes*. And if the *words*, nay *Miracles*, of *Christ*, did render the Hearts of many yet more obdurate, even to ſin againſt the *Holy Ghost*; which was the reaſon why He ſometimes refus'd to work *Miracles* among them, becauſe thereby they grew worſe and worſe; and if the Preaching of the *Gospel*, by the mouths of *Apostles*, became the ſavour of *Death* to *wicked* and

Matth. xii from v. 22. to v. 32.

and *unprepar'd* Hearts; why may not the words of *Truth* have a good Effect upon *honest* and *good* Minds, tho' spoken from the mouth of an *Hypocrite*, or of Persons, who, in other things, are greatly *Deluded*?

I have before mention'd the *Wizard* Major *Weir*, who *Bewitched* the *Presbyterians* in *Scotland*, since the *Restoration*, 1660, as much as *Simon Magus* did the *Samaritans*: And yet I suppose the more moderate of the *Quakers* will not rashly give all over to Destruction, who blindly followed him, and admir'd his *Gifts*; or will say but that some words of Truth he might drop, might have a real good Effect upon some *well meaning*, tho' grosly *Deluded* People, who followed him. Two of *Winder's Witches* (see *The Snake in the Grass*, p. 300. 2d. Edit.) were *Preachers* among the *Quakers* for Twenty years together; and thought to be as *Powerful* and *Affecting* as any others.

VI. But, the Argument will hold stronger against them, as to the *Sacraments*, than in the Office of *Preaching*; because in *Preaching* much depends upon the Qualifications of the Person, as to *Invention, Memory, Judgment*, &c. But in the Administration of an *Outward Sacrament*, nothing is requir'd, as of *Necessity*, but the lawfulness of the *Commission*, by which such a Person does Administer; and a small measure of *natural* or *acquir'd* Parts is sufficient to the *Administration*.

Therefore let us lay no stress upon the *Instrument* (more than was upon the *waters* of *Jordan* to heal *Naaman*) but trust wholly upon the *Commission*, which conveys the *Vertue* from *God*, and not from His *Ministers*: That all the *Glory* may be to *God*, and not to *Man*.

'Tis true, the *Personal* Qualifications of the *Instrument* are *Lovely* and *Desirable*; but they become a *Snare*, where we expect any part of the *Success* from them. This was the ground of the *Corinthian* Schism (1 *Cor.* i. 11.) and, tho' unseen, of ours at this Day.

VII. And the consequences of it, are of manifold and fatal Destruction.

1. This unsettles all the *Assurance* we can have in God's *Promise* to assist His own *Institution*; for, if the *Vertue*, or any part of it, lies in the *Holiness* of the *Instrument*, we can never be sure of the Effect,

Effect, as to us; because, we have no *certain* knowledge of the *Holiness* of another. *Hypocrites* deceive even *good Men*.

2. This wou'd quite disappoint the *Promise* Christ has made, *Matth.* xxviii. 20. To be with His *Ministers*, in the Execution of His Commission; to *Baptize*, &c. *always, even unto the end of the world*. For, if the *Holiness* of the *Instrument* be a *necessary* Qualification, this may fail, nay always must fail, so far as we can be *sure* of it; and consequently *Christ* has commanded *Baptism* and *His Supper* to continue, *to the end of the world*, till *his coming again*; and yet has not afforded *means* whereby they may be continu'd; which He has not done, if the *Holiness* of the *Administrator* be a *necessary* Qualification; and that He has not left us a *certain* Rule, whereby to judge of the *Holiness* of another: And thus have you rendred the *Command* of *Christ* of none Effect, thro' your Tradition.

3. This is contrary to all God's former Institutions. The *wickedness* of the *Priests*, under the *Law*, did not *excuse* any of the People from bringing of their *Sacrifices* to the *Priests:* The *Priests* were to Answer for their own Sin, but the *People* were not answerable for it, or their *Offerings* the less accepted.

But we were in a much worse condition, under the *Gospel-Administration*, if the Effect of *Christ's* Institutions, did depend either *wholly*, or in *part* upon the *Personal Holiness* of His *Priests*. This wou'd put us much more in their Power, than it is the Intention of those who make this objection to allow to them: This magnifies *Men*, more than is due to them; therefore I will apply the Apostle's words to this Case; *Let no man glory in men; who is Paul? and who is Apollo? but ministers—so then, neither is he that planteth any thing, neither he that watereth; but God who giveth the increase.*

1 Cor. iii. 21.

4. This was (with others) the Error of the Ancient *Donatists*; those Proud and Turbulent *Schismaticks*, the great *Disturbers* of the *Peace* of the Church, upon an opinion of their own *Sanctity*, above that of other Men: For which reason, they rejected all *Baptisms*, except what was performed by themselves; and *Re-baptiz'd* those who came over to them, from the *Church*; for, they said that the *Holiness* of the *Administrator* was *necessary* towards conveying the *Spiritual Graces* of *Baptism*: Thus they argu'd; *Qui non habet quod Det, quomodo Dat?* i. e. *How shall a Man give that*

(31)

to another, which he has not himself? But *Optatus* Answers them, that *God* was the *Giver*, and not *Man*, *Videte Deum esse Datorem*. And he argues Adv. Parmen. l. 5. de schismat. Donatist Ed. Paris 1631. p. 87

that it was preferring *Themselves* before *God*, to think that the *Vertue* of *Baptism* did come from *Them*; that they were nothing but *Ministers* or *Work-men*; and that, as when a *Cloth* was *Dyed*, the *change* of the *Cloth* came from the *Colours* infus'd, not from the vertue of the *Dyer*. So that in *Baptism* the *Change* of the *Baptized*, came from the *Vertue* of the *Sacrament*; not from the *Administrator*: That it was the *Water* of *Baptism*, which did *wash*, not the Person who apply'd the *Water*. That the *Personal Sanctity* of the *Administrator* signify'd nothing to the *Efficacy* of the *Sacrament*; Therefore, says he, *Nos operemur ut Ille det, qui se daturum esse promisit*, i.e. *Let us work, that God, who has promis'd it, may bestow the Effect*: And that when we work, *Humana sunt opera, sed Dei sunt Munera*, i.e. The *Work* is *Man's*, but the *Gift* is *God's*. p. 88.

And thence he exposes that Ridiculous Principle of the *Donatists*, which they advanc'd to gain *Glory* to *Themselves*; that the *Gift* in *Baptism* was of the *Administrator*, and not of the *Receiver*: *Jam illud quam Ridiculum est, quod, quasi ad Gloriam vestram, à vobis semper auditur, hoc munus Baptismatis, est Dantis, non Accipientis?* p. 89.

But he shews, that the *Gift* was conferred by *God*, proportionably to the *Faith* of the *Receiver*, and not according to the *Holiness* of the *Administrator*.

The Discourse is large, to which I refer the Reader. I have given this Tast of it, to let these see to whom I now write, that they have (tho' unaware) stumbled upon the very Notion of the *Donatists*, which divided them from the *Catholick Church*, and which, with them, has been, long since, Exploded by the whole *Christian* World; and I hope this may bring them to a more sober mind; to consider *from whence*, and *with whom* they have fallen; and to return again to the *Peace* of the *Church*, and the Participation of the Blessed *Sacraments* of *Christ*, and the Inestimable *Benefits* which He has promis'd to the *Worthy Receivers* of them.

Lastly, Let me observe that this *Error* of the *Donatists* and *Quakers*, borders near upon *Popery*; nay rather seems to exceed it. For the *Church* of *Modern Rome* makes the *Validity* of the *Sacraments* to depend upon the *Intention* of the *Priest*; but his *Intention* is much more in his own Power; and ther are more evident *Signs* of it than of his *Holiness*.

VIII. I

VIII. I wou'd not have the *Quakers* imagine that any thing I have said was meant in excuse for the ill Lives of the *Clergy* of the *Church* of *England*; as if the *Dissenters* were unblamable, but our *Clergy* wholly Prostitute to all wickedness; and that for this cause, we plead against the *Sanctity* of the *Administrator*, as Essential to the *Sacrament*.

No, That is far from the Reason: I do not love to make comparisons, or Personal Reflections. If all Men be not as they shou'd be, pray God make them so. But I think ther is no modest *Dissenter* will be offended, if I say, that ther are of our *Bishops* and *Clergy*, Men, not only of *Learning*, and *moral Honesty*, but of *Devotion*, and *spiritual Illumination*; and as much of the *Sobriety* of Religion; and can give as many *Signs* of it, Equally at least (to speak modestly) as any of our *Dissenters*, of what Denomination soever.

IX. And I hope, that what I have said will, at least, hinder the *Succession* of the *Bishops* from the *Apostles*, to be any *Objection* against them: And they being possess'd moreover of all the other *Pretences* of our *Dissenters*, the Ballance must needs lie on their side, and *security* can only be with them; because ther is *doubt* in all the other *Schemes* of the *Dissenters*, if what I have said can amount but to a *Doubt*. If the want of *Succession* and *outward Commission*, upon which *Christ* and His *Apostles*, and the whole *Christian Church*, in all Ages, till the last *Century*; and in all Places, even at this Day, except some *Corners* in the *West*; and the *Mosaical* Institution before them, did, by the Express Command of God, lay so great a stress; if all this make but a *Doubt* (it is strange that it shou'd, at least, that it shou'd not) in the mind of any considering Persons; then can they not, with *Security*, Communicate with any of our *Dissenters*; because, if he that *Eateth* and *Doubteth* is Damned, much more he that shall do so in *Religious* matters; wherein chiefly this Rule must stand, that *whatsoever is not of Faith is sin*.

Rom. xiv. 23.

X. But now, to argue a little, *ad hominem*, suppose that the *Succession* of our *Bishops* were lost; and suppose, what the *Quakers* and some others wou'd have, that the Thread being broke, we must cast a new knot, and begin again, and make an Establishment amongst our selves, the best we can. Well, When this is done, ought not that *Establishment* to be preserv'd? Ought every one to break in upon it, without just cause? Shou'd every

one

one take upon him (or *her*) to *Preach*, or *Baptize*, contrary to the *Rules* Eſtabliſh'd? This, I think, no *Society* of Men will allow; For, the Members of a *Society* muſt be ſubject to the *Rules* of the *Society*, otherwiſe it is no *Society*: And the *Quakers* of *Grace-church-ſtreet* Communion have contended as Zealouſly for this compliance as any.

Now then, ſuppoſe that the conſcientious *Quakers* to whom I ſpeak, ſhou'd lay no ſtreſs at all upon the *Succeſſion* of our *Biſhops*; and conſider our *Conſtitution* no otherwiſe than of an *Eſtabliſhment* by agreement amongſt our ſelves; yet even ſo, by their own Confeſſion, while they can find no fault with our *Doctrine* or *Worſhip*, they ought not to make a *Schiſm* in this *Conſtitution*, which they found *Eſtabliſhed*; and they ought to return to it; and if a new *Knot* was caſt upon the broken *Thread* of *Succeſſion*, at the *Reformation* from *Popery*, that *Knot* ought not to be un-loſed, without apparent and abſolute *Neceſſity*; left if we caſt new *Knots* every Day, we ſhall have no *Thread* left *un-knotted*; and expoſe our ſelves to the Deriſion of the common Adverſary.

XI. Conſider the grievous Sin of *Schiſm* and *Diviſion*; it is no leſs than the Rending of *Chriſt's Body*; and therefore *great Things* ought to be born, rather than run into it; even *all things*, except only that which is *apparently ſinful*; and that by the *Expreſs words* of *Scripture*; and not from our own Imaginations, tho' never ſo ſtrong. And tho' ther are ſome Imperfections in our *Reformation*, as to *Diſcipline*, and all the *High Places* are not yet taken away (the Lord, of His Mercy, quickly remove them) yet I will be bold to ſay, that in our *Doctrine*, *Worſhip*, and *Hierarchy*, nothing can be objected that is contrary to the *Rule* of *Holy Scripture*, or any thing Enjoyn'd, which is *There* Forbid to be done: And nothing leſs can warrant any *Schiſm* againſt our *Church*.

XII. Now, to come to a Concluſion, upon the whole matter. If you cannot get *Baptiſm* as you wou'd have it, take it as you can get it. If you cannot find Men of ſuch *Perſonal* Excellencies as the *Apoſtles*, take thoſe who have the ſame *Commiſſion* which they had, deriv'd down to them by regular *Ordination*; who *Reform'd* from *Popery*, and have been the *Eſtabliſhed Church* of this *Nation*, ever ſince: And moreover are as un-exceptionable, in their *Lives* and *Converſations*, as any others. Theſe are all the ſecurities you can have (without new *Miracles*) for Receiving the *Sacraments* from Proper hands. And therefore ther is no doubt but God will accept of your *Obedience* in Receiving them from such hands; much rather than your *Disobedience* of His Command to be *Baptized*, because you are not pleas'd with those whom His Providence has, at this Day, left in the Execution of His Commission to *Baptize*; as if the weakness of His *Minister* cou'd obstruct the Operations of His *Spirit*, in making good His part of the Covenant, which He has promised.

XIII. Ther is an Objection against *Baptism*, which is not worth an Answer; but that I wou'd condescend to the meanest, and leave nothing behind which might be a stumbling block to any.

I have heard it urg'd, that ther is no visible Effects seen by our *Baptisms*; that Men remain *wicked* and *loose* notwithstanding; and therefore some do conclude that ther is no vertue in *Baptism*.

Answ. To make this Argument of any force, it must be prov'd that *none* do receive any Benefit by it. For, if *some* do receive Benefit by it, and *others* do not, this must be charg'd upon the *Disposition* of the *Recipient*; according to the known Rule, that *whatsoever is receiv'd, is receiv'd according to the disposition of the Receiver.* Thus the same *Meat* is turn'd into *good Nourishment* in an healthy, and into *noxious Humors* in a *vitiated Stomach*. *Simon Magus* receiv'd no Benefit by his *Baptism*; and after the *Sop* the *Devil* entred into *Judas*; yet the other *Apostles* receiv'd great Benefit by it: To some it is the favour of *Life*, even the Communion of *Christ's Body* and *Blood*; to others of *Condemnation*, who *discern not the Lord's Body* in it, but receive it as a common thing: Therefore we are commanded to *examine* our selves, to *prepare* our *Hearts* for the *worthy* Receiving of it.

1 Cor. x. 16.
c. xi. 29.

v. 28.

But some say, as the *Jews* to *Christ*, *shew us a sign*: They wou'd have some *Miraculous* Effects, immediately to appear. These are Ignorant of the Operations of the *spirit*; and to these I say, in the words of *Christ*. Joh. iii. 8. *The wind bloweth where it listeth, and thou hearest the sound thereof, but canst not tell whence it cometh or whither it goeth; so is every one that is born of the Spirit.* It works *silently*, but *powerfully*; and its *Progress*, like the *growing* of our *Bodies*, is not all at once, but by Degrees; whose *motion* is Imperceptible to humane Eyes.

The true use that is to be made of this *Objection*, that so few (and yet they are not *few* who) receive the Inestimable Benefits which are convey'd in the *Sacraments* of *Christ*'s Institution, is this,

To

To take the greater Care, and the more Earnestly to beg the Assistance of God's *Grace*, to *fit* and *prepare* us, for the *worthy* Receiving of them; but by no means to neglect them: For those who *refused* to come to the *Supper* were Rejected, as well as he who came without a *Wedding Garment*.

A SUPPLEMENT.

THE stress of this *Discourse* being Founded upon *Episcopacy*; and long *Quotations* being improper in so short a method of Argument as I have taken; to supply that Defect, and, at the same time, to make it easier to the Reader, I have added, by way of *Supplement*, a short *Index* or *Collection* of *Authorities*, in the first 450 Years after *Christ*, for *Episcopacy*, with respect to the *Presbyterian* Pretences, of making a *Bishop* all one with a *Presbyter*, at least with one of their *Moderators*: And, in the next place, I have shewn the sense of the *Reformation*, as to *Episcopacy*. Take them as follows.

Some Authorities for Episcopacy, *as* distinct *from and* Superior *to* Presbytery, *taken out of the* Fathers *and* Councils, *in the first* Four Hundred and Fifty Years after Christ.

Anno Domini 70. St. *Clement* Bishop of *Rome*, and *Martyr*, of whom mention is made *Phil.* iv. 3. in his 1st. *Epist.* to the *Corinthians*, N. 42. p. 89. of the Edition at *Oxford*, 1677.

The Apostles having Preached the Gospel, thro' Regions and Cities, did Constitute the first Fruits of them, having prov'd them by the Spirit, to be *Bishops* and *Deacons* of those who shou'd

Κατὰ χώρας ἂν ἐ πόλεις κηρύσσοντες, καὶ θρεύνον τὰς Ἀπαρχὰς αὐτῶν, δοκιμάσαντες τῷ πνεύματι, εἰς Ἐπισκόπους καὶ Διακόνους τῶν μελλόντων πιστεύειν, καὶ ἕτο ἐ καινῶς, ἐκ γὰρ δὴ πολλῶν χρόνων ἐγέγραπτο

believe;

believe; and this, not as a new thing, for many Ages before it was written concerning *Bishops* and *Deacons*; for, thus faith the Scripture, in a certain place, *I will constitute their* Bishops *in Righteousness, and their* Deacons *in Faith.*

Is. lx 17.

What wonder is it then, that those who were Intrusted by God, in Christ, with this Commission, shou'd Constitute those before spoke of?

ibid. n. 44. And the *Apostles* knew by the Lord *Jesus Christ*, that Contests wou'd arise concerning the *Episcopal* Name (or Order) and for this Cause, having perfect fore knowledge (of these things) they did Ordain those whom we have mention'd before; and moreover, did Establish the Constitution, that other approved Men shou'd succeed those who Dy'd, in their Office and Ministry.

Therefore those that were Constituted by Them, or afterwards by other approved Men, with the Consent of all the Church, and have Administred to the Flock of Christ unblamably, with Humility and Quietness, without all stain of filth or naughtiness; and have carry'd a good Report, of a long time, from all Men, I think cannot, without great Injustice, be turn'd out of their Office: For, it will be no small sin to us, if we thrust those from their Bishopricks who have Holily and without Blame offer'd our Gifts (and Praiers to God.) Blessed are those

Priests

Priests who are happily Dead, for they are not afraid of being Ejected out of the Places in which they are Constituted. For, I understand that you have Depriv'd some, from their Ministry, who behaved themselves un-re-provable amongst you.

Par. 40. To the *High-Priest* his proper Offices were appointed; the *Priests* had their proper Order, and the *Levites* their peculiar Services, or *Deaconships*; and the *Lay-men*, what was proper for *Lay-men*.

Τῷ γὰρ Ἀρχιερεῖ ἴδιαι λειτουργίαι δεδομέναι εἰσὶ, & τοῖς Ἱερεῦσιν ἴδιος ὁ τόπος προςτέτακται, & Λευίταις ἴδιαι διακονίαι ἐπίκεινται· λαϊκὸς ἄνθρωπος τοῖς λαϊκοῖς προςτάγμασι δέδεται.

This, as before shewn, St. *Clement* apply'd to the Distribution of Orders in the *Christian* Church; *Bishops*, *Priests*, and *Deacons*. And the Office of the *Levites*, is here call'd by the Word Διακονία i. e. the Office of *Deacons*.

A.D. 71. St. *Ignatius*, a Glorious Martyr of *Christ*, was Constituted, by the Apostles, *Bishop* of *Antioch*, and did thereby think that he succeeded them (as all other *Bishops* do) in their full *Apostolical* Office. Thence he salutes the Church of the *Trallians*, in the *Fulness* of the *Apostolical Character*; and in his Epistle he says to them,

Be subject to your Bishop as to the Lord——

Τῷ Ἐπισκόπῳ ὑποτάσσεσθε ὡς τῷ Κυρίῳ.

And to the *Presbyters*, as to the *Apostles* of *Christ*——Likewise the *Deacons* also, being *Ministers* of the Mysteries of *Christ*, ought to please in all things.--Without these ther is no *Church* of the Elect.-He is without, who does any thing without the *Bishop*, and *Presbyters*, and *Deacons*; and such an one is Defiled in his Conscience.

Καὶ τοῖς Πρεσβυτέροις, ὡς Ἀποστόλοις Ἰησοῦ Χριστοῦ—Δεῖ δὲ & τοὺς Διακόνους ὄντας μυστηρίων Χριστοῦ Ἰησοῦ κατὰ πάντα τρόπον ἀρέσκειν· τούτων Ἐκκλησία καλεῖται.—ὁ δὲ ἐκτὸς ὢν, οὗτος & χωρὶς τοῦ Ἐπισκόπου, & τῶν Πρεσβυτέρων, καὶ τῶν Διακόνων τι πράσσων, ὁ τοιοῦτος μεμίαντ τῇ συνειδήσει.

In his *Epist. to the* Magnesians, he tells them, That they ought not to despise their *Bishop* for his youth, but to pay him all manner

Καὶ ὑμῖν δὲ πρέπει μὴ καταφρονεῖν τῆς ἡλικίας τοῦ Ἐπισκόπου, ἀλλὰ κατὰ γνώμην Θεοῦ πατρὸς πᾶσαν ἐντροπὴν αὐτῷ ἀπονέμειν καθὼς

of Reverence, according to the Commandment of God the Father. And as I know that your Holy Presbyters do———

Therefore as *Christ* did nothing without the *Father*, so neither do ye, whether *Presbyter*, *Deacon*, or *Laick*, any thing without the *Bishop*.

Some indeed call him *Bishop*; yet do all things without him; but these seem not to me to have a good Conscience, but rather to be Hypocrites and Scorners.

I Exhort you to do all things in the same mind of God, the *Bishop* Presiding in the Place of *God*, and the *Presbyters* in room of the *College* of the *Apostles*; and the *Deacons*, most beloved to me, who are intrusted with the Ministry of *Jesus Christ*.

He directs his Epistle *to the Church at Philadelphia, to those* who were in Unity with their *Bishop* and *Presbyters* and *Deacons*.

And says to them, in his Epistle, *That* as many as are of *Christ*, these are with the *Bishop*; and those who shall Repent, and Return to the Unity of the *Church*, being made worthy of *Jesus Christ*, shall partake of Eternal Salvation in the Kingdom of *Christ*.

My Brethren, be not deceived, if any shall follow him that makes a *Schism*, he shall not Inherit the Kingdom of God.

I Exhort you to partake of the one *Eucharist*; for ther is one *Body* of the Lord *Jesus*, and one *Blood* of His, which was shed for us; and one *Cup*——and one *Altar*, so ther is one *Bishop*, with his *Presbytery*, and the *Deacons*, my Fellow Servants.

Give heed to the *Bishop*, and to the *Presbytery*, and to the *Deacons*---Without the *Bishop* do nothing.

In his Epistle to the Smyrneans, he says, *Flee Divisions as the beginning of Evils.* All of them follow their *Bishops*, as *Jesus Christ* the *Father*; and the *Presbyters*, as the *Apostles*, and Reverence the *Deacons* as the Institution of *God.* Let no man do any thing of what appertains to the *Church*, without the *Bishop*, Let that *Sacrament* be judg'd Effectual and Firm, which is Difpenced by the *Bishop*, or him to whom the *Bishop* has Commited it. Wherever the *Bishop* is, there let the *People* be; as where *Christ* is, there the *Heavenly Host* is gathered together. It is not lawful, without the *Bishop*, either to *Baptize*, or celebrate the *Offices*: But what He approves of, according to the good Pleasure of God, that is firm and safe, and so we do every thing securely.

I salute your most worthy *Bishop*, your venerable *Presbytery*, and the *Deacons* my Fellow Servants.

In his Epistle to St. Policarp, Bishop *of* Smyrna, *and* Martyr, *who, together with himself, was* Disciple *to St.* John *the* Apostle, *and* Evangelist. *He gives these Directions.*

If any can remain in Chastity, to the glory of the Body of the Lord, let him remain without Boasting, if he Boast, he Perishes; and if he pretends to know more than the

Bishop,

Bishop, he is corrupted. It is the duty both of Men and Women that Marry, to be joyn'd together by the Approbation of the *Bish*. that the Marriage may be in the Lord, and not according to our own Lusts, Glory of God.

τοῖς γαμοῦσι, καὶ τ̅ γαμούσαις, μ̅τ̅ γνώμης τ̅ Ἐπισκόπȣ τ̅ν ἕνωσιν ποιεῖσθαι, ἵνα ὁ γάμȣ ᾖ κτ̅ Κύριον, καὶ μὴ κατ' ἐπιθυμίαν· πάντα εἰς τιμὴν Θεȣ γινέσθω.

Let all things be done to the Glory of God.

Give heed to your *Bishop*, that God may Harken unto you: My Soul for theirs, who subject themselves under the Obedience of their *Bishop*, *Presbyters*, and *Deacons*, and let me take my Lot with them in the Lord.

Τῷ Ἐπισκόπῳ προσέχετε, ἵνα καὶ ὁ Θεὸς ὑμῖν. ἀντίψυχον ἐγὼ τῶν ὑποτασσομένων Ἐπισκόπῳ, Πρεσβυτέροις, Διακόνοις· μετ' αὐτῶν μοι τὸ μέρος γένοιτο ἔχειν ἐν τῷ Θεῷ.

And he says to Bishop *Polycarp*, *Let nothing be done without thy sentence and approbation*.

Μηδὲν ἄνευ γνώμης σȣ γινέσθω.

A.D. 180. St. *Irenæus*, Bishop of *Lyons*, in *France*, who was Disciple of St. *Polycarp*; he flourish'd about the year of *Christ* 180.

We can reckon those *Bishops*, who have been Constituted by the *Apostles*, and their Successors all the way to our times. And if the Apostles knew hidden Mysteries, they wou'd certainly deliver them chiefly to those, to whom they committed the Churches themselves; and whom they left their own Successors, and in the same Place of Government as themselves. ---We have the Successions of the Bishops, to whom the Apostolick Church in every place was committed. All these (*Hereticks*) are much later than the Bishops, to whom the Apostles did deliver the Churches.

Advers. Hæreses. l. 3. *c.* 3.

Habemus munerare qui ab Apostolis Instituti sunt Episcopi in Ecclesiis, & successores eorum usque ad nos. Et si Recondita mysteria Scissent Apostoli, vel his maxime traderent ea, quibus etiam ipsas Ecclesias committebant; quos & successores relinquebant, suum ip'orum locum Magisterii tradentes. lib. 4. c. 63. *Habemus successiones Episcoporum quibus Apostolicam quæ in unoquoque loco est Ecclesiam tradiderunt.* l. 5. c. 20. *Omnes enim ii (Hæretici) valde Posteriores sunt, quam Episcopi, quibus Apostoli tradiderunt Ecclesias.*

The true Knowledge is the Doctrin of the Apostles, and the Ancient State of the Church, through the whole World, and the Character of the Body

L. 4. c. 6. *Agnitio vera est, Apostolorum Doctrina, & Antiquus Ecclesiæ status, in universo Mundo, & Character Corporis Christi secundum successiones Episcoporum,*

of Christ, according to the Succession of the Bishops, to whom they committed the Church that is in every Place ; and which has Descended even unto us.

quibus illi eam quæ in unoquoq; loco est Ecclesiam tradiderunt, quæ pervenit usque ad nos.

Tertullian, A.D. 203. of the Prescription of Hereticks. A.D. 203.

c. 32. Let them produce the Original of their Churches; let them shew the Order of their Bishops, that by their Succession, deduc'd from the beginning, we may see whether their first Bishop had any of the Apostles or Apostolical Men, who did likewise persevere with the Apostles, for his Founder and Predecessor. For, thus the Apostolical Churches do derive their Succession: As the Church of *Smyrna* from *Polycarp,* whom *John* (the Apostle) placed there: The Church of *Rome* from *Clement,* who was, in like manner, ordain'd by *Peter*: And so the other Churches can produce those Constituted in their *Bishopricks* by the *Apostles.*

Edant ergo Origines Ecclesiarum suarum; evolvant ordinem Episcoporum suorum, ita ut per successiones ab initio decurrentem, ut primus ille Episcopus aliquem ex Apostolis, vel Apostolicis viris, qui tamen cum Apostolis perseveraverit, habuerit Auctorem & Antecessorem. Hoc enim modo Ecclesiæ Apostolicæ census suos deferunt: sicut Smyrnæorum *Ecclesia* Polycarpum *ab* Johanne *conlocatum refert ; sicut* Romanorum, Clementem, *à* Petro *ordinatum itidem, Perinde utique & Ceteræ exhibent quos ab Apostolis in Episcopatum Constitutos Apostolici seminis traduces habeant.*

c. 36. Reckon over the Apostolical Churches, where the very Chairs of the Apostles do yet Preside in their own Places. At *Corinth, Philippi, Ephesus, Thessalonica,* &c.

Percurre Ecclesias Apostolicas, apud quas ipsæ adhuc Cathedræ Apostolorum suis locis Præsident. Corinthi, Philippi, Ephesiis, Thessalonica, *&c.*

Of Baptism, *c.* 17.

The *High-Priest,* who is the *Bishop,* has the Power of conferring Baptism; and under him the *Presbyters* and *Deacons*; but not without the Authority of the *Bishop.*

Dandi (Baptismum) jus habet summus sacerdos, qui est Episcopus, *dehinc* Presbyteri *&* Deaconi, *non tamen sine* Episcopi *Authoritate.*

Origen, Names the distinct Orders of *Bishop, Presby-*

A.D. 220. *Origenis Comment. in* A.D. 220. Matt. Rothomagi 1668. Gr. Lat. p. 255

ter, and *Deacon*. Such a Bishop (*says he, speaking of one who sought vain Glory*, &c.) doth not desire a good Work——and the same is to be said of *Presbyters* and *Deacons*.——The *Bishops* and *Presbyters* who have the Chief Place among the People.——The *Bishop* is called *Prince* in the *Churches*: And speaking of the Irreligious *Clergy*, he directs it to them, whether *Bishops, Presbyters,* or *Deacons*.

ὁ γὲν ζῶν ζῶς Ἐπίσκοπ@ ὰ καλοῦ ἔργου ἐπιθυμεῖ —— τὸ ἢ αὐτὸ καὶ περὶ πρεσβυτέρων—— καὶ Διακόνων ἐρῆ. *Ibid.* p. 443. εἰ ἢ ὡς πρεςβεύθει εἰας πεπιςευμένοι τᾶ λαῶ Ἐπίσκοποι καὶ πρεσβύτεροι. —— p. 420 ὁ ἢ ἡγέμ@, ἔτω ἢ οἶμα) ὀνομάζειν τ᾽ καλέμθον ἐν τ᾽ Ἐκκλησίαις Ἐπίσκοπον. —— p. 442. Ἐπισκόποις, ἢ πρεσβυτέροις ἢ Διακόνοις.

A.D. 240.

St. *Cyprian* Archbishop of *Carthage*, A. D. 240.

Our Lord, whose Commands we ought to Reverence and Obey, being about to Constitute the *Episcopal* Honour, and the Frame of His Church, said to Peter, *Thou art Peter,*&c. From thence the Order of *Bishops* and Constitution of the Church does descend, by the line of Succession, thro' all Times and Ages; that the Church shou'd be built upon the *Bishops*.——It is Establish'd by the Divine Law, that every Act of the Church shou'd be Govern'd by the Bishop.

Edit. Oxon. Epist. XXXIII. Lapsis.

Dominus noster, cujus Præcepta metuere & observare debemus, Episcopi honorem & Ecclesiæ suæ Rationem disponens, in Evangelio loquitur & dicit Petro, Ego dico tibi quia tu es Petrus*, &c. Inde per temporum & successionum vices Episcoporum Ordinatio & Ecclesiæ Ratio decurrit, ut Ecclesia super Episcopos Constituatur——Divina Lege fundatum est, ut omnis actus Ecclesiæ per Episcopum Gubernetur.*

To Cornelius, *then Bishop of Rome.*

We ought chiefly (my Brother) to Endeavour to keep that Unity which was Enjoyn'd by our Lord and His Apostles to us their Successors, to be carefully observ'd by us.

The *Deacons* ought to remember that it was the *Lord* who chose the *Apostles*, that is, the *Bishops*.

Christ said to the *Apostles*, and by that, to all *Bishops* or *Go-*

Ep. XLV. Cornelio.

Hoc enim vel maxime, Frater, & laboramus & laborare debemus, ut Unitatem à Domino, & per Apostolos nobis Successoribus traditam, quantum possumus obtinere curemus.

Ep. III. Rogatiano.

Meminisse autem Diaconi debent quoniam Apostolos, id est Episcopos Dominus Elegit.

Ep. LXVI. Florentio.

Dixit Christus ad Apostolos, ac

vernors

vernors of His Church, who succeed the *Apostles*, by vicarious Ordination, and are in their stead, *He that heareth you, heareth me.*

For from hence do Schisms and Heresies arise, and have arisen, while the *Bishop*, who is One, and *Governour* of the Church, by a proud Presumption is Despis'd; and that Man who is Honour'd as Worthy by God, is accounted unworthy by Man.

Nor are Heresies sprung up, or Schisms arisen from any other Fountain than from hence, that Obedience is not paid to the *Priest* of God; and that ther is not one *Priest* at a time in the Church, and one Judge for the time in the Place of Christ. To whom if the whole Fraternity did obey, according to the Divine Oeconomy, none wou'd dare to move any thing against the *Sacerdotal Colledge*----It is necessary that the *Bishops* shou'd exert their Authority with full Vigor---But if it is so, that we are afraid of the Boldness of the most Profligat; and that which these wicked Men cannot compass by the Methods of Truth and Equity, if they can accomplish by their Rashness and Despair, then is ther an end of the *Episcopal* Authority, and of their *Sublime* and *Divine Power* in Governing of the *Church*. Nor

per hoc, ad omnes Præpositos, qui Apostolis vicaria ordinatione succedunt, Qui vos audit, me audit.——

Ibid.

Inde enim Schismata & Hæreses ortæ & oriuntur, anm Episcopus qui unus est, & Ecclesiæ Præ-est, superba Præsumptione contemnitur, & homo dignatione Dei honoratus, Indignus hominibus judicatur.

Ep. LIX. Cornelio.

Neque enim aliunde Hæreses obortæ sunt, aut nata sunt schismata, quam inde quod Sacerdoti Dei non obtemperatur; *nec unus in Ecclesia ad tempus* Sacerdos, *& ad tempus* Judex vice Christi *cogitatur: Cui si secundum Magisteria Divina obtemperaret Fraternitas universa, nemo adversus* sacerdotum Collegium *quicquam moveret* ——— *vigore pleno* Episcopos *agere oportet* — *quod si ita res est ut Nequissimorum timeatur Audacia, & quod Mali vere atque equitate non possunt, Temeritate & Desperatione perficiant; actum est de* Episcopatus *vigore, & de Ecclesiæ gubernanda sublimi ac Divina Potestate. Nec Christiani ultra aut durare aut esse jam possumus, si ad hoc ventum est, ut Perditorum Minas atque Insidias pertimescamus* —

can we remain *Christians* any longer, if it is come to this, that we shou'd be afraid of the *Threats*, and *Snares* of the *wicked*---

---The Adversary of Christ, and Enemy of His Church, for this end strikes at the *Bishop* or *Ruler* of the *Church*, with all his Malice, that the *Governor* being taken away, he might Ravage the more Violently and Cruelly upon the Ship-wreck of the Church---

---Christi Adversarius & Ecclesiæ ejus Inimicus, ad hoc Ecclesiæ Præpositum sua Infestatione persequitur, ut Gubernatore sublato, atrocius atque violentius circa Ecclesiæ Naufragia grassetur.---

Is Honour then given to God, when the Divine Majesty and Censure is so Despised, that these Sacrilegious Persons say; do not think of the Wrath of God; be not afraid of His Judgment, do not knock at the Door of the Church; but without any Repentance, or Confession of their Crime, Despising the Authority of their *Bishops*, and trampling it under their feet, a False Peace is Preach'd to be had from the *Presbyters* (*Scilicet*) in their taking upon them to Admit those that were *Fallen* into *Communion*, or the *Peace* of the *Church*, without the Allowance of the *Bishop*.

Honor ergo datur Deo, quando sic Dei Majestas & Censura Contemnitur---- ut proponatur à Sacrilegis atque dicatur; ne Ita cogitetur Dei, ne timeatur Judicium Domini, ne pulsetur ad Ecclesiam Christi; sed sublata Pœnitentia, nec ulla Exomologesi Criminis facta, Despectis Episcopis atque Calcatis, Pax à Presbyteris verbis fallacibus Prædicetur?

ibid.

They imitate the coming of Anti-Christ now approaching.

Antichristi jam propinquantis adventum Imitantur.

Ep. LXXX. Successo.

Valerian (the Emperor) wrote to the Senate, that the *Bishops*, and the *Presbyters*, and the *Deacons* shou'd be prosecuted.

Rescripsisse Valerianum ad Senatum, ut Episcopi, & Presbyteri, & Diacones in continenti animadvertantur.

Firmilianus Cypriano. Ep. LXXV. p. 225.

The Power of Remitting Sins, was given to the *Apostles*, and to the *Bishops*, who have succeeded them by a vicarious Ordination.

Potestas ergo Peccatorum remittendorum Apostolis data est.--- & Episcopis qui eis Ordinatione vicaria successerunt.

What

What Danger ought we to fear from the Displeasure of God, when some *Presbyters*, neither mindful of the Gospel, nor of their own Station in the Church, neither regarding the future Judgment of God, nor the *Bishop* who is set over them; which was never done under our Predecessors, with the Contempt and Neglect of their *Bishop*, do arrogate all unto themselves? I cou'd bear with the Contempt of our *Episcopal* Authority, but ther is now no room left for Dissembling, &c.

Ep. XVI. p 36. Cyprianus Presbyteris & Diaconibus.

Quod enim periculum metuere non debemus de offensa Domini; quando aliqui de Presbyteris, nec Evangelii, nec Loci sui memores, sed neque futurum Domini Judicium, neque sibi præpositum Episcopum cogitantes, quod nunquam omnino sub Antecessoribus factum est, cum Contumelia & Contemptu Præpositi totum sibi vendicent? Contumeliam Episcopatus nostri dissimulare & ferre possum———— sed dissimulandi nunc locus non est.

Optatus Milevitanus, Bishop of *Mileve*, or *Mela* in *Numidia* in *Africa*. A. D. 365.   A.D. 365.

In his 2d. Book against *Parmenian*. The Church has her several Members, *Bishops, Presbyters, Deacons*, and the Company of the Faithful.

l. 2. Contra Parmenianum. *Certa Membra sua habet Ecclesia*, Episcopos, Presbyteros, Diaconos, *& turbam Fidelium.*

You found in the Church, *Deacons, Presbyters, Bishops*, you have made them *Lay-men*; acknowledge that you have Subverted Souls.

Invenistis Diaconos, Presbyteros, Episcopos. *fecistis Laicos; agnoscite vos animas evertisse.*

St. *Ambrose* Bishop of *Milan*. A. D. 370. upon *Eph.* iv. 11. *Speaking of the several Orders of the Church. And he gave some* Apostles, and some Prophets, and Evangelists, &c. Says, that by the *Apostles* there were meant the *Bishops*; by *Prophets*, the Expounders of the *Scriptures*; and by the *Evangelists*, the *Deacons*. But says that they all met in the *Bishop*; for that he was the *Chief Priest*, that is,

Quosdam dedit Apostolos, quosdam Prophetas, &c. *Apostoli*, Episcopi *sunt: Prophetæ* Explanatores *sunt Scripturum sicut* Agabus---*Evangelistæ* Diaconi *sunt, sicut fuit* Philippus————*.*Nam in Episcopo *omnes ordines sunt; quia* Princeps Sacerdos *est, hoc est,* Princeps *est* Sacerdotum, *&* Propheta, *&* Evangelista, *& cætera adimplenda officia Ecclesiæ in Ministerio Fidelium.* A.D. 370.

(says

(*says he*) the *Prince* of the *Priests*, and both Prophet and *Evangelist*, to supply all the Offices of the Church for the Ministry of the Faithful.

And upon 1 *Cor.* xii. 28. says that *Christ* Constituted the *Apostles Head* in the *Church*; and that these are the *Bishops*.

Caput in Ecclesia Apostolos posuit———*Ipsi sunt* Episcopi.

And upon *v.* 29. *are all Apostles?* i. e. all are not *Apostles*. This is true (*says he,*) because in the Church ther is but one *Bishop*.

Verum est, quia in Ecclesia unus Episcopus *est*.

And because all things are from one God the Father, therefore hath He appointed that one *Bishop* shou'd Preside over Each Church.

Quia ab uno Deo Patre sunt omnia, singulos Episcopos, singulis Ecclesiis Præ-esse Decrevit.

In his Book of the *Dignity* of the *Priesthood*, c. 3. he *says*, That ther is nothing in this World to be found more *Excellent* than the *Priests*, nothing more *Sublime* than the *Bishops*.

De Dignat. Sacerdot. c. 3. ut ostenderemus nihil esse in hoc seculo Excellentius Sacerdotibus, *nihil Sublimius* Episcopis *reperiri.*

And speaking of what was Incumbent upon the several Orders of the *Church*, he does plainly distinguish them: For, says he, in the same place;

God does require one thing from a *Bishop*, another from a *Presbyter*, another from a *Deacon*, and another from a *Lay-man*.

Aliud est enim quod ab Episcopo *requirit Deus & aliud quod à* Presbytero, *& aliud quod à* Deacono, *& aliud quod à* Laico.

A.D. 380.

St. *Jerom*, A. D. 380. In his Comment upon the Ep. to *Titus*.

When it began to be said, *I am of Paul, I of Apollos*, &c. and every one thought that those whom he Baptized, belong'd to himself, and not to Christ; it was Decreed thro' *The whole Earth*, that one Chosen from among the *Presbyters* shou'd be set over the rest, that the Seeds of *Schism* might be taken away.

Postquam unusquisque eos quos Baptizabat suos putabat esse non Christi, IN TOTO ORBE *Decretum est, ut unus de* Presbyteris *Electus superponeretur Cæteris, ut Schismatum semina tollerentur.*

In his *Epist.* to *Evagrius.*

From *Mark* the *Evangelist* to *Heraclas*, and *Dionysius* the *Bishops*, the *Presbyters* of *Egypt* have

A Marco *Evangelista ad* Heraclum *usq; ad* Dionysium *Episcopos,* Presbyteri *Ægypti semper unum ex se Electum, in Cesiori Gra-*
always

(47)

always chosen out one from among themselves, whom having plac'd in an higher Degree than the rest, they called their Bishop.

He that is Advanc'd, is Advanc'd from less to greater.

The Greatness of Riches, or the Humility of Poverty does not make a *Bishop* greater or less, seeing *all* of them are the *Successors* of the *Apostles*.

That we may know the Apostolical Oeconomy to be taken from the Pattern of the Old Testament, the same that *Aaron*, and his *Sons*, and the *Levites* were in the *Temple*, the *Bishops*, *Presbyters*, and *Deacons* are in the *Church* of *Christ*.

To *Nepotianus*.

Be subject to your *Bishop* or *Chief-Priest*; and receive him as the Father of your Soul.

Against the *Luciferians*.

The safety of the Ch. depends upon the Dignity of the *High-Priest*, to whom unless a sort of absolute and eminent Power be given above all, ther will be as many *Schisms* in the *Church* as ther are *Priests*. Thence it is, that without the Command of the *Bishop*, neither a *Presbyter*, nor a *Deacon*, have Power to Baptize——And the *Bishop* is to impose his Hands upon those who are Baptized by *Presbyters* or *Deacons*, for the Invocation of the Holy Spirit.

And Comforting *Heliodorus*, a *Bishop*, upon the Death of *Nepo-*

dis collocatum Episcopum *Nominabant.*

Qui provehitur, à Minori ad Majus provehitur.

Potentia Divitiarum & Paupertatis Humilitas, sublimiorum vel inferiorem Episcopum *non facit, Ceterum Omnes* Apostolorum *Successores sunt.*

Ut sciamus Traditiones Apostolicas sumpt.is de veteri Testamento: Quod Aaron, *& Filii ejus atq; Levitæ in* Templo *fuerunt, hoc sibi* Episcopi, Presbyteri, *& Deaconi, vendicent in Ecclesia.*

Ad Nepotianum.

Esto sujectus Pontifici *tuo; & quasi animi* Parentem *suscipe.*

Advers. Luciferianos.

Ecclesiæ salus in summi Sacerdotis *Dignitate pendet, cui nisi exors quædam & ab omnibus Eminens detur Potestas, tot in Ecclesia efficientur Schismata quot Sacerdotes. Inde venit, ut sine* Episcopi *jussione neque* Presbyter *neque* Diaconus *jus habeant Baptizandi——Ad eos qui per* Presbyteros *&* Diaconos *Baptizati sunt,* Episcopus *ad Invocationem sancti Spiritus manum Impositurus excurrat.*

Epitaphium Nepotiani *à* Heliodorum. *Episcopum venerebatur——*
tian-

tian his **Presbyter** and his Nephew, he Commends *Nepotian* in that he *Reverenc'd his Bishop*. He Honour'd *Heliodorus*, in publick as his *Bishop*, at home as his Father, and *Co-equals*, he was the first in and Co-equals, he was the first in	*In publico* Episcopum, *domi Patrem noverat. —Inter* Presbyteros *& Co-æquales, primus in opere,* &c. But among his Presbyters his Vocation; &c.
Upon the 60th. of *Isa*. He calls the future *Bishops, Princes* of the Church.	*Principes futuros Ecclesiæ* Episcopos *Nominavit*.
Of the Ecclesiastical Writers. Concerning *James*.	*In script. Ecclesiast. De* Jacobo.
James, after the Passion of our Lord, was immediatly, by the Apostles, ordained Bishop of *Jerusalem*. The like he tells of the first Bishops of other Places.	*Jacobus post Passionem Domini statim ab Apostolis Hierosolimorum* Episcopus *est ordinatus*.
Epist. 54. against *Montanus*.	*Ep.* 54, *contra* Montanum.
With us the *Bishops* hold the Place of the *Apostles*.	*Apud nos* Apostolorum *locum* Episcopi *tenent*.
A.D. 420. St. Augustine *Bishop* of *Hippo* in Africa, A. D. 420. Epistle 42.	
The Root of the Christian Society is diffus'd throughout the World, in a sure Propagation, by the Seats of the *Apostles*, and the Succession of the *Bishops*.	*Radix Christianæ Societatis per sedes* Apostolorum *& Successiones* Episcoporum *certa per orbem Propagatione diffunditur*.
Quest. veter. & novi Test. N. 97.	
Ther is none but knows that our Saviour did Constitute *Bishops* in the Churches; for before He Ascended into Heaven, He laid His Hands upon the *Apostles* and Ordained them *Bishops*.	*Nemo ignorat Salvatorem* Episcopos *Ecclesiis Instituisse; Ipse enim priusquam Cœlos Ascenderet, Imponens Manus* Apostolis *ordinavit eos*.Episcopos, *Quod dixit* Clarus *à Muscula in Concilio* Carthag. *Repetit* August. *de Baptismo contra* Donatist.
l. 7. c. 43. The Sentence of our Lord Jesus Christ is clear, who sent His Apostles, and gave to *Them alone* that Power which He had Received from His Fa-	*Manifesta est sententia Domini nostri* Jesu Christi *Apostolos suos mittentis, & ipsis solis Potestatem à Patre sibi traditam permittentis; quibus nos ther;*

Father; to whom we have Succeeded, Governing the Church of God by the same Power.

Ep. 162. *speaking of the* Bishops *being call'd* Angels. *Rev.* 2. *he says*, By the voice of God, the Governour of the Church is Praised, under the Name of an *Angel*.

Of the words of our Lord, Serm. 24.

If He said to the Apostles alone, *he that despiseth you, despiseth me*, then despise us: But if those words of His come down. even unto us, and that He has Called us, and Constituted us in their Place, see that you do not despise us.

Against *Faustus*.

We embrace the Holy Scripture, which from the Times of the Presence of Christ himself, by the Disposition of the Apostles, and the Successions of other *Bishops* from their Seats, even to these Times, has come down to us, safely kept, commended and honour'd through the whole Earth.

Against Petilian.

What has the Chair of the Church of *Rome* done to thee, in which *Peter* sat, and in which, at this day, *Anastasius* sits; or of the Church of *Jerusalem*, in which *James* did sit, and in which *John* does now sit.

Against Julian.

Irenæus, Cyprian, Reticius, Olympius, Hilary, Gregory, Ba-

nos Successimus, eadem Potestate Ecclesiam Domini Gubernantes.

Divina voce sub nomine Angeli Laudatur Præpositus Ecclesiæ.

De verbis Domini, Serm. 24.

Si solis Apostolis dixit, Qui vos spernit, me spernit, *spernite nos: Si autem Sermo Ejus pervenit ad nos, & vocavit nos, & in eorum loco Constituit nos, videte ne spernatis nos.*

Contra Faust. *Lib.* 33. *cap.* ult.

Scripturam amplectimur quæ ab Ipsius Presentia Christi temporibus, per Dispensatione Apostolorum, *& cæteras ab eorum sedibus Successiones Episcoporum, usque ad hæc tempora toto Orbe terrarum custodita, commendata, clarificata pervenit.*

Lib. 2. *contra Literas Petiliani* C. 51.

Cathedra quid tibi fecit Ecclesiæ Romanæ *in qua* Petrus *sedit, & in qua hodie* Anastasius *seaet; aut Ecclesiæ* Hierosolimitanæ *in qua* Jacobus *sedit, & in qua hodie* Joannes *sedet.* [*Vid. contra* Crescon. *l.* 2. *c.* 37.]

Contra Julianum, *l.* 2, *cap.* ult.

Irenæus, Cyprianus, Reticius, Olympius, Hilarius, Gregorius, fil, sil, John, Ambrose—these were *Bishops*, Grave, Learned, &c.

Basilius, Joannes, Ambrosius, isti erant Episcopi, Docti, Graves, &c. *in Ecclesiæ Regimine Clari.*

Questions upon the Old Testament. Quest. 35.

The *King* bears the Image of *God*, as the *Bishop* of *Christ*. Therefore while he is in that Station, he is to be Honour'd, if not for himself, yet for his Order.

Quest. ex vet. Test. qu. 35. *Dei enim Imaginem habet* Rex, *sicut &* Episcopus Christi. *Quamdiu ergo in ea traditione est, Honorandus est, si non propter se, vel propter Ordinem.*

Let this suffice as to the Testimonies of particular *Fathers* of the Church, tho' many more may be produc'd, in that compass of time, to which I have confin'd our present Inquiry. And now (that no Conviction might be wanting) I will set down some of the *Canons* of the *Councils* in those times, to the same purpose; whereby it will appear, that *Episcopacy*, as *distinct* from, and *superior* to *Presbytery*, was not only the Judgment of the first Glorious *Saints* and *Martyrs* of *Christ*; but the current *Doctrin*, and *Government* of the *Church*, both *Greek* and *Latin*, in those early Ages of *Christianity*.

In the *Canons* of the *Apostles*, the distinction of *Bishop*, *Presbyter*, and *Deacon* is so frequent, that it is almost in vain to give *Citations*. The 1*st*. and 2*d. Can.* shew the difference to be observ'd in the *Ordaining* of them.

Let a *Bishop* be Consecrated by two or three *Bishops*.

Ἐπίσκοπος χειροτονείσθω ὑπὸ Ἐπισκόπων δύο ἢ τριῶν.

Let a *Presbyter* and *Deacon* be Ordained by one *Bishop*.

πρεσβύτερος ὑπὸ ἑνὸς Ἐπισκόπου χειροτονείσθω, & Διάκονος.

See the same Distinction of these Orders. *Can.* 3. 4, 5, 6, 7, 8. 17, 18. 25. 27, 28, 29. 32, 33. 36. 42. 44, 45. 51, 52, 53. 63. 68, 69, 70. 83. *Can.* 15. shews the Jurisdiction of the *Bishops* over the *Presbyters* and *Deacons*.

If any *Presbyter* or *Deacon*, or any of the *Clerical* Order, shall leave his own Parish, and go to another, without the *Bishop's* leave, he shall officiate no longer; especially if he obey not the *Bishop*, when he exhorts him to Return, persisting in his Insolence

Εἴ τις πρεσβύτερος, ἢ Διάκονος, ἢ ὅλως ὁ καταλόγου τῶ Κληρικῶν, ἀπολείψας τὴν ἑαυτοῦ παροικίαν, εἰς ἑτέραν ἀπέλθῃ, καὶ παντελῶς μεταςὰς διατρίβῃ ἐν ἄλλῃ παροικίᾳ παρὰ γνώμην τοῦ ἰδίου Ἐπισκόπου· τοῦτον κελεύομεν μηκέτι λειτουργεῖν, εἰ μάλιςα προσκαλουμένου αὐτὸν τοῦ Ἐπισκόπου αὐτοῦ,

and

and disorderly Behaviour, but he shall be reduc'd there to Communicate only as a *Lay-man*.

And *Can.* 31. If any *Presbyter*, despising his own *Bishop*, shall gather Congregations apart, and erect another Altar, his *Bishop* not being Convict of Wickedness or Irreligion, let him be Depos'd as an Ambitious Person; for, he is a Tyrant: And likewise such other *Clergy* or *Laity*, who shall joyn themselves to him shall be Excommunicated. But, let this be after the first, second, and third Admonition of the *Bishop*.

Can. 39. Let the *Presbyters* and *Deacons* do nothing without the Consent of the *Bishop*; for it is He to whom the People of the Lord are committed, and from whom an account of their Souls will be Requir'd.

Can. 41. We Ordain the *Bishop* to have power of the Goods of the Church--- And to Administer to those who want, by the hands of the *Presbyters* and *Deacons*.

Can. 55. If any *Clergy-man* shall Reproach his *Bishop*, let him be Depos'd: For, *Thou shalt not speak Evil of the Ruler of the People.*

After the *Canons* of the *Apostles*, I produce next a Great Council of 87 Bishops held at *Carthage*, in the Year of *Christ*, 256. under St. *Cyprian*, Archbishop of that Place, which is Published in St. *Cyprian*'s Works before quoted, p. 229. where he tells us,

That besides the *Bishops*, there met there both *Presbyters* and *Deacons*, and great Numbers of the *Laity*.

Episcopi plurimi cum Presbyteris & Diaconibus, &c.

The

The Council of *Eliberis* in *Spain*, about the Year of *Christ* 305. Cap. 18. and 19.

Bishops, Presbyters, and *Deacons* are Nam'd distinct. And c. 32. *Presbyters* and *Deacons* are forbid to give the Communion to those who had grievously offended, without the Command of the Bishop.

Episcopi, Presbyteri, & Diaconi, &c. *Non est Presbyterorum, aut Diaconorum Communionem talibus præstare debere, nisi eis jusserit Episcopus.*

c. 75. Of those who shall falsly accuse a *Bishop, Presbyter,* or *Deacon.*

Si quis Episcopum, Presbyterum, vel Diaconum falsis Criminibus appetierit, &c.

c. 77. It is ordained that those who are Baptiz'd by a *Deacon,* without the *Bishop* or *Presbyter,* shall afterwards be Confirm'd by the *Bishop.*

Si quis Diaconus, sine Episcopo vel Presbytero aliquos Baptizaverit; Episcopus eos per Benedictionem perficere debebit.

The Council of *Arles* in *France,* about the Year of *Christ* 309. c. 18. It is ordain'd that the *Deacons* shou'd be subject to the *Presbyters:* And c. 19.

That the *Presbyters* shou'd be subject to their *Bishop,* and do nothing without his consent.

Presbyteri sine Conscientia Episcopi nihil faciant.

A.D 315.

The Council of *Ancyra,* A. D. 315.

c. 1. and 2. Having Prohibited those *Presbyters* and *Deacons* who had, in times of Persecution, Offer'd to Idols, from the Execution of their Office, says, that notwithstanding the *Bishop* sees their Repentance sincere; the *Bishop.*

Ἐι μέντοι τινὲς τῶν Ἐπισκόπων τάξοις συνίδοιεν ταπείνωσίν τινα ἢ ταπείνωσιν προσόπῳ, ἐθέλοιεν πλέον τι διδόναι ἢ ἀφαιρεῖν, ἐπ᾽ αὐτοῖς εἶ τὴν ἐξουσίαν.

may Dispence with them if he for that this Power is lodg'd in

A.D. 321.

The Council of *Laodicea,* A. D. 321.

Can. 41. That no Clergy-man ought to Travel, without the consent of his *Bishop.*

Ὅτι ὐ δεῖ Ἱερατικὸν ἢ Κληρικὸν ἄνευ κελεύσεως Ἐπισκόπου ὁδεύειν.

Can. 56. That the *Presbyters* ought not to go into the Church, and sit in their Stalls, till the *Bishop* come, and to go in with the *Bishop.*

Ὅτι ὐ δεῖ Πρεσβυτέρους πρὸ τῆς εἰσόδου τῦ Ἐπισκόπου εἰσιέναι & καθέζεσθαι ἐν τῷ βήματι, ἀλλὰ μετὰ τῦ Ἐπισκόπου εἰσιέναι.

The

The First and Great Council of *Nice*, A. D. 325.

Can. 16. That if any *Presbyters* or *Deacons* leave their own Churches, they ought not to be receiv'd into another Church: And that if any shall ordain such in his Ch. as belong to another, without the consent of his proper *Bishop*, let such Ordination be void.

Πρεσβύτεροι ἢ Διάκονοί οἱ ἀναχωρήσουσι τῆς ἐκκλησίας, οὐδαμῶς δεκτοὶ ὀφείλουσιν εἶναι ἐν ἑτέρᾳ ἐκκλησίᾳ—— εἰ δὲ καὶ τολμήσειέν τις ὑπαρπάσαι τῶν ἑτέρῳ διαφέροντα, καὶ χειροτονῆσαι ἐν τῇ αὐτοῦ ἐκκλησίᾳ, μὴ συγκαταθεμένου τοῦ ἰδίου Ἐπισκόπου—— ἄκυρος ἔστω ἡ χειροτονία.

The Council of *Gangra*, 326.   A.D. 326.

Can. 6. If any have private Meetings out of the Church, without their *Presbyter*, let 'em be Anathematiz'd by the Sentence of the *Bishop*.

Εἴ τις παρὰ τὴν ἐκκλησίαν κατ' ἰδίαν ἐκκλησιάζει—— μὴ συνόντος τοῦ Πρεσβυτέρου, κατὰ γνώμην τοῦ Ἐπισκόπου, ἀνάθεμα ἔστω.

Can. 7. If any will take or give of the Fruits offer'd to the Church, out of the Church, without leave of the *Bishop*, let him be *Anathema*.

Εἴ τις καρποφορίας ἐκκλησιαστικὰς ἐθέλοι λαμβάνειν, ἢ διδόναι ἔξω τῆς ἐκκλησίας, παρὰ γνώμην τοῦ Ἐπισκόπου—— Ἀνάθεμα ἔστω.

The Council of *Antioch*, A.D. 341.   A.D. 341.

Can. 3. If any *Presbyter* or *Deacon*, leaving his own Parish, shall go to others; and refuse to return, when his own *Bishop* shall summon him, let him be Depos'd.

Εἴ τις Πρεσβύτερος ἢ Διάκονος, καταλειπὼν τὴν ἑαυτοῦ Παροικίαν, εἰς ἑτέραν ἀπέλθῃ, εἰ μάλιστα καλοῦντι τῷ Ἐπισκόπῳ τῷ ἰδίῳ ἐπανελθεῖν εἰς τὴν παροικίαν τὴν ἑαυτοῦ καὶ παραμένειν μὴ ὑπακούει—— παντελῶς αὐτὸν καθαιρεῖσθαι τῆς λειτουργίας.

Can. 4. If any *Bishop* being Depos'd by a *Synod*, or a *Presbyter* or *Deacon* being Depos'd by his own proper *Bishop*, shall presume to exercise his Function, let no room be left them, either for Restauration or Apology.

Εἴ τις Ἐπίσκοπος ὑπὸ Συνόδου καθαιρεθεὶς, ἢ Πρεσβύτερος, ἢ Διάκονος ὑπὸ τοῦ ἰδίου Ἐπισκόπου. Τολμήσειέν τι περὶ ξαι τῆς λειτουργίας, μηδὲ ἀποκαταστάσεως, μηδὲ ἀπολογίας χώραν ἔχειν.

Can. 5. If any *Presbyter* or *Deacon*, despising his own *Bishop*, shall separate himself from the Church, and gather a Congre-

Εἴ τις Πρεσβύτερος ἢ Διάκονος, καταφρονήσας τοῦ Ἐπισκόπου τοῦ ἰδίου, ἀφώρισεν ἑαυτὸν τῆς Ἐκκλησίας, καὶ ἰδίᾳ συνήγαγε, καὶ Θυσια-
gation

(54)

gation of his own, and set up a different Altar; and shall refuse to submit himself to his *Bishop*, calling him the first and second time, let him be absolutely Depos'd.

Can. 12. If any *Presbyter* or *Deacon*, being Depos'd by his own proper *Bishop*, or a *Bishop* by the *Synod*, dare Appeal to the *King*, seeing his Appeal lies to a greater *Synod* of more *Bishops*, where he is to expect the Examination of his Cause, and to referr the Decision to them; But if, making light of these, he trouble the *King* with it, such an one is worthy of no Pardon, nor ought to be admitted to make any sort of Apology, or to have hopes of his being ever Restor'd any more.

Can. 22. That a *Bishop* ought not to Ordain *Presbyters* or *Deacons* in another *Bishop*'s Diocess, without his leave.

θήριον ἔπηξε, καὶ τῦ Ἐπισκόπου πρῶτον καὶ δεύτερον καλοῦντι ἀπειθοίη, ἐῦτον καθαιρεῖθαι παντελῶς.

Εἴ τις ὑπὸ τῦ ἰδίε Ἐπισκόπου καθαιρεθεὶς πρεσβύτερ Θ᾽ ἢ Διάκονος, ἢ ἐξ Ἐπίσκοπος ὑπὸ Σωόδε, ὀχλήσῃ τολμήσειε ταῖς βασιλικαῖς ἀκοαῖς, δέον ἐπὶ μείζονα Ἐπισκόπων Σωόδον τρέπεσθαι, ᾗ ἀνομίζῃ δίκαια ἔχειν προσαναφέρειν πλείοσιν Ἐπισκόποις, ἑ τ᾽ παρ᾽ αὐτῷ ἐξέτασίν τε ἑ ἀκριβῆ ἀκρίβωσιν αὐδέχεδαι. εἰ δὲ τοῦτων ὀλιγωρήσας ἐνοχλήσειε τῷ βασιλεῖ, καὶ τούτον μηδὲ μιᾶς συγγνώμης ἀξιοῦσθαι, μηδὲ χώραν ἀπολογίας ἔχειν. μηδὲ ἐλπίδα μελλούσης ἀποκαταστάσεως προσδοκᾶν.

Ἐπίσκοπον μὴ καθιστᾶν Πρεσβύτερον ἢ Διάκονον εἰς τόπες ἑτέρῳ Ἐπισκόπῳ ὑποκειμένες, εἰ μὴ ἄρα μ᾽ γνώμης τῦ οἰκείου τ᾽ χώρας Ἐπίσκοπου.

In the Council of *Carthage*, A. D. 348.

C. xi. The Case is put where a *Deacon* being accus'd, shall be Try'd by *three* Neighbouring *Bishops*, a *Presbyter* by *six*, and a *Bishop* by *twelve*.

A tribus vicinis Episcopis, si Diaconus est arguatur; si Presbyter, à sex, si Episcopus à duodecim Consacerdotibus audiatur.

The second *Oecumenical Council* of *Constantinople*, A. D. 381.

Can. 6. Ranks those with *Hereticks*, who, tho' they profess the true Faith, yet run into *Schism*, and gather Congregations apart from, and in opposition to our Canonical *Bishops*.

Αἱρετικὰς ἢ λέγομβυ, τάς τε πάλαι τῆς ἐκκλησίας ἀποκηρυχθέντας πρὸς ἢ τούτοις καὶ τὰς τ᾽ πίστιν μβυ τὴν ὑγιῆ προσποιεμένες ὁμολογεῖν, ἀποσχίθέντας δὲ καὶ ἀντισυνάγοντας τοῖς κανονικοῖς ἡμῶν Ἐπισκόποις.

The Council of *Carthage*, A. D. 419.

Can. 3. Mentions the three distinct

Τὰς τρεῖς βαθμὰς——Φησὶ δὲ

ſtinct *Orders* of *Biſhop*, *Presbyter*, Ἐπισκόπας, πρεσβυτέρας, καὶ Διά-
and *Deacon*; and compares them κόνας, ὡς πρώτῳ ἑστὼς. Ἐπισκόποις,
to the *High-Prieſt*, *Prieſts*, and ὣ Ἱερεῦσι Θεῷ, ὣ Λευίταις.
Levites.

In the ſame manner they are as diſtinctly mention'd,

Can. 4. *Biſhop*, *Presbyter* and   Ἐπίσκοπ<i>Ⓖ</i>, πρεσβύτερ<i>Ⓖ</i>, καὶ
Deacon; and their Powers di-   Διάκον<i>Ⓖ</i>.
ſtinct. For,

Can. 6. It is declar'd not to be lawful for *Presbyters* to *Conſe-
crate Churches*, or Reconcile *Penitents*; but if any be in great Danger, and deſirous to be Reconcil'd in the abſence of the *Biſhop*,

The *Presbyter* ought to con-   Ὀφείλει εἰκότως ὁ πρεσβύτερ<i>Ⓖ</i>
ſult the *Biſhop*, and receive his   ἐρωτῆσαι τ̄ Ἐπίσκοπον.
Orders in it, as is declar'd in the 7. *Can*.

Can. 10. If any *Presbyter*, be-   Ἐὰν τις Πρεσβύτερ<i>Ⓖ</i>, ἐκ τοῦ ἰδίου
ing puff'd up with Pride, ſhall   Ἐπισκόπου φυσιωθεὶς σχίσμα ποιήσῃ,
make a *Schiſm* againſt his own   Ἀνάθεμα ἔςω.
proper *Biſhop*, let him be *Anathema*.

Can. 11. Gives leave to a *Presbyter*, who is Condemn'd by his
Biſhop, to Appeal to the Neighbouring *Biſhops*; but if, without
this, he flies off, and makes a *Schiſm* from his *Biſhop*, it confirms
the *Anathema* upon him.

Can. 12. Orders what is before Recited out of *Can*. xi. of the
Council of *Carthage*.

That a *Biſhop* who is Accus'd   Ἐπίσκοπ<i>Ⓖ</i> ὑπὸ δώδεκα Ἐπισ-
ſhall be try'd by *twelve Biſhops*,   κόπων ἀκυσθῇ, καὶ ὁ πρεσβύτερ<i>Ⓖ</i>
if more may not be had; a *Pres-   ὑπὸ ἓξ Ἐπισκόπων, καὶ τοῦ ἰδίου, ὁ Διά-
byter* by *ſix Biſhops*, with his own   κον<i>Ⓖ</i> ὑπὸ τριῶν.
Biſhop; and a *Deacon* by *three*.

Can. 14. Orders that in *Tripoli*, becauſe of the ſmaller number of *Biſhops* in thoſe Parts, a   Ὁ πρεσβύτερ<i>Ⓖ</i> ἀκεῖτε ὑπὸ πέντε
Presbyter ſhall be judg'd by   ἀκυσθῇ Ἐπισκόπων, καὶ Διάκον<i>Ⓖ</i>
Five Biſhops, and a *Deacon* by   ὑπὸ τριῶν, οὗ ἰδίου αὐτοῦ Ἐπισκόπου
Three, his own proper *Biſhop*   προκαθημένε.
Preſiding.

Can. 46. That a *Presbyter*   Πρεσβύτερος ἄνδρα γνώμην τοῦ
ſhall not Reconcile a Penitent,   Ἐπισκόπου μὴ καταλλάσσει με-
without the knowledge of the   τανοῦντα· εἰ μηδὲν ἀνάγκης συνω-
Biſhop; unleſs upon neceſſity,   θείης ἐν τῇ ἀπουσίᾳ τοῦ Ἐπισκόπου.
in the abſence of the *Biſhop*.

Can.

Can. 59. That one *Bishop* may ordain many *Presbyters*; but that it was hard to find a *Presbyter* who was fit to be made a *Bishop*.

Δύναται δὲ εἷς Ἐπίσκοπος πολλοὺς χειροτονεῖν Πρεσβυτέρους· πρεσβύτερος δὲ πρὸς Ἐπισκοπὴν ἐπιτήδειος δυσχερῶς εὑρίσκεται.

Can. 65. That a *Clergy man*, being Condemned by the *Bishops*, cannot be deliver'd by that *Church* to which he did belong, or by any Man whatsoever.

Κληρικὸν τῇ τῶν Ἐπισκόπων κρίσει καταδικασθέντα, μὴ ἐξεῖναι τὸν αὐτὸν εἴτε παρὰ τῆς ἐκκλησίας, ἧς ὑπῆρχεν, εἴτε ἀπὸ οἱουδήποτε Ἀνθρώπου διεκδικεῖσθαι ποινῆς.

Can. 126. That *Presbyters* and *Deacons* may Appeal from their own *Bishop* to the Neighbouring *Bishops*, chosen by consent of their own *Bishop*, and from them to the *Primate* or *Provincial Synod*; but not to any *Trans-marine* or *Forraign* Jurisdiction, under pain of Excommunication.

Πρεσβύτεροι, καὶ Διάκονοι, ἐν αἷς ἔχουσιν αἰτίαις, ἐὰν περὶ τῆς ψήφου τοὺς ἰδίους Ἐπισκόπους μέμφωνται, οἱ γειτνιῶντες Ἐπίσκοποι τούτων ἀκροάσωνται, καὶ τὰ μεταξὺ τούτων περατωσάτωσαν οἱ παρ' αὐτῶν κατὰ συναίνεσιν τῶν ἰδίων αὐτῶν Ἐπισκόπων προσλαμβανόμενοι· ἐὰν δὲ καὶ ἀπ' αὐτῶν ἐκκαλέσασθαι θελήσωσιν, μὴ ἐκκαλέσωνται, εἰ μὴ πρὸς τὰς τῆς Ἀφρικῆς συνόδους, ἢ πρὸς τοὺς Πρωτεύοντας τῶν ἰδίων αὐτῶν ἐπαρχιῶν. πρὸς δὲ τὰ πέραν τῆς θαλάσσης ὁ βουλόμενος ἐκκαλέσασθαι, ὑπὸ μηδενὸς ἐν Ἀφρικῇ δεχθείη εἰς κοινωνίαν.

The Council of *Chalcedon*, being the Fourth General Council *A. D.* 451.

Can. 9. If any *Clergy-man* have a Cause of complaint against another *Clergy-man*, let him not leave his own proper *Bishop*, and have Recourse to the *Secular* Courts--Whoever does otherwise shall be put under the Canonical Censures.

Εἴ τις κληρικὸς πρὸς κληρικὸν πρᾶγμα ἔχει, μὴ ἐγκαταλιμπανέτω τὸν οἰκεῖον Ἐπίσκοπον, καὶ ἐπὶ κοσμικὰ δικαστήρια μὴ κατατρεχέτω—— εἰ δέ τις παρὰ ταῦτα ποιήσοι, Κανονικοῖς ἐπιτιμίοις ὑποκείσθω.

Can. 13. That a Forreign *Clergy-man*, and not known shall not officiate in another City, without Commendatory Letters from his own *Bishop*.

Ξένους κληρικοὺς καὶ ἀγνώστους ἐν ἑτέρᾳ πόλει, δίχα συστατικῶν γραμμάτων τοῦ ἰδίου Ἐπισκόπου μηδόλως μηδαμοῦ λειτουργεῖν.

Can. 18. If any of the *Clergy* shall be found Conspiring, or Joyning in *Fraternities*, or Contriving any thing against the *Bishops*, they shall fall from their own Degree.

Can. 29. To reduce a *Bishop* to the Degree of a *Presbyter*, is Sacrilege.

Εἴ τινες τοίνυν κληρικοὶ ἢ Μονάζοντες εὑρεθεῖεν ἢ συνομνύμενοι ἢ φρατριάζοντες, ἢ κατασκευάζας τυρεύοντες ἐπισκόποις, ἢ συγκληρικοῖς, ἐκπιπτέτωσαν παντῃ τοῦ οἰκείου βαθμοῦ.

Ἐπίσκοπον εἰς πρεσβυτέρου βαθμὸν φέρειν Ἱεροσυλία ἐςτὶν.

These Authorities are so plain and full as to prevent any Application, or Multiplying of further Quotations, which might easily be done: For, if these can be answer'd, so may all that can possibly be produc'd, or framed in words.

And ther is no Remedy left to the *Presbyterians*, and other Dissenters from *Episcopacy*, but to deny all these by whole-sale, to throw off all *Antiquity*, as well the first Ages of Christianity, even that wherein the *Apostles* themselves Liv'd and Taught, as all since; and to stand upon a New Foundation of their own Invention.

But this only shews the Desperatness of their Cause; and the Impregnable Bulwork of *Episcopacy*; which (I must say it) stands upon so *Many*, *Clear*, and *Authentick Evidences*, as can never be overthrown, but by such *Topicks* as must render *Christianity* it self Precarious.

And if from the *Etymology* of the Words *Bishop* and *Presbyter*, any Argument can be drawn (against all the Authorities Produc'd) to prove them the same, we may, by this way of Reasoning, prove *Cyrus* to be *Christ*, for so he is call'd, *Isa.* XLV. 1.

Or if the *Presbyterians* will have their *Moderator* to be a *Bishop*, we will not Quarrel with them about a word. Let us then have a *Moderator*, such as the *Bishops* before describ'd, viz. A *Moderator*, as a standing Officer, during *Life*, to whom all the *Presbyters* are to be obedient as to *Christ*, *i.e.* to the *Moderator*, as Representing the Person of *Christ*: That nothing be done in the *Church* without Him: That He be understood as the *Principle* of *Unity* in His *Church*; so that, they who unjustly break off from his *Communion*, are thereby in a *Schism*: That he shew his *Succession*, by Regular Ordination, convey'd down from the *Apostles*. In short, that He have all that *Character* and

Authority, which we see to have been Recogniz'd in the *Bishops*, in the very Age of the *Apostles*, and all the succeeding Ages of *Christianity*, and then call Him *Moderator, Superintendent*, or *Bishop*: For, the Contest is not about the *Name*, but the *Thing*.

And if we go only upon the *Etymology* of the *Word*, how shall we prove *Presbyters* to be an *Order* in the *Church*, more than *Bishops*? as *Athanasius* said to *Dracontius* of those who persuaded him not to accept of a *Bishoprick*.

Why do they persuade you not to be a Bishop, when they themselves will have Presbyters?

Διὰ τί συμβελεύουσί σοι μὴ ἀντιλαμβάνεσθαι σε τῆς Ἐπισκοπῆς, αὐτοὶ θέλοντες ἔχειν πρεσβυτέρους ;

I will end this Head, with the Advice of that great *Father* to this same *Dracontius*.

If the Government of the Churches do not please you; and that you think the Office of a *Bishop* has no Reward, thereby making your self a Despiser of our *Saviour*, who did Institute it; I beseech you surmise not any such things as these, nor do you Entertain any who advise such things; for that is not worthy of *Dracontius*: For what things the Lord did Institute by His *Apostles*, those things remain both good and sure.

Εἰ δὲ τῆς Ἐκκλησίας ἡ Διάταξις οὐκ ἀρεστή σοι, οὐδὲ νομίζεις δ' τῆς Ἐπισκοπῆς λειτέργημα μισθὸν ἔχει, ἀλλὰ καταφρονεῖς τε ταῦτα διαταξαμένε Σωτῆρ@ πεποίηκας σαυτὸν, παρακαλῶ, μὴ τοιαῦτα λογίζου, μνδὲ ἀνέχου τῷ ταῦτα συμβελόντων. οὐ γὰρ ἄξια Δρακοντίου ταῦτα. ἃ γὰρ ὁ Κύρι@ διὰ τῇ ἀποςόλων πέπωκε, ταῦτα καλὰ καὶ βέβαια μένει.

Athanas. Epist. ad *Dracont*.

II. Having thus Explain'd those Texts of *Scripture* which speak of *Episcopacy*, by the Concurrent sense of those who liv'd with the *Apostles*, and were taught the Faith from their Mouths; who liv'd zealous *Confessors*, and dy'd glorious *Martyrs* of *Christ*; and who Succeeded the *Apostles* in those very *Churches* where themselves had sat *Bishops*: And having deduc'd their Testimonies, and of those who Succeeded them down for Four Hundred and Fifty Years after Christ (from which time, ther is no doubt rais'd against the Universal Reception of *Episcopacy*) and this not only from their *Writings* apart, but by their *Canons* and *Laws*, when Assembl'd together in *Council*; which one wou'd think sufficient Evidence, against none at all on the other side, that is, for the *Succession* of *Churches*

Churches in the *Presbyterian* Form, of which no one Inftance can be given, fo much as of any one *Church* in the *world* fo Deduc'd, not only from the days of the *Apoſtles* (as is ſhewn for *Epifcopacy*) but before *Calvin*, and thofe who *Reform'd* with him, about 160 Years laſt paſt: I ſay, tho' what is done is ſufficient to ſatisfie any *Indifferent* and *Un-byaſs'd* Judgment, yet ther is one *Topick* yet behind, which, with our *Diſſenters*, weighs more than all *Fathers* and *Councils*; and that is, the late *Reformation*, from whence fome Date their very *Chriſtianity*. And if even by this too *Epifcopacy* ſhou'd be *witneſſed* and *Approv'd*, then is ther nothing at all in the World left to the Oppofers of *Epifcopacy*, nothing of *Antiquity*, *Precedent*, or any *Authority* but their own *wilful will* againſt all *Ages* of the whole *Catholick Church*, even that of the *Reformation* as well as all the Reſt.

Let us then Examine. Firſt, for the *Church* of *England*, that is thrown off clearly by our *Diſſenters*, for that was *Reform'd* under *Epifcopacy*, and continues fo to this day.

And as to our Neighbour Nation of *Scotland*, where the *Presbyterians* do boaſt that the *Reformation* was made by *Presbyters*; that is moſt *Clearly* and *Authentically* Confuted by a Late Learned and worthy Author (already mention'd) in his *Fundamental Charter of Presbytery*, Printed 1695. fo as to ſtop the Mouths of the moſt Perverfe, who will not be Perfuaded tho' they are Perfuaded.

Go we then abroad, and fee the ſtate of the *Reformed* Churches there.

The *Lutherans* are all cut off, as the Church of *England*; for they ſtill Retain *Epifcopacy*, as in *Denmark*, *Sweden*, &c.

Ther remains now only the *Calviniſts*. Here it is the *Presbyterians* fet up their Reſt! This is their ſtrong *Foundation*!

And this will fail them as much as all the other: For, be it known unto them (however they will receive it) that *Calvin* himſelf, and *Beza*, and the reſt of the Learned *Reformers* of their Part, did give their Teſtimony for *Epifcopacy* as much as any. They counted it a moſt unjuſt *Reproach* upon them, to think that they condemn'd *Epifcopacy*; which they ſay they did not throw off, but cou'd not have it there, in *Geneva*, without coming under the *Papal Hierarchy*: They highly *Applauded* and *Congratulated* the *Epifcopal Hierarchy* of the *Church* of *England*, as in their feveral

ral Letters to Q. *Elizabeth*, to the *Arch-bishop* of *Canterbury*, and others of our *English Bishops*: They Pray'd heartily to God for the Continuance and Preservation of it: Bemoan'd their own unhappy Circumstances, that they cou'd not have the like, because they had no *Magistrate* to Protect them; and wished for *Episcopacy* in their *Churches*, the want of which they own'd as a great *Defect*; but call'd it their *Misfortune* rather than their *Fault*. As the Learned of the *French Hugonots* have likewise pleaded on their Behalf.

As for their *Excuse*, I do not now meddle with it, for I think it was not a good one. They might have had *Bishops* from other Places, tho' ther were none among themselves, but those who were *Popish*: And they might as well have had *Bishops* as *Presbyters*; without the Countenance of the *Civil-Magistrate*. It might have rais'd a greater *Persecution* against them; but that is nothing as to the *Truth* of the thing. And if they thought it a *Truth*, they ought to have *suffer'd* for it.

But whatever becomes of their *Excuse*, here it is plain, that they gave their *Suffrage* for *Episcopacy*; which who so pleases may see at large in Dr. *Durel's View of the Government and Worship in the Reformed Churches beyond the Seas*, (who was himself one of them) Printed. 1662.

So that our Modern *Presbyterians* have departed from *Calvin* as well as from *Luther*, in their Abhorrence of *Episcopacy*, from all the *Christian* World, in all Ages; and particularly from all our late *Reformers*, both of one sort and other.

Calvin wou'd have *Anathematiz'd* all of them, had he liv'd in our times. He fay's ther were none such to be found in his time, who oppos'd the *Episcopal Hierarchy*, but only the *Papal*, which Aspir'd to an *Universal Supremacy* in the *See* of *Rome* over the whole *Catholick Church*, which is the *Prerogative* of *Christ* alone. But, says he,

If they wou'd give us such a *Hierarchy*, in which the *Bishops* shou'd so Excell, as that they did not refuse to be subject to *Christ*, and to depend upon Him, as their *only* Head, and refer all to Him; then I will confess that they are worthy of all *Anathemas*, if any such shall be	*Talem si nobis Hierarchiam exhibeant, in qua sic Emineant Episcopi, ut Christo subesse non Recusent, & ab Illo tanquam unico Capite pendeant, & ad Ipsum referantur*, &c. *Tum vero nullo non Anathemate dignos fatear si qui erunt qui non Eam Revereantur, summaque Obedientia observ-*

found,

found, who will not Reverence it, and submit themselves to it, with the utmost Obedience. *vent. Calvin. De necessitat. Ecclef. Reformand.*

See, he says, *si qui erunt*, if ther shall be any such, which supposes that he knew none such; and that he own'd none such amongst his *Reformers*: And that if ever any such thou'd arise, he thought ther were no *Anathemas* which they did not deserve, who shou'd refuse to submit to the *Episcopal Hierarchy*, without such an *Universal Head*, as Excludes *Christ* from being the *only* Universal *Head*; for if ther be *another*, (tho *substitute*) He is not *only*. Thus He is called the *Chief Bishop*, but never the *only Bishop*, because ther are others deputed under Him. But He calls no *Bishop* the *Universal Bishop*, or *Head* of the *Catholick Church*; because He has appointed no *Substitute* in that *supreme* Office; as not of *Universal King*, so neither of *Universal Bishop*.

And *Beza* supposes as Positively as *Calvin* had done, that ther were none who did oppose the *Episcopal Hierarchy* without such an *Universal Head* now upon Earth; or that oppos'd the *Order* of *Episcopacy*; and condemns them as *Mad-men*, if any such cou'd be found. For thus says he,

If ther be any (which you shall hardly persuade me to believe) who reject the whole Order of *Episcopacy*; God forbid that any Man, in his wits, shou'd assent to the *Madness* of such Men.

Si qui sunt autem (quod sane mihi non facile persuaseris) qui omnem Episcoporum ordinem Rejiciant, absit ut quisquam satis sanæ mentis furoribus illorum assentiatur. Beza. ad Tractat. de Minist. Ev. Grad. ab Hadrian. Sarav. Belga Editam. c. 1.

And particularly as to the *Church* of *England*, and her *Hierarchy* of *Archbishops* and *Bishops*, he says, that he never meant to oppugne any thing of that; but calls it a *singular Blessing of God*; and wishes that she may ever enjoy it.

Fruatur sane ista singulari Dei beneficentia, quæ utinam sit illi Perpetua. Ibid. c. 18.

So that our Modern *Presbyterians* are disarm'd of the Precedent of *Calvin*, *Beza*, and all the *Reformers* abroad; by whose Sentence they are *Anathematiz'd* and counted as *Mad-men*.

Here then, let us consider and beware of the Fatal Progress of *Error*! *Calvin* and the *Reformers* with him, set up *Presbyterian* Government, as they pretended, by *Necessity*; but still kept up and
Pro-

Profess'd the highest Regard to the *Episcopal Character* and *Authority*: But those who pretend to follow their Example, have utterly Abdicated the whole *Order* of *Episcopacy*, as *Anti-Christian* and an *Insupportable Grievance*! While, at the same time, they wou'd seem to pay the greatest Reverence to these *Reformers*; and much more to the *Authority* of the *First* and *Purest* Ages of *Christianity*; whose *Fathers* and *Councils* spoke all the *High* things, before Quoted, in behalf of *Episcopacy*; far beyond the *Language* of our later *Apologists* for that *Hierarchy*; or what durst now be Repeated, except from such *unquestionable Authority*.

In this they imitate the hardness of the *Jews*, who Built the *Sepulchers* of those *Prophets*, whom their *Fathers* slew; while, at the same time, they Adher'd to, and out-did the Wickedness of their *Fathers*, in Persecuting the *Successors* of those *Prophets*.

FINIS.

ERRATA.

Pag. 3. col. 2. l. 11. r. *καταρδωσιν*. p. 39. col. 1. l. 10, 11. r. All of you follow your Bishops, col. 2. *penult*. r. ἑὰν. p. 40. l. 16. A. D. 180. shou'd be on the Margent; p. 42. col. 2. l. 3. dele —— after Πρεσβυτέρων. and r. ἱερεὺς. p. 44. col. 2. l. 14. r. Ira. p 45. col. 2. l. 28. r. *scripturarum*. p. 47. col. 2. *penult*. r. *ad Heliodorum*. p. 51. col. 1. l. 11, 12, 13, 14. r. As likewise such other *Clergy*, and as many as shall join with him: but the *Lay-men* shall be Excommunicated.

ADVERTISEMENT.

Whereas I have plac'd the *Apostolical Canons* in the Front of the *Councils* before Quoted, I thought fit (to prevent needless Cavil) to give this Advertisement, that I do not contend, they were made by the *Apostles* themselves, but by the Holy *Fathers* of the *Church*, about the end of the Second and beginning of the *Third Century*, as a *Summary* of that *Discipline*, which had been transmitted to them, by Un-interrupted Tradition, from the *Apostles*; whence they have justly obtain'd the Name of *The Apostolical Canons*; and, as such, have been Receiv'd and Reverenc'd in the succeeding Ages of Christianity.

The *Councils* Quoted after these *Canons*, bear their Proper Dates; and ther can be no Contest about them.

And what is Quoted of St. *Ignatius* and the other *Fathers*, is from the most Uncontroverted Parts of their Works, to obviate the Objection of *Interpolations*, and *Additions*, by the Noise of which our Adversaries endeavour to throw off, or enervate their whole Authority; and quite to dis-arm us of all that *Light* which we have from the *Primitive Ages* of the *Church*; because it makes all against them. Though they fail not to Quote the *Fathers* on their side, whensoever they can Screw them to give the least seeming Countenance to their *Novelties* and *Errors*: Yet *Boldly* Reject them All, when brought in Evidence against them, and that they can no otherwise struggle from under the weight of their Authority.

A Catalogue of Books Printed for Charles Brome *at the* Gun *at the West-End of St.* Paul's Church-yard.

THE Snake in the Grass: Or, Satan transform'd into an Angel of Light. Discovering the Deep and Unsuspected Subtilty which is couched under the Pretended Simplicity of many of the Principal Leaders of those People call'd Quakers. The Second Edition, with Additions.

Some

Some Seasonable Reflections upon the Quakers Solemn Protestation against *George Keith*'s Proceedings at *Turner's-Hall*, 29. *April* 1697. Which was by them Printed, and sent thither, as the Reasons of their not Appearing to defend themselves. Herein annex'd Verbatim By an Impartial Hand.

Satan Dis-rob'd from his Disguise of Light: Or, the Quakers Last Shift to Cover their Monstrous Heresies, laid fully open. In a Reply to *Thomas Ellwood*'s Answer (Published the End of last Month) to *George Keith*'s Narrative of the Proceedings at *Turner's-Hall*, *June* 11. 1696. Which also may serve for a Reply (as to the main Points of Doctrine) to *Geo. Whitehead*'s Answer to The Snake in the Grass; to be Published the End of next Month, if this prevent it not.

A Discourse proving the Divine Institution of Water-Baptism: Wherein the Quaker Arguments against it, are Collected and Confuted. With as much as is needful concerning the Lord's Supper. These Four Books are Written by the Author of: The Snake in the Grass.

The Quakers set in their True Light, in order to give the Nation a clear sight of what they hold concerning Jesus of *Nazareth*, the Scriptures, Water-Baptism, the Lord's Supper, Magistracy, Ministry, Laws, and Government: Historically collected out of their most approved Authors, which are their best Construing-Books, from the year of their Rise 1650 to the year of their Progress 1696. By *Francis Bugg*, Sen.

An Essay concerning Preaching: Written for the Direction of a Young Divine; and useful also for the People, in order to Profitable Hearing.

Crums of Comfort, and Godly Prayers; With Thankful Remembrances of God's wonderful Deliverances of this Land.

www.ingramcontent.com/pod-product-compliance
Lightning Source LLC
Chambersburg PA
CBHW021836230426
43669CB00008B/990